Contemplating the Future
of Moral Theology

Contemplating the Future of Moral Theology

Essays in Honor of
Brian V. Johnstone, C.Ss.R.

EDITED BY
Robert C. Koerpel
AND
Vimal Tirimanna, C.Ss.R.

FOREWORD BY
Charles Curran

☙PICKWICK *Publications* • Eugene, Oregon

CONTEMPLATING THE FUTURE OF MORAL THEOLOGY
Essays in Honor of Brian V. Johnstone, C.Ss.R.

Copyright © 2017 Wipf and Stock Publishers. All rights reserved. Except for brief quotations in critical publications or reviews, no part of this book may be reproduced in any manner without prior written permission from the publisher. Write: Permissions, Wipf and Stock Publishers, 199 W. 8th Ave., Suite 3, Eugene, OR 97401.

Pickwick Publications
An Imprint of Wipf and Stock Publishers
199 W. 8th Ave., Suite 3
Eugene, OR 97401

www.wipfandstock.com

PAPERBACK ISBN: 978-1-5326-0335-8
HARDCOVER ISBN: 978-1-5326-0337-2
EBOOK ISBN: 978-1-5326-0336-5

Cataloguing-in-Publication data:

Names: Koerpel, Robert C., editor. | Tirimanna, Vimal, editor. | Curran, Charles E., foreword.

Title: Contemplating the future of moral theology : essays in honor of Brian V. Johnstone, C.Ss.R. / edited by Robert C. Koerpel and Vimal Tirimanna ; foreword by Charles Curran.

Description: Eugene, OR : Pickwick Publications, 2017 | Includes bibliographical references.

Identifiers: ISBN 978-1-5326-0335-8 (paperback) | ISBN 978-1-5326-0337-2 (hardcover) | ISBN 978-1-5326-0336-5 (ebook)

Subjects: LCSH: Johnstone, Brian V. | Christian ethics.

Classification: BJ1251 .C66 2017 (print) | BJ1251 .C66 (ebook)

Manufactured in the U.S.A. 05/17/17

Contents

List of Contributors | vii

Foreword by Charles Curran | ix

Introduction | xv

1. Faith, Conscience, and the Threefold Way | 1
   —Dennis J. Billy, C.Ss.R.

2. Where Moral Theology Begins: "*Aditus ad Universam Moralem Theologiam*" | 21
   —Raphael Gallagher, C.Ss.R.

3. Should the Church Change Its Teaching on Sexual Morality? | 38
   —Gerald Gleeson

4. Gift as a Principle of Moral Action | 55
   —Aristide Gnada

5. Natural Law Debates and the Forces of Nature | 71
   —James F. Keenan, S.J.

6. Jesus Ascends: An Expanding Horizon | 88
   —Anthony J. Kelly, C.Ss.R.

CONTENTS

7. The Rise and Fall of Normative Ethics in Recent
   Catholic Moral Theology | 105
   —Terrence Gerard Kennedy, C.Ss.R.

8. Moral Theology and Practice in Anglican-Roman Catholic
   Dialogue: Difference, Convergence, and Diversity | 118
   —Charles Sherlock

9. The Process of Formulating Official Catholic Teachings:
   Consulting the Laity and *Sensus Fidelium* | 130
   —Vimal Tirimanna, C.Ss.R.

10. Las "Obras de Misericordia" y la Teología Moral:
    La "Corrección Fraterna" | 151
    —Marciano Vidal

Bibliography for Brian Johnstone, C.Ss.R. | 171

Contributors

Dennis J. Billy, C.Ss.R., John Cardinal Krol Professor of Moral Theology at St. Charles Borromeo Seminary in Wynnewood, Pennsylvania and Karl Rahner Professor of Catholic Theology at the Graduate Theological Foundation in Mishawaka, Indiana.

Raphael Gallagher, C.Ss.R., Retired Professor from the Alphonsian Academy, Rome. He has contributed to theological journals, including *Studia Moralia*, *Irish Theological Quarterly*, and *Revue d'éthique et de théologie morale*.

Gerald Gleeson, *Professor Ordinarius* (Philosophy) in the Ecclesiastical Faculty at the Catholic Institute of Sydney, Honorary Research Fellow of Australian Catholic University, a member of the Plunkett Centre for Ethics in Health Care (Sydney), and Fellow of St John's College within the University of Sydney. He has published articles on moral philosophy, metaphysics, philosophy of language, bioethics, and theology in such journals as *Sophia*, *Pacifica*, *The Australasian Catholic Record*, *Literature and Aesthetics*, *Compass Theology Review*, and *Bioethics Outlook*.

Aristide Gnada, Professor of Fundamental Moral Theology at the Alphonsian Academy, Rome. His publications include *L'Harmattan: Le principe Don en éthique sociale et théologie morale. Une implication de la philosophie du don chez Derrida, Marion et Bruaire* (2009); and *Le concept de don. Ce qui dit l'être personnel et l'agir moral* (2013).

CONTRIBUTORS

James F. Keenan, S.J., Canisius Chair, Director of the Jesuit Institute and Director of the Gabelli Presidential Scholars Program at Boston College. His most recent book is *University Ethics: How Colleges Can Build and Benefit from a Culture of Ethics* (Rowman and Littlefield, 2015).

Anthony J. Kelly, C.Ss.R., Professor of Theology at Australian Catholic University, member of the Institute for Religion and Critical Inquiry, and Distinguished Fellow in the Directorate of Identity and Mission. His most recent books are *The Resurrection Effect: Transforming Christian Life and Thought*; and *Upward: Faith, Church and the Ascension of Christ*.

Terence Gerard Kennedy, C.Ss.R., Professor of Fundamental Moral Theology at the Accademia Alfonsiana, Rome. He is the author of the two-volume manual of moral theology, *Doers of the Word*.

Charles Sherlock, Anglican priest in Melbourne, Australia and an Honorary Research Fellow of the University of Divinity, Australia.

Vimal Tirimanna, C.Ss.R., Professor of Moral Theology at the National Seminary of Our Lady of Lanka, Kandy, Sri Lanka and the Pontifical Alphonsian Academy, Rome. He has written articles for international theological periodicals, such as *New BlackFriars, Concilium, Studia Moralia, Segno, Review for Religious, Studies in Interreligious Dialogue, Homo Dei, Asian Christian Review, Vidyajyoti Journal of Theological Reflection, Asia Focus, Asian Horizons,* and *Asia Journal of Theology.*

Marciano Vidal, Ordinary Professor la Universidad Pontificia Comillas, Madrid, El Instituto Superior de Ciencias Morales, Madrid, and Extraordinary Professor at the Academia Alfonsiana, Rome.

Foreword

In this foreword, I have been asked to introduce Brian V. Johnstone to the reader. All of the contributors to this volume and most other Catholic moral theologians are quite familiar with the role and contributions that Brian has played in contemporary moral theology. This book by definition is a grateful testimony from colleagues and former students about his significant work. What I might be able to add here is my own experience in working with Brian as a colleague and the fact that I was instrumental in bringing Brian to the United States and the theology faculty at the Catholic University of America.

Almost forty years later and with a diminished memory, I might not remember all the details, but the basic outlines of the experience are quite clear. Either in the fall of 1980 or the spring of 1981, our theological faculty at the Catholic University of America was looking for another person to teach moral theology. In a chance conversation with a colleague at the Kennedy Institute of Ethics at Georgetown University, I learned that Father Brian V. Johnstone, a Redemptorist priest from Australia, had applied to the Kennedy Institute as a visiting scholar in the 1981-82 academic year since he was going to be on sabbatical. I had heard of Brian Johnstone and was very impressed by his curriculum vitae that he submitted for the position at the Kennedy Institute. Our faculty talked about the possibility of offering him a one-year visiting professorship at our institution. I then called Brian at the Redemptorist house associated with the Theological Union at Yarra where he was teaching. Recall that in those days there was no internet and long-distance telephone calls between Australia and the United States were not all that common. As I recall, I reached him at meal time and in the conversation broached to him the possibility of his coming to our faculty for the 1981-82 school year to teach moral theology. I do not recall all the subsequent correspondence and development, but Brian received permission from the Redemptorist superiors in Australia to accept our offer. The fact that there was a Redemptorist college or residence very close to Catholic University was also a significant factor in his coming.

Since there was no opportunity for an in-depth interview of Brian with the faculty, it was agreed that the original contract would be for a one-year visiting professor. However, as that year evolved the faculty became more and more interested in offering Brian a full time academic position. After discussions by the various committees of the faculty and the final vote of the entire faculty, a full time position was offered to Brian. Again after consultation with Redemptorist superiors, Brian accepted our invitation. He stayed at Catholic University until 1987 having received continuous tenure on the basis of his superior research, teaching, and faculty service. As I recall, there was not a negative vote in his regard.

His faculty colleagues greatly appreciated his person and his work. All recognized his serious contribution to scholarship and teaching. He was also a delightful colleague who never seemed to take himself too seriously. There was a bit of the absent minded professor about Brian that only endeared him all the more to his colleagues. One story stands out. Occasionally there were some problems and even robberies in the area of Catholic University. One day near the Redemptorist college Brian was held up. The thief took his watch and the book he was carrying. Whenever Brian retold the story, he lamented much more the loss of the book than the loss of the watch. It was a book by David Tracy that he was reading and heavily marking up. He could understand why the thief might be interested in his watch, but he had no idea what the thief was going to do with a book by David Tracy!

I personally was very happy to have Brian as a colleague in our discipline of moral theology. He did not always agree with all my positions, and likewise I did not always agree with his, but we both appreciated the ability to share and dialogue. He was willing to express his own position but always in a very quiet and non-provocative way. This aspect of his personality made him a most valued colleague for all of us. Brian was deeply appreciated and even loved by his colleagues. He was a quiet introvert who did not have a boastful bone in his body. Wherever he has taught, Brian has always engaged in some pastoral work. In Washington he worked quite extensively with the Teams of Our Lady which were originally founded in France by Father Henri Caffarel but came to the United States in 1958. Brian's commitment to his scholarship and the Church was recognized by all. Because of a sudden change in Catholic University in 1986, four doctoral students were left stranded without a director. Brian graciously stepped into the breach and made sure that all ultimately finished their degrees.

Brian received tenure at Catholic University but by then the Accademia Alfonsiana wanted him to join their faculty in Rome. The Accademia Alfonsiana is an institute of moral theology started by the Redemptorists in Rome, which from 1960 has been able to give the Church recognized doctoral and licentiate degrees in moral theology. The Accademia has been a major source for training Catholic moral theologians from all over the world. The Accademia was a logical extension of the work and interest of St. Alphonsus, the patron of Catholic moral theologians and the founder of the Redemptorist order. Brian, because of his own Redemptorist commitment, was honored by being asked to join this faculty. He taught at the Alfonsiana from 1987 to 2005. At the Alfonsiana his influence became more global. He has made significant contributions to moral theology in Australia, the United States, Rome, and the world.

I was very pleased that Brian went to the Alfonsiana. I received my own doctorate in moral theology there and was quite proud of the fact that I was the first person awarded the doctoral degree from the Alphonsiana in 1961. I greatly appreciated my education and have tried to show my gratitude by supporting the institution over the years. I was convinced that Brian would make a significant contribution to the work of my alma mater.

Once Brian went to the Alfonsiana, we were no longer in regular contact. By that time I too had left Catholic University. Our paths would cross sporadically over the years, but I was able to follow his writings. Most of his scholarly essays appeared in *Studia Moralia*, the official journal of the Alfonsiana. I have been a subscriber to this journal ever since its inception in 1963, and it was quite easy for me to follow Brian's writings.

The depth and breadth of his writing in moral theology has been impressive. He has recognized the importance of both the theological and the philosophical aspect of our discipline. In two articles in *The Thomist* in the 1980s, he explored the meaning of proportional reason and the structures of practical reason in light of the contemporary debates. In later writings he dialogued with Jacques Derrida and Jean Luc Marion. From a theological perspective, he insisted on conversion and the role of the resurrection in Catholic moral theology. While some moral theologians emphasized either the philosophical or the theological aspects of the discipline, Brian Johnstone recognized the need for both. Later writings have emphasized the importance of gift and the centrality of the concept of gift in moral theology, bringing together both the theological and the philosophical aspects of the question. He is also very knowledgeable about the historical tradition and development of moral theology often bringing in the work of Thomas Aquinas and Alphonsus Liguori. In addition, Brian Johnstone has addressed many of the individual moral problems that have arisen for both the Church and the world. He has devoted many essays to the critical issue of peace and war, strongly stressing the presumption in the Catholic tradition against violence.

Brian returned to the Catholic University of America in 2005 and permanently retired in 2012. Even though I had left Catholic University many years before, I had a very minor role in his return. I wrote a letter in support of Catholic University of America's petition for an immigrant visa for Brian Johnstone based on his standing as an "Alien of Extraordinary Ability in the Field of Theology and Religious Studies." My three-page letter mentioned there is no doubt that Brian Johnstone has made significant and major contributions to the field of moral theology that are recognized throughout the world. There are few scholars, if any, who have published more in international scholarly journals than he. The letter then goes on to give reasons supporting my judgment about Brian.

Soon after he returned to Catholic University, he called me to ask my advice on a question. The theology faculty at Catholic University urged him to apply for the Warren Blanding Chair of Religion and Culture, an endowed chair at the university. Brian said he was somewhat hesitant to apply, because he did not think he was worthy of such an endowed chair since he had never published a monograph in moral theology. The call was vintage Brian—he did not think he was worthy of an endowed chair. I patiently explained to him the reasons why he was a very viable candidate for such a chair in light of his many contributions to moral theology. He was truly a respected senior scholar in moral theology, recognized as such in many parts of the world. His ultimate appointment to that chair not only was an honor for him, but it also brought distinction to Catholic University. In a press release announcing Brian Johnstone's appointment to the chair, the dean referred to him as a world renowned theology scholar.

There have been some indications that in his retirement he wants to write a systematic moral theology based on the concept of gift. I hope he will do so, but it is not all that necessary in light of his many contributions to the discipline. One major reason Brian was never able to write such a monograph in his teaching career is his strong commitment to his own students. While he was teaching at the Alfonsiana, he directed the dissertations of 71 doctoral students. Brian was never a hands-off director, in fact if anything he was on the scrupulous side in his working with doctoral candidates. He dedicated himself to his doctoral students at the expense of his own writing in moral theology. This is only one more reason why his colleagues and students are in such debt to Brian Johnstone.

Charles E. Curran

Elizabeth Scurlock University Professor of Human Values
Southern Methodist University

Introduction

Professor Brian V. Johnstone, C.Ss.R., has been contributing to the intellectual life of Catholicism, especially in the field of moral theology, for nearly four decades. Born and raised in Brighton, Australia, in 1958 he was professed as a Redemptorist, one of the main apostolates of the religious congregation founded by the official Roman Catholic patron of confessors and moral theologians, St. Alphonsus Maria de Liguori (1696–1787). After completing his studies at the Redemptorist Major Seminary in Ballarat, Australia, he was ordained to priesthood in 1965. From 1967 to 1968 he studied for his licentiate at the Pontifical Atheneum of Sant'Anselmo in Rome, and proceeded to Germany for further studies and research in theology at Katholisch-Theologische Fakultaet der Universität Bonn and at Fachbereich Katholische Theologie der Universität Tübingen (1968–1970). From 1971 to 1972 he pursued doctoral studies at Katholieke Universität Leuven, Belgium, and wrote his doctoral dissertation on the relationship between eschatology and ethics.

He has taught moral theology at various institutions around the world, spending significant portions of his teaching career at the Redemptorist Major Seminary in Ballerat, Australia, Yarra Theological Union, Box Hill, Australia, Catholic Theological College, Clayton, Australia, *Accademia Alfonsiana* in Rome (1987–2006), and The Catholic University of America (1981–1987 and 2006–2012). He has published numerous theological articles on many topics, including biomedical ethics, peace and war, and fundamental moral theology. Thus, it is no exaggeration to say that he has dedicated his entire life to teaching and writing theology.

INTRODUCTION

As Emeritus Professor at Australian Catholic University he is now spending the evening of his life in his Redemptorist community in Melbourne, Australia. This felicitation volume (*festschrift*) honors his scholarship and teaching with original articles written by internationally recognized theologians. It is the product of two of his former students from Rome and Washington, DC. Along with those who have contributed essays to this volume, it is their effort to honour him for his collegiality, commitment and contribution to the science of moral theology.

In "Faith, Conscience, and the Threefold Way," Dennis Billy, C.Ss.R., shows how faith purifies, illumines, and elevates our rational faculty. Weakened as it is by the anthropological dissonance resulting from humanity's primeval fall from grace, our natural power of reason is neither autonomous nor absolute. Even in its redeemed and elevated state, its heightened powers stem not from itself, but from its deeper participation in the higher reason of the Divine Logos. As creatures, everything we have comes from God and is meant to return to him and add to his glory. This holds true for every aspect of our human makeup: the physical, the emotional, the intellectual, the spiritual, and the social. Billy argues that conscience, our ability to distinguish good from evil and make judgments concerning it in concrete situations, is not exempt from this fundamental truth of God's creative, redemptive, and sanctifying plan.

Raphael Gallagher, C.Ss.R., examines the pastoral role of conscience in the moral theology of Saint Alphonsus de Ligouri and observes how unlike his contemporaries Ligouri begins his moral system with a tract on conscience that considers conscience a first principle of practical reason, but as a "practical judgment about the object of the choice to be made rather than the act of applying speculative knowledge to an analysis of the case in point." Often mistakenly categorized as a "casuist" or "probabilist," Gallagher makes the case that Ligouri's moral theory is best understood as "pastoral prudence," a moral theory that participates in the broader redemptive relationship God has with the world of which divine mercy is the defining feature. Gallagher sees Ligouri's pastorally prudent approach as a way forward for contemporary moral theology, especially after Vatican II.

In "Should the Church Change Its Teaching on Sexual Morality?" Gerald Gleeson delves into a controversial topic of Catholic sexual ethics. From the classical virtue perspective, Gleeson explores the deep metaphysical issue of body-soul unity of the human person and its implications for "gay marriage." From this perspective, Gleeson asks if it reasonable to affirm the goodness of non-marital uses of sex.

Aristide Gnada, C.Ss.R., explores the concept of the gift as the origin, norm, and finality of moral action. In the light of gift as the fundamental experience of the human persons, the moral life could be understood as a giving of oneself for the other in analogy with the divine self-giving to humanity and the gift itself as that principle of moral action. In its conceptual and formal reality, the gift reveals itself as an ethical norm which orientates the human being in his/her action and expresses the fundamental precept of natural moral law to do good and avoid evil. The gift presents itself as an anthropological and theological reality which gives meaning to the actions of the human being who is called to realize in himself/herself according to his/her own being as gift. For Gnada, the gift serves as a criterion for a theological-moral dialogue within the perspective of universal ethics, as well as an ethics of love based on the example of Jesus Christ and in the image of the One and Triune God.

Drawing on Bernard Lonergan's distinction between the classicist and historicist worldviews, James Keenan, SJ explores the natural law's relation to these approaches and the implications this relationship has for moral epistemology. The "historicist, natural law" approach Keenan advocates charts a middle course between the classicist approach, as it comes to expression in the modern tendency to absolutize universal and unalterable moral prescriptions and prohibitions, and the older high-Scholastic view of the natural law as an integral part of cultivating prudential judgment and promoting human flourishing. Keenan's approach offers a renewed understanding of nature and human reason's participation in the wisdom of God, the Creator, that is capable of critical dialogue with the sciences.

Basing his conviction that the ascension and exaltation of Christ are the horizon in which the whole New Testament is set, Anthony Kelly, C.Ss.R., shows the link between the resurrection and ascension in the gospels of Luke and John, and the Pauline writings, before demonstrating through the imagination of faith that ascension is the high-point of Christ's very mission in the sense that He returns to the Father, sends the Holy Spirit, and promises of His future return. He is now "out of this world" in the sense that His absence, presence, and return are now defined only by the infinite creativity of the Spirit. By understanding the Incarnation as an event expanding into the Resurrection and Ascension we appreciate the full reality of Incarnation and avoid needless distortions of it. Kelly's article offers a holistic theology that dynamically connects the five articles of the creed concerning the Incarnation, Crucifixion, Resurrection, Ascension and the promise of His return to the single Christ-event.

The history of moral theology since the Second Vatican Council remains unwritten. However, Terrence Kennedy, C.Ss.R., takes a first step toward writing this history by tracing the historical and conceptual development of Catholic moral theory in his article "The Rise and Fall of Normative Ethics in Recent Catholic Moral Theology." He observes post-conciliar shifts in thought toward the "new natural law theory" and explores the debates surrounding the controversial "proportionalism," while examining in detail key figures associated with the post-conciliar movements such as John Finnis and Germain Grisez.

In "Moral Theology and Practice in Anglican-Roman Catholic Dialogue: Difference, Convergence, and Diversity," Charles Sherlock explores the common moral and doctrinal issues and real historical differences that unite and divide Anglicans and Roman Catholics. While Anglican and Roman Catholic dialogue has come a long way since the Second Vatican Council, recent developments over same-sex issues have seen the convergence between these two Christian Communions shift towards exploration of the limits of reconciled diversity.

Vimal Tirimanna, C.Ss.R., highlights how traditionally Christian theology has upheld the fact that all the baptized are anointed by the Holy Spirit and consequently, the Christian community as a whole will not be allowed to fall into error by the same Spirit with regard to its faith and morals. Vatican II officially resurrected this traditional belief through the concept of *sensus fidelium* as expressed explicitly in *Lumen Gentium* No: 12. However, during the post-conciliar era the practical implications of this concept remain unexplored and the process of arriving at official Church teaching in and through the participation of all the baptized has not been followed. The result is a glaring gap between the teachings of the clerical hierarchy and the practice and belief of the rest of the Church. Tirimanna insists that while the majority or public opinion cannot be equated to *sensus fidelium*, there is an indispensable need to consult and listen to the laity if the Church's teaching is to be credible in the eyes of the contemporary believers.

In his article "Las 'Obras de Misericordia' Y La Teología Moral", Marciano Vidal, C.Ss.R., offers a reflection on the traditional Christian works of mercy, paying particular attention to fraternal correction, the third spiritual work of mercy. In going about his task, he first gives a brief but comprehensive history of the works of mercy in moral theology. He also points out how these works of mercy (though accentuated within Vatican II documents) have had little impact on theological reflection in recent times. Vidal discusses the ethical nature of fraternal correction and suggests how it is possible to fraternally correct superiors, institutions, and structures, as has been done by Pope Francis.

This felicitation volume covers a wide range of themes in the Christian moral life with the intention of challenging the reader to reflect upon the present while contemplating the future of moral theology, just as Professor Brian Johnstone's work has guided his readers, colleagues, and students through the present while pointing a way forward for the future. It seems fitting that this volume of essays in honor of him follow the same course he has charted throughout his career.

Robert Koerpel and Vimal Tirimanna, C.Ss.R.

1

Faith, Conscience, and the Threefold Way

Dennis J. Billy, C.Ss.R.

Catholic theology looks to faith *and* reason, to revelation *and* natural law, for guidance in solving the pressing moral issues of the day. In doing so, it recognizes that such issues must take into account two important facets of reality: the human and the divine, the spheres of the natural and supernatural. These spheres "mutually support each other" by offering "a purifying critique and a stimulus to pursue the search for deeper understanding."[1] What is more, they relate to one another in a unique way. Man is *capax Dei* ("capable of God").[2] Human beings can be aware of God and enter into relationship with him. "Grace," moreover, "perfects nature."[3] It changes nature not by destroying it and starting anew, but by transforming it from the inside out.

These fundamental insights of Catholic theology have special relevance for the moral life. Human reason is not an autonomous arbiter of moral action, but an active participant in a higher, eternal power that has implanted a desire for the good in the human heart and left a knowledge of that good in the inclinations of human nature fully revealed in the person of Jesus, the Eternal Wisdom of the Father and Incarnation of the Divine

---

1. John Paul II, *Faith and Reason*, no. 100.
2. See Aquinas, *Summa Theologica*, I–II, q. 113, a. 10, resp.
3. Ibid., I, q. 1, a. 8, ad 2m. See also The International Theological Commission, *In Search of a Universal Ethic*, no. 101.

Logos.⁴ Faith puts us in close contact with the Risen Christ, whose Spirit renews our minds and hearts, interiorizes the law for us, and enables us to live the moral life.⁵ It reforms reason and elevates conscience by lifting it from its fallen state to redeem, sanctify, and ultimately divinize it.

What Is Conscience?

Conscience is a moral compass that gives us the proper bearings to find our way to our final end and destination. At its most basic level, it is "an imprint on us of the divine light,"⁶ a lantern that lights the way ahead and warns us of dangers lurking in the darkness. It is an instrument for helping us make our way safely through life to the secure harbor on other side. It is the voice of God within our hearts that enables us to find our way home, a law imprinted in our hearts that helps us to distinguish good from evil. "The voice of conscience," John Paul II tells us, "has always clearly recalled that there are truths and moral values for which one must be prepared to give up one's life."⁷ That voice gives witness to the truth and is a participation in the Eternal Wisdom of God. This participation can be numbed and dulled, covered over by any number of internal and external factors (e.g., bad habits, one's upbringing, a lack of moral education, bad company, sin), but it can never be fully extinguished.⁸ Like a fire that has been left unattended, it may, at times, seem to have burned out, but a tiny spark always remains buried beneath the smoldering coals and ashes to be kindled anew and set aflame.

Conscience enables us to distinguish authentic goods from apparent goods and to orient them toward God, our ultimate good. It urges us on to do and actively pursue what is good. Its ability to distinguish good from evil stems from its participation in a higher reason, which perfectly reflects the goodness of God himself and is, in fact, the Word of God. Conscience is ultimately "knowledge with" (*con-scientia*) Christ. It is a participated

---

4. See The International Theological Commission, *In Search of a Universal Ethic*, nos. 103–9.

5. See John Paul II, *The Splendor of Truth*, nos. 83, 103.

6. Aquinas, *Summa Theologica*, I–II, q. 91, a. 2, resp.; John Paul II, *The Splendor of Truth*, no. 42.

7. John Paul II, *The Splendor of Truth*, no. 94.

8. Aquinas, *Summa Theologica*, I–II, q. 79, a. 12, resp.; I–II, q. 94, a. 6, resp. See also Second Vatican Council, *The Pastoral Constitution*, no. 16.

knowledge given to every human being in the depths of his heart. As the Apostle Paul attests: "They [the Gentiles] show that what the law requires is written on their hearts, to which their own conscience also bears witness" (Rom 2:15).[9] As the fathers of the Second Vatican Council assert, "man has in his heart a law written by God; to obey it is the very dignity of man; according to it he will be judged."[10] Through conscience, the finger of God touches the soul, inscribes his law in it, and thus empowers it to distinguish good from evil. It derives this power not from itself, but by means of a participated theonomy in the wisdom and goodness of God, the one and only Absolute.[11]

More specifically, conscience is a cohesive, unified whole with three singular (albeit related) dimensions: capacity, process, and judgment.[12] It is a *capacity* insofar as it represents our ability to know the fundamental principles of the natural law and hold them (contain them, if you will) in an ongoing, lasting manner. In Thomistic terminology, this dimension is represented by the habit of the practical intellect known as synderesis.[13] This habit is a natural disposition of reason that, once it receives the necessary data from sense experience and understands the concepts they represent, immediately recognizes as a self-evident principle that *good* must be done and *evil* avoided. This habitual knowledge extends not only to this primary principle of the natural law, but also to the basic inclinations of human nature: *self-preservation*, which man has in common with all substances; *sexual union* and the *rearing of offspring*, which is has in common with the rest of animal world; and the desire for *truth* and *life in society*, which it possesses by virtue of its rational side of his nature.[14]

If conscience is a capacity by virtue of its ability to assess and maintain continual contact with the fundamental principles of the natural law, it is also a *process*, because it also involves a sustained, back-and-forth movement of deliberation. Unlike angels, whose knowledge is whole, entire, and immediately intuitive, human beings exercise their rational power in

9. All Scripture quotations come from The Holy Bible: New Revised Standard Version with Apocrypha.

10. Second Vatican Council, *The Pastoral Constitution*, no. 22.

11. John Paul II, *The Splendor of Truth*, no. 41.

12. See *Catechism of the Catholic Church*, no. 1780; O'Connell, *Principles of Catholic Morality*, 110–12; Gula, *Reason Informed by Faith*, 132.

13. Aquinas, *Summa Theologica*, I, q. 79, a. 12, resp.

14. Ibid., I-II, q. 94, a. 2, resp. See also Pinckaers, *The Sources of Christian Ethics*, 400–56.

a largely discursive manner.[15] That is to say, they carefully weigh the pros and cons of a moral dilemma before reaching a conclusion. In Thomistic terminology, a human act is one of deliberated will, an action that involves a linear, discursive movement of reason that arrives at a conclusion and is freely accepted and executed by the will. The deliberating side of this equation represents this second level of conscience. Although Aquinas prefers the twofold nomenclature of synderesis/conscience in his presentation of our basic moral knowledge, he devotes a considerable amount of time and space to the process of deliberation (*deliberatio*) in his analysis of the human act.[16] For him, moral deliberation flows from the habitual moral knowledge held by synderesis, applies that knowledge to concrete situations, and draws a conclusion about what is to be done.

Conscience (*conscientia*) is also a *judgment*, one that flows from our stable pool of fundamental moral principles (*synderesis*) and represents the conclusion of a process of rational deliberation (*deliberatio*) about what good must be pursued by applying these principles and those derived from them in a given situation. Aquinas calls conscience an act of the practical reason: it offers witness about whether good or evil has been done; it incites or binds by offering a judgment about whether something should or should not be done; and it excuses, accuses, or torments by determining whether or not something has been well done.[17] For Basil of Caesarea, it is "the natural power of judgment" and for John of Damascus, it is the "law of our intellect."[18] When seen in this light, it is an act that flows from the power of the practical reason, is sustained by the habit of synderesis, and refined by the process of deliberation. It represents the final interface between man's internal judgment about good and evil and the choices before him. Its purpose is to make judgments about the goodness of particular ends and to insure that they are properly oriented toward man's ultimate end in God.

---

15. Ibid., I, q. 58, a. 3, resp.

16. Ibid., I, q. 79, aa. 12–13; I–II, q. 14, aa. 1–6. See also, Ratzinger, *On Conscience*, 30–38; O'Connell, *Principles of Catholic Morality*, 110–12; Gula, *Reason Informed by Faith*, 132.

17. Aquinas, *Summa Theologica*, I, q. 79, a. 13, resp.

18. Cited by Aquinas in ibid.

Humanity's Anthropological Dissonance

As comprehensive and insightful as it may seem, this presentation limits itself to the natural order and therefore remains incomplete. A proper understanding of conscience comes only when it is examined against the graced backdrop of the Christian narrative of humanity's creation, fall, and redemption: "Only in the mystery of Christ's Redemption do we discover the 'concrete' possibilities of man."[19] For this reason, we must not focus on "man dominated by lust," but on "man redeemed by Christ."[20]

In its doctrine of original sin, the Catholic Church affirms that humanity's primeval fall from the graced innocence and goodness of its created state had serious repercussions throughout its entire anthropological makeup.[21] Whatever happened at that momentous event at the dawn of human history, every dimension of our nature—physical, emotional, intellectual, spiritual, social—was seriously damaged. The deep harmony of our interior life was disrupted and led us to become out of sync with ourselves, others, and God. Our intellects became darkened, our wills weakened, our passions unruly, our bodies subject to death, our relationships tense and troubled.[22] If the Christ-event is to be taken seriously, it must be understood in the context of some deliberate and chosen evil on the part of our collective humanity at the dawn of time. God entered our world, because sin had already done so. The New Adam was born to offset the Old (cf. Rom 5:12–21; 1 Cor 15:21–22).[23]

This anthropological dissonance manifests itself most profoundly in our ability to distinguish good from evil. The account of the Fall in Genesis uses figurative language to say that man abused his freedom by taking for himself what belonged properly to God alone: the power to decide what is good and what is evil (cf. Gen 2:17).[24] This temptation "to be like God" (Gen 3:5) is deeply rooted in the human psyche and leads us to place ourselves at the center of our moral universe.[25] Even today, our weakness of nature resulting from this primeval fall from grace impedes our ability to focus

19. See John Paul II, *The Splendor of Truth*, no. 103.
20. Ibid.
21. See *Catechism of the Catholic Church*, no. 390; Denzinger, *Enchiridion*, (D2b) 1234–35 [The lettered-numbered references are to Denzinger's systematic index].
22. *Catechism of the Catholic Church*, nos. 402–9, 1264.
23. Ibid., no. 411.
24. See also John Paul II, *The Splendor of Truth*, nos. 35, 102.
25. Ibid., no. 86.

our lives entirely on God. As a result, we time and again put apparent goods in the place of our ultimate end and true good. We worship false gods—pleasure, power, and possessions (to name but a few)—and lose touch with God's providential plan for our lives (cf. Matt 4:1–11; 1 Tim 6:9–10).[26]

This original wound at the dawn of time has wreaked havoc not only on us, but also on the whole created world. Because we stand at the summit of God's creation, our primeval choice for evil has had a ripple effect throughout the universe. These repercussions manifest themselves in a number of concrete ways, and can be understood especially if we think of humanity as a microcosm of the universe. The results of this fall from grace are still experienced to this day:

- We have lost God's friendship.
- We feel alienated from ourselves, others, and creation.
- Our minds have become enfeebled.
- Our wills have been weakened.
- Our passions and emotions have become disordered.
- We experience work as a burden.
- We become ill and suffer disease of every kind.
- We grow feeble with time and age without grace.
- We encounter death, are afraid of it, and dread its coming.[27]

Our capacity to distinguish good from evil, as well as authentic goods from merely apparent goods, and to place ourselves instead of God at the center of things has darkened our minds and inhibited our ability to see the way to God. The fire of divine light that once burned brightly in our minds and hearts has dwindled to a small, smoldering ember. The light which once illumined our minds has dwindled to a mere spark. As a result, we see things dimly; reason's eyes are covered with cataracts. We do not see the world as we should. We make mistakes in judgments. We stumble and fall. We lose our way. The forms of conscience guiding people today (e.g., true, erroneous, certain, doubtful, perplexed, scrupulous, lax, probable, etc.)[28]

26. See also Michael, *An Introduction to Spiritual Direction*, 67–71.

27. On the effects of original sin, see Aquinas, *Summa Theologica*, I-II, q. 85, aa. 1–6; II-II, q. 164, aa1–2. See also Ott, *Fundamentals of Catholic Dogma*, 112–14; Denzinger, *Enchiridion* (2b), 1234–35; Billy, *Evangelical Kernels*, 65–76.

28. For a manualist treatment of these various forms of conscience, see Davis, *Moral and Pastoral Theology*, 65–80.

are but symptoms of our fragmented humanity and ultimately derive from humanity's primeval fall from grace that has resulted in the dimming of reason's light. The fire has lost much of its fuel and is a mere remnant of its former glory—that is, until the coming of Christ

Humanity's Re-creation

God's remedy for this primordial human sinfulness is to initiate a new creation through the Incarnation and Paschal Mystery of his Son, the Divine Logos and Eternal Word of the Father. This new creation does not destroy the old, but heals it of its wounds and elevates it to new heights. Jesus, our Redeemer, is the New Adam, the firstborn of the new creation. Through Him, human pride is overcome by divine humility. The cross becomes the new tree of life. Death is cast out of both tomb and heart. Humanity is reborn. We have cast off the old self and put on the new (cf. Eph 4:22–24). Our human nature is divinized by Christ's selfless, redeeming love. The abiding presence of the Spirit begins in us a gradual process of transformation that gives us the freedom of the sons and daughters of God and new life in the Risen Lord. Through Christ's gift of his Spirit, the New Law of grace overcomes the Old Law of sin and death. Conscience, our *scintilla animae* ("spark of the soul") and guiding moral lantern, is flooded with divine light.[29] We are empowered not only to distinguish good from evil with ease, but also to do and pursue goodness and truth with all our heart, mind, soul, and strength. The words of the Apostle Paul ring true: "It is no longer I who live, but it is Christ who lives in me" (Gal 2:20). Christ continues to live out his paschal mystery in the members of his body, the Church.[30]

In Luke's Gospel, Jesus says, "I have come to bring fire to the earth, and how I wish it were already kindled" (Luke 12:49). In the Gospel of John, he calls himself the "light of the world" (John 8:12). In the Acts of the Apostles, his Spirit hovered over the heads of his disciples in the form of "tongues of fire" at the birth of the Church at Pentecost (Acts 2:3). The image of fire is an apt metaphor for the moral-spiritual life. Fire purifies, enlightens, warms, and attracts. If tended properly, it can do much good; if left untended, it can wreak havoc and destruction, or simply dwindle in size and peter out. In the words of Hebrews, "Jesus Christ is the same yesterday

---

29. See Aquinas, *Summa Theologica*, I–II, q. 108, a. 1, resp.; John Paul II, *The Splendor of Truth*, no. 59.

30. See Marmion, *Christ*, 406–10; Billy, *Evangelical Kernels*, 17–31.

and today and forever" (Heb 13:8). Conscience—whether in its created, fallen, or redeemed form—is a reflection of the light of Christ. Jesus came to redeem to world and, in doing so, heal our broken and troubled consciences: "For my yoke is easy, and my burden is light" (Matt 11:30).

In the Gospel of John, Jesus says "I have come as light into the world, so that everyone who believes in me should not remain in darkness" (John 12:46). Faith in Christ is the lantern that lights the way for us. In the Gospels, Jesus emphasizes the importance of having faith in him. In Matthew's Gospel, he says that if the faith of a mustard seed can move mountains (cf. Matt 17:20). In Mark's Gospel, he observes the faith of those who bring their paralyzed friend to him and decides not only to heal him, but also to forgive him his sins (cf. Mark 2:1–12). In the Gospel of Luke, he tells the woman who kisses his feet and anoints them with oil that her faith has saved her (cf. Luke 7:50). Later, he heals a blind man and tells him the same thing (cf. Luke 18:42). The centrality of faith in Christ permeates much of the New Testament. In the Acts of the Apostles, Peter says that it was by faith in the name of Jesus Christ that a man lame from birth was made to walk (Acts 3:16). In his letter to the Romans, Paul says that the righteous one lives by faith (Rom 1:17). In First Corinthians, he identifies faith as one of the three things that last (cf. 1 Cor 13:13). The letter of James emphasizes the complementarity of faith and works (cf. Jas 2:17). These are but a few of the New Testament verses that emphasize the centrality of faith in Christ for the Christian life.

Faith is an infused theological virtue of our faculty of reason; along with other theological virtues of hope and charity, it forms the foundation of the Christian moral life.[31] It is, in the words of John Paul II, "a lived knowledge of Christ, a living remembrance of his commandments, and a truth to be lived out."[32] It strengthens human reason and enables us to see the world through the eyes of Christ. It prepares us for the Spirit's gifts of wisdom, understanding, and knowledge. It builds on nature and gives rise to the supernatural organism by opening a person up to receiving other infused virtues and beginning a gradual process of transformation that conforms a person more and more unto the person of Christ. Through faith, we commit ourselves entirely to God and accept all that the Church proposes for our belief. As Christians, we are called to keep the faith, live it,

---

31. See Aquinas, *Summa Theologica*, I–II, q. 62, a. 3, resp.; *Catechism of the Catholic Church*, nos. 1812–16; Aumann, *Spiritual Theology*, 247–75.

32. John Paul II, *The Splendor of Truth*, no. 88.

profess it, bear witness to it, and spread it. If we do not acknowledge faith in Christ before men, he will not acknowledge us before God the Father. John Paul II warns of the "destructive dichotomy . . . which separates faith from morality" and challenges Christians to "rediscover *the newness of faith and its power to judge* a prevalent and all-intrusive culture."[33] Without the light of faith, we are unable to make our way home to God.[34]

The Threefold Way

"The light of faith," as Pope Francis reminds us, "is capable of illuminating every aspect of human existence."[35] It is born of "an encounter with the living God."[36] It steeps us in God's love and transforms us in such a way that it gives us "new eyes to see" and "a great promise of fulfillment."[37] What is more, it follows a threefold path of purgation, illumination, and union. In the encyclical *Deus caritas est*, Pope Benedict XVI says this about this threefold influence:

> Faith by its specific nature is an encounter with the living God—an encounter opening up new horizons extending beyond the sphere of reason. But it is also a purifying force for reason itself. From God's standpoint, faith liberates reason from its blind spots and therefore helps it to be ever more fully itself. Faith enables reason to do its work more effectively and to see its proper object more clearly.[38]

In this passage, the pope emeritus ties reason specifically to this threefold spiritual-moral journey. Faith *purifies* reason by freeing it of its blind spots and helping it to become itself more fully. As the fathers of the Second Vatican Council remind us, authentic human values "are often wrenched from their rightful function by the taint in man's heart, and hence stand in need of purification."[39] At its most basic level, a blind spot overlooks something,

---

33. Ibid.

34. See Matt 10:32–33; *Catechism of Catholic Church*, no. 1816; Pieper, *Faith. Hope. Love*, 91–98.

35. Francis, *The Light of Faith*, no. 4.

36. Ibid.

37. Ibid.

38. Benedict XVI, *Deus caritas est*, no. 28. For the purification of reason by faith, see Hahn, "Bringing Theologians," 21–24.

39. Second Vatican Council, *The Pastoral Constitution*, no. 11.

because it has not been directly (or even indirectly) observed. Depending on what is not taken into account, this failure to see can have minimal or dire consequences. When applied to reason, these blind spots depend to a large extent on the concept of rationality employed in a particular instance. One such blind spot revolves around the claim that reason itself has a history and is shaped by that narrative.[40] Some scholars would deny this claim and ascribe reason a purely transcendental, ahistorical nature; others would embrace it fully and say that it is completely shaped by historical consciousness; still others would ascribe only a limited validity to the claim and say that it has a fixed nature that adapts to historical circumstances and changes over time. In some ways, the history of Western philosophy represents a movement from myth to analogy to univocal thinking to equivocation, deconstruction, and relativity.[41] While Pope Benedict has a historical sensibility and recognizes the impact of history on how reason is understood by philosophers, he would insist on its transcendent character and its existence apart from human thought and hence its freedom from the tradition within which it is passed on and humanity's own subjective experience of it and that tradition.[42] The purification of reason takes place by seeking out the natural law inherent in all of creation and finding its fulfillment in the new law of grace.[43]

Faith does not merely purify reason; it also *illumines* it by helping it "to see its proper object more clearly."[44] As the fathers of the Second Vatican Council assert, it "throws a new light on everything, manifests God's design for man's total vocation, and thus directs the mind to solutions which are fully human."[45] John Paul II agrees, it "sharpens the inner eye, opening the mind to discover in the flux of events the workings of Providence."[46] Abba Philimon, one of the early desert fathers puts it this way: ". . . just as the eye is attentive to sensible things and is fascinated by what it sees, so the purified intellect is attentive to intelligible realities and becomes so rapt

---

40. See MacIntyre, *After Virtue*, 204–25.

41. See Billy, "The Unfolding of a Tradition," 9–31.

42. See Ratzinger, *On Conscience*, 64–70; Odozor, *Moral Theology*, 123–27, 132.

43. See The International Theological Commission, *In Search of a Universal Ethic*, no. 99.

44. Benedict XVI, *God is Love*, no. 28. See also John Paul II, *The Splendor of Truth*, nos. 88–89.

45. Second Vatican Council, *The Pastoral Constitution*, no. 11.

46. John Paul II, *Faith and Reason*, no. 16.

by spiritual contemplation that it is hard to tear it away."[47] St. Bonaventure tells us that meditation enlightens our darkened minds.[48] Similarly, St. Alphonsus de Liguori asserts: "He who does not make mental prayer has but little light and little strength."[49] Authentic prayer requires faith. Reason's true enlightenment comes not in a false autonomy that narrows reason's scope and separates it from the life of faith, but by a fundamental openness to the transcendent that purifies it, enlightens it, and helps it to recognize its of own proper limits.

Faith opens up new horizons that extend beyond the sphere of reason. It invites reason to accompany it in examining unexplored frontiers of the human person in a mutually beneficial way. Reason is not autonomous, but a participation in a much larger reality that it shares with faith. It is "the voice and interpreter of some higher reason to which our spirit and our freedom must be subject."[50] It flows from the same source as faith and is destined to find its way back to that same source. In its present state, reason shares in humanity's fallen state and needs to be healed by the transforming and sanctifying grace of the Spirit. For some, this fundamental truth may itself be a blind spot, since humanity in its present state is generally blind to the realities of faith. Like God himself, however, who chose to enter our world and encounter us through our own experience, these realities penetrate the mind and promise to transform all those who seek the truth with a sincere heart. In the words of the fathers of the Second Vatican Council: "the Holy Spirit in a manner known only to God offers to every man the possibility of being associated with this paschal mystery."[51]

Faith ultimately leads to *union*. It purifies and illumines reason to enable us to enter into a deeper and more intimate encounter with the living God. It leads us into this personal encounter by directing our attention away from undue attachments, correcting and strengthening our spiritual vision, and enabling us to stand in right relationship with the very ground of our existence. By outlining the limits of our natural powers of reason, it opens up new horizons which, left to ourselves, we would be unaware of and unable to pursue. It opens up for us the possibility of knowing God personally

---

47. See McGinn, *The Philokalia*, 127.
48. Bonaventure, *The Triple Way*, 69.
49. Liguori, *The Dignity and Duties of Priests*, 290–91.
50. John Paul II, *The Splendor of Truth*, no. 44.
51. Second Vatican Council, *The Pastoral Constitution*, no. 22; Denzinger, *Enchiridion* (C4fi), 1215.

and living in close communion with him. It is a grace-filled disposition that renews our minds and hearts. It opens up the door of friendship that leads to a mutual indwelling of hearts. This mutual indwelling effects a gradual transformation of our humanity that divinizes us and enables us to share in the very life of God himself. "God became man," we are told, "so that man might become divine."[52] This soteriological principle lies at the heart of the Christian message and has relevance for every dimension of our human makeup: the physical, emotional, intellectual, spiritual, and social. It tells us that every part of us will all be transformed in Christ, the New Man and firstborn of the New Creation. By taking on our wounded humanity and hanging it on the cross, Christ opened up the heavens and allowed the divine light to shed its light once more in the darkened recesses of the human heart. In doing so:

- He reestablishes our friendship with God.
- He heals our relationship with ourselves, others, and creation.
- He renews our minds.
- He strengthens our wills.
- He orders our passions and emotions.
- He helps us find meaning and joy in our work.
- He accompanies us in suffering and heals us in due time.
- He is present to us at all stages of our lives.
- He gives us the courage to face death and look beyond it.[53]

Because of his Incarnation, passion, death, and resurrection, the spark of divine love has been rekindled in our hearts and our wounded humanity placed on the road to recovery. Jesus' love for us, however, does not stop there: he promises not only to heal us of our wounds, but also to share in his divinity. He does so by lifting us beyond our earthly horizons and inviting to enter into intimate fellowship with the divine. As a result, those

---

52. See 2 Pet 1:4; Irenaeus, *Against the Heresies*, 448–49; Athanasius, *On the Incarnation of the Word*, 8.54; *Catechism of the Catholic Church*, no. 460.

53. On the work redemption in Christ, see Aquinas, *Summa Theologica*, III, q. 49, aa. 1–6. See also Ott, *Fundamentals of Catholic Dogma*, 175–90; Denzinger, *Enchiridion* (D7b), 1238–39; Billy, *Evangelical Kernels*, 95–108.

who walk the path of holiness, the Church's saints, "light up every period of history by reawakening its moral sense."[54]

Observations

As grace builds on nature, so faith transforms conscience by divinizing it and enabling it to function on an elevated plane. The remarks that follow seek to elicit some of the implications of this transformative process in our moral knowledge.

1. To begin with, faith in Christ reshapes secularized Western culture's narrative concerning reason's progressive (and autonomous) march toward enlightenment and scientific development by calling it back to a much earlier narrative, one rooted in humanity's recognition of its anthropological dissonance and need for redemption. If the narrative of the Enlightenment has run its course and been displaced with postmodernism and its deconstructionist assault on reason, the resulting sea of relativistic uncertainties offers even less solace than the narrative it has displaced. The faith-based narrative of salvation history invites the secularized West to retrieve its past and face its future with hope. When seen in this light, faith offers reason hope, and hope inspires conscience to see, judge, and act toward an ultimate good and end in God.[55]

2. The Catholic faith recognizes an intimate relationship between being and action. Action flows from being—and vice versa. Actions informed by a deep faith life reverberate both outwardly and inwardly. They not only the world without, but also a person's inner life. Actions, in other words, help shape the soul. Those who practice their faith with sincere hearts deepen it and, in doing so, develop a deeper capacity to see, judge, and act in the world in a Christian manner. "Putting on the mind of Christ" (Cf. Rom 13:14; Gal 3:27; 1 Cor 2:16; Phil 2:5–11) means seeking to view the world as Jesus did. It involves using our faith as a point of departure for everything we do. This "spirituality of practice" sharpens our spiritual eyes and enables us to see what needs to be done in a particular situation with more clarity

---

54. John Paul II, *The Splendor of Truth*, no. 93.

55. On the generation of hope by faith, see Aquinas, *Summa Theologica*, I–II, q. 62, a. 4, resp. See also Pieper, *Faith. Hope. Love*, 103.

and accuracy. It shapes the Christian conscience and draws us more deeply into the life of the Church by enabling us to think and act in communion with the other members of Christ's body.[56]

3. Catholic theology maintains a delicate balance between faith and reason. It recognizes that human beings capable of good and therefore capable of God.[57] It draws an intimate connection between morality and spirituality and concludes that the moral question is essentially a religious one.[58] God is the Ultimate Good: all other goods derive their goodness from Him and are destined to return to Him. Human beings have their beginning and end in God. During our earthly sojourn, we yearn for Him and seek to make our way toward Him. He is the one thing that matters. In the words of St. Augustine of Hippo: "you have made us for yourself, and our hearts are restless until they can find peace in you."[59] For Catholics, faith is not opposed to reason, but meets it on its own ground, guides it, and ultimately perfects it.

4. Conscience makes judgments about the past, present, and future. It must have recourse to the internal senses of memory and imagination, both of which have themselves been affected by the anthropological dissonance of humanity's fall from grace. Through faith in Christ, grace gradually transforms these internal senses and enables to remember the past, experience the present, and imagine the future in the light of God's salvific love. As a result, these senses empower conscience to make its judgments concerning the past, present, and future with a deeper sense of God's loving presence in a person's life. Conscience, in other words, begins to see Christ as the true Lord of history who works at all times to bring good out of evil and who allows nothing to escape his providential plan for the world.

5. A life of faith deepens our relationship with Christ, who identifies himself as "the way, the truth, and the life" (John 14:6). This relationship deepens our appreciation of the intrinsic relationship between conscience and truth. Christ is the truth, and truth is the guardian of conscience. The person of Christ is absolute truth against which we judge what must be done or not done. Conscience is determined not

---

56. See John Paul II, *The Splendor of Truth*, no. 71.
57. Ibid., no. 9.
58. Ibid., nos. 9, 98.
59. Augustine, *Confessions*, 17.

by individual opinion, or majority rule, or a statistical compilation of the social sciences, but by the intimate dialogue with Christ that takes place in the depths of our hearts in concert with the Church's teaching authority. The Spirit guides us from within and without by means of a participated theonomy. In Christ, God has given us a concrete example of what it means to live according to the law of love. Christ's Spirit empowers us to live by this law as members of his body. The freedom of conscience is a freedom in the truth and a freedom in the faith. It manifests itself by means of a close adherence to the truth as embodied in the person of Christ.[60]

6. Because builds on nature, it follows that faith transforms the three dimensions of conscience—capacity, process, and judgment—and elevates them to new heights. It does so by deepening our ability to delve beneath appearances of things, thus sensing the reality of the spiritual world. It helps us to recognize the true value of created things. It sets us on a course of undue attachment to these things so that we can focus more fully on our true and ultimate good. It enhances out ability us to distinguish between true and apparent goods. It enables us to make judgments in our daily lives that clearly distinguish between true goods and merely apparent goods. Faith deepens out capacity for God and involves us in a journey that ultimately brings us to a face-to-face encounter with God. It heals our wounded nature, restores our reasoning powers to their former heights, and deepens our participation in that higher reason in which it shares.

7. Faith works in conjunction with other theological virtues to enable the whole person to see God, focus on him as our ultimate end, and enter into intimate relationship with him. All three of these virtues—faith, hope, and love—work together in a circular manner to draw a person ever more deeply into the mystery of the divine. That mystery involves not only seeing God's will for us, but also implementing it in our daily lives. Through the grace of the Spirit, these virtues impact our naturally acquired virtues—prudence, justice, fortitude, and temperance —by empowering them to function on a divinized, supernatural level. In doing so, they transform our conscience, which resides with the practical intellect and thus closely associated with the virtue of prudence. The infused virtue of prudence presupposes faith

---

60. See John Paul II, *The Splendor of Truth*, nos. 41, 54–64.

and the other theological virtues and empowers us to make sound judgments that lead to God in a free and spontaneous manner, as if it were a second nature for us to do so.[61]

8. Faith purifies conscience, illumines it, and brings it to an even deeper encounter with the voice of God. It does so by opening us to the movement of the Spirit in our lives and allowing its gifts and promptings to transform us so that our minds will be more and more conformed to Christ's. If the grace of the Spirit is the New Law given us by virtue of Christ's paschal mystery, then the gifts of the Spirit are the fullness of that Law in that they perfect our rational and appetitive powers. The gifts of the Spirit most closely associated with reason are wisdom, knowledge, understanding, and counsel. Those associated with the appetite are fortitude, piety, and fear of the Lord. These gifts are infused by God and dispose us to be more open to divine inspiration. They assist our capacity to make sound judgments in different ways and enable us to see God more clearly and follow him more spontaneously.[62]

9. We deepen and intensify our life of faith by turning to God with heartfelt prayer. The Apostle Paul exhorts us to "pray without ceasing" (1 Thess 5:17). Constant prayer develops in us an attitude of trust in God and helps us to invite us into the smallest details of our lives. What could be easier than to say, "Lord, help me!" or "Lord come to my assistance!"[63] Prayer is nothing more than lifting our hearts and minds to God.[64] It is morally necessary for our salvation.[65] When we enter into dialogue with God in a constant and ongoing manner, our minds and hearts are gently shaped by the encounter. The practice of heartfelt prayer brings us closer to God by shaping our souls and its powers of reason and will to become more attuned to him. A life of prayer makes deepens our faith and contributes to its purifying, enlightening, and unifying effects on our conscience. Through the various types of prayer—vocal, mental, contemplative, liturgical—we direct every part of our human makeup toward God. God, in turn,

---

61. See Aquinas, *Summa Theologica*, I-II, q. 62, a. 4, resp.; q. 63, a. 3, resp., a.4, resp.; II-II, q. 47, a. 14, resp.

62. Ibid., I-II, q. 68, a. 1. resp.

63. See Liguori, *Prayer*, 98.

64. See John of Damascus, *On the Orthodox Faith*, 3.24; *Catechism of the Catholic Church*, no. 2559.

65. Liguori, *Prayer*, 98.

orients his entire self in us by sending his Spirit to dwell in our hearts and deepening our understanding of the divine mysteries.

10. Finally, faith enables us to focus our lives on the person of Jesus Christ, "the Alpha and Omega, the first and the last, the beginning and the end" (Rev 22:13). This focus on the person of Jesus Christ personalizes history by turning philosophical teleology into faith-based eschatology. It enables us to view the movement of history not merely in terms of an abstract end, but in terms of our personal relationship with God. It also helps us to view our lives not merely in terms of our movement toward God, but also in terms of God's movement toward us. What took place in the mystery of the Incarnation was the beginning of a much larger process by which Christ recapitulates all things in himself. Faith helps us to see this process at work, even in our individual actions. It shows us that natural law has it beginning and end in Christ, the Eternal Law, that conscience, in the end, is ultimately "knowledge with" Christ, and that the goal of our lives is to live in Christ and for Christ to live in us.

These observations draw out some of the implications of faith's impact on conscience formation and the moral life. While in no way exhaustive, they point out the intimate relationship between spirituality and morality in the life of the Christian and offer a number of important insights into faith's transforming effect on our knowledge of the good and attempt to embody it in our lives. If nothing else, they encourage to take to heart the words of the Apostle Paul: "we walk by faith, not by sight" (2 Cor 5:7).

Conclusion

Faith purifies, illumines, and elevates our rational faculty. Weakened as it is by the anthropological dissonance resulting from humanity's primeval fall from grace, our natural power of reason is neither autonomous nor absolute. Even in its redeemed and elevated state, its heightened powers stem not from itself, but from its deeper participation in the higher reason of the Divine Logos. As creatures, everything we have comes from God and is meant to return to him and add to his glory. This holds true for every aspect of our human makeup: the physical, the emotional, the intellectual, the spiritual, and the social. Conscience, our ability to distinguish good from evil and make judgments concerning it in concrete situations, is not exempt from this fundamental truth of God's creative, redemptive, and sanctifying plan.

Faith transforms conscience on every level of its makeup: its *capacity* for the good, the *process* it goes through to distinguish good from evil, and the *judgments* it makes regarding the action to be done. It expands reason's horizons to see that human beings are capable not merely of good, but of God and that questions concerning the good to be done are essentially religious at their source. It reshapes the narrative underlying reason's functioning from one of continual enlightened progress to one rooted in Christ's redemptive mystery. It reshapes our memory and imagination to assist reason in interpreting the past, present, and future in the light of God's redemptive love. It helps reason to recognize it limitations and, as a result, its need for assistance in interpreting God's Word and applying it to the issues facing the world today.

Faith enlightens every dimension of human existence. As grace builds on nature, so faith elevates reason. Conscience is a part of this transformation, since it is a specific function of our practical reasoning and represents that dimension of our rational faculty, which makes practical decisions about the concrete steps we must make in our journey. Faith brings into focus our journey's end, the goal toward which our actions are to tend. It heightens the teleological dimension of the moral life and connects it to the spiritual quest. It reminds reason that it is called to a participation in an even deeper vision and that life on earth is oriented toward a life to come. In the end, it reminds us that conscience is meant to bring us to a "knowledge with" God, one that involves not merely "knowledge about," but an intimate union of hearts.

Bibliography

Aquinas, Thomas. *Summa Theologica*. Translated by Fathers of the English Dominican Province. New York: Benzinger, 1947. http://www.ccel.org/ccel/aquinas/summa.i.html.

Augustine. *The Confessions*. Translated by Rex Warner. New York: New American Library, 1963.

Athanasius. *On the Incarnation of the Word*. In *Athansius: Selected Works and Letters*, edited by Philip Shaff and Henry Wace. Nicene and Post-Nicene Fathers of the Christian Church, Second Series 4. Edinburgh: T. & T. Clark, 1885. http://www.ccel.org/ccel/athanasius/incarnation.

Aumann, Jordan. *Spiritual Theology*. London: Sheed & Ward, 1980.

Benedict XVI. *God is Love* (*Deus caritas est*). Encyclical Letter, December 25, 2005. http://w2.vatican.va/content/benedict-xvi/en/encyclicals/documents/hf_ben-xvi_enc_20051225_deus-caritas-est.html.

Billy, Dennis J. *Evangelical Kernels: A Theological Spirituality of Religious Life*. Staten Island, NY: Alba, 1993.

———. "The Unfolding of a Tradition." In *Spirituality and Morality: Integrating Prayer and Action*, edited by Dennis J. Billy and Donna Orsuto, 9–31. New York: Paulist, 1996.

Bonaventure. *The Triple Way*. In *Mystical Opuscula*. Translated by José de Vinck. Paterson, NJ: St. Anthony Guild, 1960.

Catechism of the Catholic Church. Vatican City: Libreria editrice Vaticana, 1994. http://www.vatican.va/archive/ENG0015/_INDEX.HTM.

Davis, Henry. *Moral and Pastoral Theology*. Vol. 1, *Principles*. London: Sheed & Ward, 1935.

Denzinger, Heinrich. *Enchiridion symbolorum definitionum et declarationum de rebus fidei et morum*. Edited by Peter Hünermann. 43rd ed. San Francisco: Ignatius, 2012.

Francis. *The Light of Faith* (*Lumen fidei*). Encyclical Letter, June 29, 2013. http://w2.vatican.va/content/francesco/en/encyclicals/documents/papa-francesco_20130629_enciclica-lumen-fidei.html.

Gula, Richard. *Reason Informed by Faith*. Mahwah, NJ: Paulist, 1989.

Hahn, Scott W. "Bringing Theologians to Their Knees: Theology as a Spiritual Science in Pope Benedict XVI." In *Eschatology*, edited by Elizabeth Shaw, 3–32. Pittsburgh: Fellowship of Catholic Scholars, 2015.

The Holy Bible: New Revised Standard Version with Apocrypha. Oxford: Oxford University Press, 1989. http://www.biblestudytools.com/apocrypha/nrsa/.

The International Theological Commission. *In Search of a Universal Ethic: A New Look at Natural Law*. Published document, 2009. http://www.vatican.va/roman_curia/congregations/cfaith/cti_documents/rc_con_cfaith_doc_20090520_legge-naturale_en.html.

Irenaeus. *Against the Heresies*. In *The Apostolic Fathers, Justin Martyr, Irenaeus*, edited by Alexander Roberts and James Donaldson. Ante-Nicene Fathers of the Christian Church. Edinburgh: T. & T. Clark, 1867. http://www.ccel.org/ccel/schaff/anf01.ix.html.

John of Damascus. *On the Orthodox Faith*. In *Hilary of Potiers, John of Damascus*, edited by Philip Shaff and Henry Wace. Translated by S. D. F. Salmond. Nicene and Post-Nicene Fathers of the Christian Church, Second Series 9. Edinburgh: T. & T. Clark, 1885. http://www.ccel.org/ccel/schaff/npnf209.iii.i.html.

John Paul II. *Faith and Reason* (*Fides et ratio*). Encyclical Letter, September 14, 1998. http://w2.vatican.va/content/john-paul-ii/en/encyclicals/documents/hf_jp-ii_enc_14091998_fides-et-ratio.html.

———. *The Splendor of Truth* (*Veritatis splendor*). Encyclical Letter, August 6, 1993. http://w2.vatican.va/content/john-paul-ii/en/encyclicals/documents/hf_jp-ii_enc_06081993_veritatis-splendor.html.

Liguori, Alphonsus de. *Dignity and Duties of Priests*. Edited by Eugene Grimm. The Complete Works of St. Alphonsus de Liguori 12. Toronto: Redemptorist Fathers, 1927.

———. *Prayer, The Great Means of Salvation*. Edited by Eugene Grimm. The Complete Works of St. Alphonsus de Liguori 3. Toronto: Redemptorist Fathers, 1927.

MacIntyre, Alasdair. *After Virtue: A Study in Moral Theory*. 2nd ed. London: Duckworth, 1985.
Marmion, Columba. *Christ, The Life of the Soul*. Translated by Alan Bancroft. Bethesda, MD: Zaccheus, 2005.
McGinn Bernard, ed. *The Philokalia: "Discourse on Abba Philimon."* In *The Essential Writings of Christian Mysticism*, 125–30. New York: Modern Library, 2006.
Michael, Chester P. *An Introduction to Spiritual Direction: A Psychological Approach for Directors and Directees*. Mahwah, NJ: Paulist, 2004.
O'Connell, Timothy. *Principles of Catholic Morality*. San Francisco: Harper & Row, 1990.
Odozor, Paulinus Ikechukwu. *Moral Theology in an Age of Renewal*. Notre Dame, IN: University of Notre Dame Press, 2003.
Ott, Ludwig. *Fundamentals of Catholic Dogma*. Edited by James Canon Bastible. Translated by Patrick Lynch. 4th ed. Rockord, IL: Tan, 1974.
Pieper, Josef. *Faith. Hope. Love*. San Francisco: Ignatius, 2012.
Pinckaers, Servais. *The Sources of Christian Ethics*. Translated by Mary Thomas Noble. Edinburgh: T. & T. Clark, 1995.
Ratzinger, Josef. *On Conscience*. San Francisco: Ignatius, 2007.
Second Vatican Council. *The Pastoral Constitution on the Church in the Modern World (Gaudium et spes)*. The Pastoral Constitution on the Church in the Modern World, December 7, 1965. http://www.vatican.va/archive/hist_councils/ii_vatican_council/documents/vat-ii_const_19651207_gaudium-et-spes_en.html.

— 2 —

Where Moral Theology Begins
"Aditus ad Universam Moralem Theologiam"

RAPHAEL GALLAGHER, C.Ss.R.

It is well known that Saint Alphonsus de Liguori (1696–1787) begins his Moral Theology with a tract on conscience. Moral theology, as it developed since Vatican 2, does not seem to favour this starting point.[1] However, commencing with conscience as the first step in moral decisions is not *per se* problematic for a catholic theologian, as the resignation speech of Emeritus Pope Benedict 16th indicates.[2] This contribution seeks to reconstruct the primacy[3] of conscience from a textual analysis of Saint Alphonsus, with a concluding projection on the possibility of a pastorally oriented moral theology.

The Question

The fact that he was one of the few Doctors of the Church not quoted at Vatican 11 could indicate that the moral theology of Alphonsus is *passé*. Despite a number of significant studies on his moral theology in the last 20 years,[4] the theological jury is unconvinced about his continued relevance.

---

1. O'Gorman, "Vatican 2," 27–42.
2. "Conscientia mea iterum atque iterum coram Deo explorata ad cognitionem certam perveni vires meas ingravescente aetate non iam aptas esse ad munus Petrinum aeque administrandum" (Benedict XVI, "Declaratio," lines 1–3).
3. I am taking "primacy" in the literal sense of "in the first place."
4. Vidal, *La morale*; Rey-Mermet, *Moral Choices*; Capone, *La proposta morale*.

That he was a significant moral theologian in his own epoch is not queried, and this historical importance has been bolstered by magisterial[5] and papal approval.[6] These encomiums do not, however, address the question posed in this contribution, which is concerned with the starting point of moral theological reflection. This question depends on a prior one: what moral theology are we talking about? Alphonsus' conception of moral theology as a scientific discipline to prepare future priests to be valid administrators of the sacrament of penance, consonant with the Council of Trent (1545–1563), has no direct linear roots in either patristic or scholastic theology, and could be considered obsolete.[7] One could speculate whether it might be better leave it without progeny as well. The promulgation of the Council documents, especially *Gaudium et spes*, has contributed to the current taut period of moral theological debate.[8] One of the few consensus points is that there can be no return to the manual form of moral theology associated with Saint Alphonsus. All other main points—the nature, methodology, scientific structure and purpose of moral theology—are disputed.[9] Why add the question of the starting point to an already congested list of *quaestiones disputatae*?

The argument is of necessity narrow and focussed. It depends on explaining what Alphonsus meant by calling conscience the *aditus ad universam moralem Theologiam*[10] and, subsequently, indicating whether this has any importance for moral theology today. The first step involves proof that I am generally faithful to the overall project of the Saint.[11] The second question must probe whether the possible applications are compatible with the project of Vatican 2 and subsequent clarifications.[12] The aim of

---

5. Amarante and Marrazzo, *Santo Dottore e Patrono*. Vidal, *La morale*, 224–40, updates this with magisterial statements from 1950 to 2000.

6. Benedict XVI, "Catechesis."

7. For this article, I confine myself to citations from two of the major moral works of Alphonsus de Liguori, *Theologia Moralis* and *Pratica del Confessore*. The translations are my own.

8. Bordeyne and Villemin, *Vatican II et la théologie*.

9. Bonandi, *Il difficile rinnovamento*.

10. Liguori, *Theologia Moralis*, 1, 1, Monitum.

11. My views could be tested against those presented by Vereecke, *Alphonse de Liguori*, and Forte, *L'Uno per l'Altro*, 37–58.

12. An overview of these debates can be found in Pesch, *Il Concilio Vaticano Secondo*.

this contribution is to consider one possible starting point for moral theology and it is not proposed as an *a priori* exclusion of other valid moral theologies.[13]

The Question in the Context of a System

Though the focus of this contribution is on conscience as the entry point to moral theology, it is important to note the immediate context in which Alphonsus introduces the question. He is presenting his system of moral theology. The use of the term "system" in theology dates from the 1600s and would broadly correspond to what we would now call theological methodology. The elaboration of his system was a slow and painful process for Alphonsus. He began his study of moral theology with the rigid textbook of François Genet (1640–1702), only to abandon it when he judged it unsuitable for the ministerial problems faced by the first generation of the religious congregation he founded in 1732 (the Redemptorists). By 1748, he had the first edition of his own moral theology ready for printing, and he re-published it nine times between then and 1785. The path from personal study, through ministerial experience, to formulating his own system was not linear. His system is, originally, more intuitive than explored point by point. It was only when his views were contested that he felt compelled to explain his system, which he clarified in a series of important works from 1762. We can talk of a mature presentation of his system from the sixth edition of his moral theology in 1767. The abandonment of one system (that of Genet) was due to the maturing insights from dealing with intricate moral issues in practice, and Alphonsus published his moral theology when he was 52 years of age. Only later, now in his 60s, does he give a coherent explanation of his system.[14] Alphonsus did not first develop a system, in theory, which was then to be applied in practice. The theory he started with proved inadequate in practice and this failure was the catalyst for a new theory.

---

13. No particular theological system is obligatory, in line with Pope John Paul II, *Veritatis Splendor*, 29.

14. A full list of these technical works, mainly an explanation of probabilism, is to be found in Ferrero and Boland, "Las obras impresas," 485–583.

The Choice of Conscience as the Starting Point of the System

The fact that Alphonsus begins with the tract on conscience is the most important characteristic of his system. Unlike many contemporaries, he does not start with a discrete discussion on law. The conscience tract of Alphonsus' moral system is its characteristic feature and the one in which he invested the most substantial personal time and energy.

Alphonsus wrote his moral theology with a particular understanding of that discipline, as noted above and he did so for a particular audience. He wrote for the students of the first generation of the Redemptorists because, in the principal work of the Congregation (that of preaching parish missions), these students would be confronted with intricate problems in moral instruction and hearing confessions. Moral theology was considered the science of moral doctrine, communicated through instructions, and the art of leading people to and keeping them in a state of grace, sustained in particular by the celebration of the sacrament of confession. Alphonsus did not set out to write a self-standing treatise on conscience: his aim was to write a complete moral theology, but it is of pivotal significance that he insists that the entry point to this science is the tract on conscience: *aditus ad universam moralem Theologiam*.[15] His resources are often from Saint Thomas, as presented by the masters of the "Second Thomism." Crucially, however, his interpretation of Thomas on conscience develops a particular nuance. This was because of the need to form the young Redemptorists in a moral theology capable of putting into practice the motto Alphonsus gave to his Congregation: *With Him* (that is, Christ) *there is Plentiful Redemption*. Alphonsus notes in the preface to the *Theologia Moralis* that he undertook this arduous task because he could not find any moral theologian who did so adequately. He considered the manual of H. Busenbaum (1600–1668) close enough to his requirements, and used it as a basis for his first edition, which can be considered as a presentation of Busenbaum with the personal glosses of Alphonsus.

The focal idea is that Alphonsus considers conscience as the practical verdict of reason by which we judge what we should do, here and now, to achieve what is good and to avoid what is evil. He emphasises the practical and immediate nature of the act of conscience in making a judgment about the object to be chosen. Two points are notable. Firstly, it is a different focus

---

15. Liguori, *Theologia Moralis*, I, Monitum.

to saying that conscience is primarily the knowledge of general principles such as *obey God* or *do unto others what you would have done unto you*. Secondly, it illustrates how Alphonsus, though still generally following Saint Thomas, gives preference to one component rather than another in the Thomistic texts.[16] Conscience, for Alphonsus, is the practical act of judgment about the object of the choice to be made, rather than the act of applying speculative knowledge to an analysis of the case in point. Why this preference for Alphonsus? The simple explanation is the correct one: the emphasis on conscience as a practical judgment on the object to be chosen is the typical question that arises in the sacrament of confession and moral instruction.[17]

This decisional focus explains a vital point in Alphonsus' tract on conscience that was disputed in his own day, and still causes much puzzlement. Honest error of conscience does not constitute sin for Alphonsus. Theologians who view conscience as a *theoretic* exposition of the knowledge that is acquired in order to lead to moral action will never understand this. For them, right reason never fails. Those theologians who see conscience as the *practical* analysis of the object of the moral choice to be made here and now will understand it effortlessly. For them, right reason often fails because of a variety of circumstances and human conditions:

> In the second place, we say that a person who has an invincibly erroneous conscience not only does not sin when acting in accordance with it, but is indeed bound to follow it. The reasoning here has two elements. The person does not sin because, though the action itself is not good, however it is good according to the conscience of the person who acts. Thus, the person is always bound to follow such a conscience if conscience, which is the proximate rule of action, advises the person to act in this way. Indeed, not only does a person not sin who acts according to an invincibly erroneous conscience, but more probably gains merit by doing so ... the reasoning is that, in order to call an action good, or at least not flawed, it suffices that the action be guided by the dictate of reason and prudence...[18]

Alphonsus deals with the practical problems that can arise, such as scruples, ignorance, and doubts. Further, in explaining his own system, he had to

---

16. Aquinas, *Summa Theologiae*, 1a 11ae.

17. These were not the primary considerations for Thomas, but they had some importance. Cf. Gilby, *Principles of Morality*.

18. Liguori, *Theologia Moralis*, 1, 5–6.

deal with the systems discussed by other theologians. These discussions are now mainly of historical interest. More important, for my purposes here, is to recall the definition of a formed conscience that, interestingly, Alphonsus takes from the Chancellor of Paris University Jean Gerson (1363–1429):[19]

> A conscience ... is formed when finally, that is after deliberation and discernment, one comes to a definitive judgment of reason and it is decided, and agreed to, that something is to be done or avoided ... to act against such a formed conscience is a sin ...[20]

Such is the conscience that Alphonsus proposes as the entry point for moral theology. This affirmation, however, implies deeper strata of reflection in order to understand the fuller impact of the choice of Alphonsus.

A Particular Theological Anthropology of Human Liberty

The placing of conscience as the entry point is a consequence of his theological evaluation of human liberty as expounded in the latter part of the tract. An error in explaining the system of Alphonsus is to imply that he uses reflex principles (such as *a doubtful law does not bind* or *when in doubt possession is the stronger position*) as epistemological criteria. Alphonsus, trained as a lawyer, was familiar with such principles and he uses them, but in a specific way. They are principles to be applied in the act of judgment with regard to the object of the choice to be made. It is incorrect to say that Alphonsus uses these principles, often associated with the philosophical position of probabilism, as anything more than part of the reflection needed in coming to the judgment of conscience. The motive why this assessment of Alphonsus seems correct can be demonstrated by his theological analysis of human liberty. Such liberty is anterior to all law, including divine law. The human person is created as a free being: freedom is the person's fundamental quality before God. Given that many of the people Alphonsus would have had pastoral contact with were illiterate, up to 85% in some estimates, the intricate reflex principles could hardly have been of much use to them. Their application, limited but necessary, was to assist the

---

19. Gerson would seem *prima facie* an unlikely theological source for Alphonsus, given the Chancellor's negative view of papal infallibility, a doctrine staunchly defended by Alphonsus. The appeal of Gerson for Alphonsus lies in his pastoral spirituality and his engagement with the idea of moral certainty.

20. Liguori, *Theologia Moralis*, 1, 1, 19.

priest in helping the penitent to arrive at a judgment in conscience about what to do here and now. This depended on the acceptance that the penitent, though illiterate, had a prior dignity because of their creation as free children of God. It is the liberty of the person that is to be most sacredly guarded. Law receives its moral validity, not from external promulgation, but because it is promulgated in the conscience of an individual whose freedom is theologically determinative:

> From all that has been said, it can be inferred (a) that if a law has been doubtfully formulated or doubtfully promulgated it does not oblige, because possession is not on its side, but on the side of liberty. Likewise, it can be said that if it to be doubted whether it has been understood as promulgated, then there is no burden attached to it. Thus, we are not held to fulfil the law since, for that part of the law in which the law is doubtful, the law is not in possession . . .[21]

The argument of Alphonsus on this point is compact, and to an extent analogical. Remembering his initial training in jurisprudence, Alphonsus would have been thoroughly familiar with the idea of "possession," as in the ownership of material goods. In his moral system, Alphonsus moves from the primacy of possession in legal contracts (*possession is nine-tenths of the law,* as the popular saying goes) to extend this idea of possession to the virtue of justice in general. In the final and more analogical part of his argument, Alphonsus moves the idea of "possession" to that of human liberty.[22] This argument is convincing for Alphonsus because, if there is a doubt about the promulgation of the law, then the law cannot be said to be "in possession" and we thus move to what is certainly prior to an unclear law, that is, the possession of human liberty:

> Every time that a doubtful law minimally obliges a person, the person remains unbound and is free from the obligation of the law. In such a case, he is at liberty to use his freedom, of which he is truly in possession, since the law is doubtful . . . no one can deny that the principle of the person in possession is always the superior one. In the case in which the law is in possession, then we stand by the law. If, truthfully, liberty is in possession, then we stand by liberty . . .[23]

21. Ibid., 1, 1, 27.

22. Though in part superseded by later research, the best general source on the juridical training of Saint Alphonsus and its implications for his moral system is the unpublished thesis of Freda, "De institutione et eruditione."

23. Liguori, *Theologia Moralis,* 1, 1, 26.

Intrinsic Authority Preferred

The first impression from reading Alphonsus' moral theology would suggest otherwise. He was a casuist. It is interesting, however, that he does not try to solve every case: he offers solutions to about 500 of the 4000 questions he poses in the *Theologia Moralis*, less than 15%. His interest in cases of conscience is to educate his reader in the art of reasoning in moral matters. He is explicit in the Preface to the Moral Theology:

> However, in the selection of opinions, it has always been my major concern to prefer reason to authority. Moreover, before I offer my judgment . . . I was careful to remain indifferent about individual questions and to free myself from every flash of passion . . .[24]

Undeniably, Alphonsus quotes extensively from others: 800 authors are referenced in the *Theologia Moralis*. The purpose of these quotations is, however, not to simply clinch an argument by external authority, but to show that he has examined all sides of a question before he comes to offer his own opinion. Since Pascal's damning critique of casuistry, it has been commonplace to paint all casuists with the same negative brush. There is sufficient recent scholarship to show that the nature of high casuistry needs to be reassessed[25] and, in particular, that Alphonsus is a casuist who argues theologically from intrinsic reasoning.[26] This depends on a proper assessment of the technique of a theological casuist, such as Alphonsus. "Technique" refers to the use of reasonable arguments in reaching a conclusion. The method of the best of the casuists is, admittedly, more implicit than explicit. I take three of the implicit elements in Alphonsus to support my view that (in the main) he prefers intrinsic to extrinsic authority. Casuists, both rigid and benign, give the first consideration to norms. Norms are comprehended as the obligations known to reason, deriving directly from divine law or indirectly from natural, ecclesial or civil law:

> No one can doubt that in (moral) action we are bound to seek the truth and to follow it. Is it therefore licit to ask if there is any other way we can know the truth unless it is through coming to know the truth under the guidance of human reason? It must, therefore,

---

24. Ibid., Praefatio.

25. Jonsen and Toulmin, *Abuse of Casuistry*. Useful also is Keenan and Shannon, *Context of Casuistry*.

26. I am in the debt of Hurtubise, *La casuistique* for the following paragraphs.

be said that the truth which is followed and embraced is that truth which is shown to us, and placed before our eyes, by reason . . .[27]

The normative component of casuistry is followed by a second technical moment that we can call the narrative one. Again, the casuists, of whatever system, give pronounced attention to this. Because the casuist, by definition, is dealing with "cases," it is understandable that the elements of the case in question be explained, often in the greatest detail. Otherwise, it would be impossible to know whether the norms, known through reason, apply to this particular case or not:

> We now deal with the scrupulous conscience . . . a conscience is scrupulous when, for a frivolous reason and without a rational basis, there is a fear of sin, even though in reality there is no sin at all. A scruple is a defective understanding of something. These are the signs of a scrupulous conscience. (a) obstinacy of judgment . . . (b) frequent changes of judgment . . . (c) having irrelevant ideas about the various circumstances that were, or could have been, present in some action. (d) a fear of sin in everything, and obstinately holding out against advice, even against one's own judgment . . .[28]

After the normative and narrative parts the casuist comes to the most delicate element of his technique, the dialectical resolution of the case. This involves the practice of rhetoric and is often the distinguishing mark between the skilled and unskilled casuist. It highlights whether the theological casuistry used is rigorist or benign. In the case of Alphonsus, it will come as no surprise that he uses a dialectic of mild benignity:

> There are some who boast they are educated and theologians of skill but who refuse to read the moral theologians, whom they refer to with the pejorative name of 'casuists'. They say that it is sufficient, in hearing confessions, to know the general principles of morality because, with these, they can resolve all the particular cases. Who will deny that, in the resolution of cases, one needs to use principles? However, here is the difficulty: how do you apply the appropriate principles to particular cases? This cannot be done without a thorough discussion, as there are points to be clarified on one side and on the other. It is precisely to this issue that the moral theologians devote their time. They seek to clarify which are

---

27. Liguori, *Theologia Moralis*, 1, 2, 173.
28. Ibid., 1, 1, 11.

the principles to be used in the resolution of many particular cases (of conscience)...[29]

A Particular View of Pastoral Prudence

It is important to note, further, that giving the first place to conscience in moral theology is not a type of reductionism. Seeking the moral truth was the central concern for Saint Alphonsus. How he approaches this task says much about his reliance on St. Thomas[30] and the implications for a moral theology that starts with conscience:

> The proper choice of opinions more conformable to the truth, in any particular question, took an enormous amount of work (on my part). For many years, I went through the various volumes of the classic authors, both those of a rigid and of a benign approach ... but most especially I took care in annotating the doctrine of the Divine Thomas, and I sought to study these in their proper sources. Besides, for the more intricate questions, I also consulted the more recent learned scholars...[31]

Why not a straightforward commentary on Saint Thomas, and why does he consult other scholars who, in fact, may not have been Thomistic in orientation? Alphonsus sought to complement his primary source (Thomas) with a recognition that new problems had arisen since the time of the Angelic Doctor (explained by "the more recent scholars"). The combination of these two sources provides a particular interpretation of prudence in the moral system of Saint Alphonsus. It was important, for him, not only to be faithful to Saint Thomas but also to present a moral theology that was pastorally positive in the new circumstances of his own day. With this developmental view, Alphonsus can be categorised as using a theory of pastoral prudence.[32]

Alphonsus is not embracing a two-track approach to moral truth: one that deduced through the theoretic study of prudence (as in Saint Thomas) and one that is arrived at by examining new moral experiences (as in the more recent authors). I call his attitude pastoral prudence. Truth

---

29. Liguori, *Praxis Confessarii*, 1, 17.
30. O'Meara, *Thomas Aquinas*, 154.
31. Liguori, *Theologia Moralis*, Praefatio.
32. Cf. Damen, "S. Alfonsus Doctor Prudentiae," 1–27.

is univocal, but its articulation depends on how one comes to see the one truth in a variety of different circumstances. The truth that interests Saint Alphonsus is that which leads to salvation. Prudence, for him, is essentially pastoral because it serves the finality of salvation:

> Dear reader, my intention in writing this Moral Theology, which has a strictly practical goal, was not to present you with a heavy scholastic treatise on human actions. Rather, wanting to be of assistance in the salvation of souls, I believed myself obliged to choose only those questions which, in this area, I deem to be the most necessary and useful to know for the proper practice (of Christian life). Had I acted in any other way, not only would I have wasted a lot of lamp-oil with my efforts, but you would also be wasting your time in reading such useless observations . . .[33]

The theory of prudence, as explained by Saint Thomas, is of central importance for Saint Alphonsus. The application of this theory, in practice, is not the creation of another "truth" but its insertion into the broader intention of God who wishes only the salvation of people. It is this assessment that allows one to call Alphonsus a proponent of pastoral prudence.

In the various controversies surrounding Saint Alphonsus, none has been more intricate or difficult to resolve than this understanding of pastoral prudence.[34] There can be an impression of inconsistency on the central questions of moral truth and experience. It is important, once again, to underline how Alphonsus' choice of conscience as the *aditus ad universam moralem Theologiam* involves the further anthropological statements on human liberty and appeal to reason: conscience is where the journey into moral truth begins, not where it ends.[35]

---

33. Liguori, *Theologia Moralis*, 5, Tractatus Praeambulus.

34. An very different interpretation is to be found in the influential article of Deman, "Probabilisme." Deman's view of the lack of consistency between Saint Alphonsus and Saint Thomas is repeated in Pinckaers, *The Pinckaers Reader*, 77.

35. I referred in note (2) to the resignation speech of Emeritus Pope Benedict XVI. Note how the process begins with conscience and then moves to a personal appropriation of what has been learned through interrogating conscience. It is not the isolated conscience that decides, but the person who has internalized the process of interrogating conscience.

The Emphasis on Conscience as Part of Conversion

Though the focus of this contribution has been a precise point in a specific text from Alphonsus (conscience as the entry point to all of moral theology), a consideration of other texts can be a useful way of concluding this analysis. Alphonsus was a prolific writer—on prayer, spiritual direction, the devout life, the duties of one's state in life, as well as a voluminous correspondence with the early Redemptorist confreres and others who sought his counsel.[36] Part of his accent on conscience is linked to this: Alphonsus did not conceive moral theology as a science separated from other spiritual and doctrinal concerns. When he stresses that conscience is the *aditus ad universam moralem Theologiam* it is plausible to surmise that he considers conscience to be the entry point to the overall Christian life. Admittedly, he accepted the then normal pedagogical divisions between the study of moral, dogmatic and ascetic theology. However, one can sense from these other writings an inner coherence that gives an additional emphasis to his theology of conscience.

The spirit to be found in these other writings is already indicated in his main moral work:

> Epikeia means an exception to the case (from the general law) when, in a given situation, it can be concluded with certainty, or at least with great probability, that the lawgiver did not intend to include it under the law ... This epikeia has its application not only to human laws, but also to the natural law when, because of the circumstances of the action which is contrary to such a law, there is no malice.[37]

Such a view is possible because of a deep understanding that mercy is God's supreme attribute. God is the eternal judge, certainly, but He shows his quality as judge by exercising His mercy when, in strict justice, He is not bound to do so.[38] This merciful quality of God is mirrored in the moral system of Saint Alphonsus because of his particular theology of conversion.

In this work for missionary conversion, most evident in the main apostolate of the Redemptorists as preachers of the God of Loveliness, was a desire to encourage people to restructure their personal lives. Subtly, we

---

36. The digital library IntraText contains most of the important works.
37. Liguori, *Theologia Moralis*, 1, 2, 201.
38. Congar, *Les Voies du Dieu Vivant*.

are again brought back to conscience as the entry point of the process. A vengeful God inspires only the desire to conform externally to the presumed order of God in the universe: the attraction of a loving God is to arouse in people a desire to restructure their life in a grace-filled way. Alphonsus did not write a moral system adapted to the encouragement of social change, as we now understand the term. Nevertheless, he does call for a restructuring of personal identity. Moreover, this is possible only if we allow the love of God to be the prime mover in this process.[39]

An extended quotation from a sermon of Saint Alphonsus underlines the importance of the loving appeal to a free conscience. The sermon was preached in 1745 during a mission in the southern Italian city of Foggia. Heavily damaged during an earthquake about 15 years previously, the restored city of Foggia was developing another, and less endearing, reputation: a centre for prostitution, illegal trading in banned books, and of social unrest because of migration. Alphonsus himself preached the opening sermon of the mission:

> On this first night of the mission, before I address you, my dear people, allow me first to speak to God . to ask Him what he wishes me to say to you . . . What do you wish me to say to this ungrateful city and to these, your ungrateful servants? . . . You are disgusted with them, and rightly so . . . You have terrified them with chastisements . . . You threatened them with a plague epidemic . . . you threatened them with the sufferings of war . . . and with death under the destruction of the earthquake. And, Lord, what has been their response? Nothing. They have become worse than before . . . If you wish me to tell them what I feel I will tell them to prepare themselves for all the punishments they deserve. I shall tell them that they should no longer seek or hope for compassion and pardon because they no longer deserve it. Lord, do you wish me to speak to them in this way? No, dear friends, no . . . God does not wish me to speak to you of justice and punishments but of peace and pardon if only you will stop offending Him.[40]

The tone is rhetorical, quite different to the more analytic arguments of other quotations I have given. However, the "moral system" underlying it is the same. The moral life is a call in conscience, to the free person, to consider carefully the choices to make. The call comes from a God of mercy

---

39. The most readable of the writings of Alphonsus de Liguori on this aspect is *Pratica di amar Gesù Cristo*.

40. Jones, *Alphonsus de Liguori*, 180–81.

and forgiveness, not from a vengeful and cruel judge. The response to the call is given where the call is first heard, in our conscience.

Concluding Projection

When Alphonsus was composing his moral theology, it was a time of cultural unrest, intellectual confusion, political uncertainty and divisions within the Church. The French Revolution began just two years after he died. The relative success of his system was its capacity to communicate the Christian moral message in an attractive and convincing way. There can be no return, in literal terms, to that system. Alphonsus wrote a manual for future priests in a Church shaped by the Council of Trent. We, too, are living through a (different) period of cultural unrest, intellectual confusion, political uncertainty and divisions within the Church. The benchmark for a renewed moral theology is no longer Trent, but the Second Vatican Council, especially the Pastoral Constitution on the Church in the Modern World *Gaudium et spes* (1965).[41]

My motivation in writing this contribution is a concern that moral theology, as it has developed in the last fifty years, has become a speculative discipline with an oblique relationship to pastoral concerns. People involved in direct ministry often express a sense of disappointment that moral theologians have "abandoned" them, either because of lack of interest or out of fear of the reactions of a bureaucratically authoritarian church. If conscience can be the *aditus ad universam moralem Theologiam* in one expression of the manual tradition (Alphonsus de Liguori) it should not be impossible to have an analogous starting point for one expression of the moral tradition as it is developing after Vatican 11. The challenge, as framed by Pope Francis, is substantial:

> Not infrequently an opposition between theology and pastoral ministry emerges, as if they were two opposite, separate realities that had nothing to do with each other. We not infrequently identify doctrine with conservatism and antiquity: and, on the contrary, we tend to think of pastoral ministry in terms of adaptation, reduction, accommodation, as if they had nothing to do with each other. A false opposition is generated between theology and pastoral ministry, between Christian reflection and Christian life

---

41. Cf. Bordeyne, *L'homme et son angoisse,* and Thomasset, "Dans la fidélité au Concile."

... The attempt to overcome this divorce between theology and pastoral ministry, between faith and life, was indeed one of the main contributions of Vatican Council 11.[42]

Conscience seems an appropriate locus to start rectifying this divorce. To express the possibilities and limits of my projection, I conclude by entering some *caveats*. The definition of conscience in Alphonsus, with its emphasis on the practical judgment about what is to be done here and now, needs be updated in the light of insights regarding consciousness at the heart of a person's self-awareness.[43] The foundational arguments in Alphonsus' tract about human liberty and intrinsic consistency should be an encouragement to re-evaluate the role of probability in moral certainty.[44]

The practical discernment of the gradual journey towards conversion can be facilitated by results from the human sciences.[45]

With these *caveats,* conscience could still function as the *aditus ad universam moralem Theologiam.* This could be a significant contribution to the scientific credibility of a pastorally oriented moral theology.

Bibliography

Amarante, Alfonso, and Antonio Marazzo, eds. *Santo, Dottore e Patrono. I quatrri documenti pontifici sulla glorificazione di Sant'Alfonso Maria di Liguori.* Materdomini, Italy: Valsele, 2009.

Aquinas, Thomas. *Summa Theologiae.* Oxford: Blackfriars, 1966.

Benedict XVI. "Catechesis." *L'Osservatore Romano*, March 31, 2011.

———. "Declaratio." http:w2vaticana.va/DECLARATIO.

---

42. Francis, "Video Message."

43. Alphonsus discusses conscience in the overall context of the celebration of the Sacrament of Confession. Even if one grants (as I do) that Alphonsus is not a rigid casuist, the juridical remnants of confessional practice remain in his work. This is not an insuperable problem if we consider the broader tradition of the Christian tradition of conscience, such as outlined in Strohm, *Conscience*. A particular difficulty in the catholic presentation of conscience is the relationship between the internal authority of conscience in relationship to external church authority. By widening the concept of conscience to include consciousness, part of this antipathy may lessened.

44. The *forma mentis* of Alphonsus was shaped by his jurisprudential training: as mentioned in note 22 above. The recovery of a more philosophical understanding of probable moral certainty would be a welcome counterpoint for today's discussions, as suggested by Fleming, *Defending Probabilism*.

45. Given the lengthy treatment given by Alphonsus to scruples, an interesting example of a contribution from the human sciences is Ciarocchi, *The Doubting Disease*.

Bonandi, A. *Il difficile rinnovamento. Percorsi fondamentali della teologia morale postconciliare.* Assisi: Cittadella, 2003.

Bordeyne, P. *L'homme et son angoisse. La théologie morale de Gaudium et Spes.* Paris: Cerf, 2004.

Bordeyne, P., and L. Villemin, eds. *Vatican II et la théologie. Perspectives pour le XXIè siècle.* Paris: Cerf, 2006.

Capone, D. *La proposta morale di Sant'Alfonso. Svilupppo e attualità.* Edited by J. S. Botero and S. Majorano. Rome: Edacalf, 1997.

Ciaroccchi, J. W. *The Doubting Disease: Help for Scrupulosity and Religious Compulsions.* Mahwah, NJ: Paulist, 1995.

Congar, Y. *Les voies du Dieu vivant.* Paris: Cerf, 1962.

Damen, C. "S. Alfonsus Doctor Prudentiae." *Rassegna di Morale e Diritto* 4 (1939–40) 1–27.

Deman, T. "Probabilisme." In *Dictionnaire de théologie catholique*, edited by A. Vacant and E. Mangenot, 13:417–619. Paris: Letouzey et Ané, 1936.

Fererro, F., and S. J. Boland, "Las obras impresas por S. Alfonso Maria de Liguori." In *Studia et subsidia de vita et operibus S. Alfonsi Mariae de Ligorio*, edited by F. Ferrero and S. J. Boland, 485–543. Rome: Collegium S. Alfonsi, 1990.

Fleming, J. *Defending Probabilism: The Moral Theology of Juan Caramuel.* Washington, DC: Georgetown, 2006.

Forte, B. *L'Uno per l'Altro. Per un'etica della trascendenza.* Brescia: Morcelliana, 2003.

Francis. "Video Message to the Second International Congress of Theology in Buenos Aires September 4, 2015." http://www.news/popes-video-messasage.

Freda, A. "De institutione et eruditione juridica S. Alphonsi M. de Ligorio." STD Thesis, Pontifical Lateran University, 1939.

Gilby, T. *Principles of Morality: Summa Theologiae 1a11ae.* Cambridge: Blackfriars, 1966.

Hurtubise, P. *La casuistique dans tous ses états. De Martin Azilcueta à Alphonse de Liguori.* Ottawa: Novalis, 2006.

John Paul II. *Veritatis Splendor.* Rome: Libreria Editrice Varticana, 1993.

Jones, F. M. *Alphonsus de Liguori: The Saint of Bourbon Naples.* Dublin: Gill and Macmillan, 1993.

Jonsen, A., and S. Toulmin. *The Abuse of Casuistry: A History of Moral Reasoning.* Berkeley: University of California, 1995.

Keenan, J., and T. Shannon. *The Context of Casusitry.* Washington, DC: Georgetown, 1995.

Liguori, Alphonsus de. *Opera Omnia S. Afonso Maria de Liguori.* Intratext Digital Library CD, no. IXTCDIGITAP00034. May 2003.

———. *Pratica del Confessore (Praxis Confessarii).* Frigente: Mariana, 1987.

———. *Pratica di amar Gesù Cristo.* Rome: Città Nuova, 1996.

———. *Theologia Moralis.* Rome: Ex Typografia Vaticana, 1905.

O'Gorman, K. "Vatican 2 on Moral Theology: Fifty Years Later." *Doctrine and Life* 65 (2015) 27–42.

O'Meara, T. *Thomas Aquinas: Theologian.* Notre Dame: University of Notre Dame Press, 1997.

Pesch, O. H. *Il Concilio Vaticano 2. Preistoria e svolgimento, risultati, storia post-conciliare.* Brescia: Morcelliana, 2005.

Pinckaers, S. *The Pinckaers Reader: Renewing Thomistic Moral Theology.* Edited by J. Berkman and C. Steven Titus. Washington, DC: Catholic University of America Press, 2005.

Rey-Mermet, Theodule. *Moral Choices: The Moral Theology of Saint Alphonsus Liguori.* Liguori, MO: Liguori, 1998.
Strohm, P. *Conscience: A Very Short Introduction.* Oxford: Oxford University Press, 2011.
Thomasset, A. "Dans la fidelité au Concile Vatican 11. La dimension herméneutique de la théologie morale." *Revue d'Ethique et de théologie morale* 263 (2011) 31–61.
Vereecke, L. *Alphonse de Liguori. Pasteur et Docteur.* Paris: Beauchesne, 1987.
Vidal, M. *La morale de Sant'Alfonso. Dal rigorismo alla benignità.* Rome: Edacalf, 2006.

3

Should the Church Change Its Teaching on Sexual Morality?

Gerald Gleeson

In his later writings Brian Johnstone proposed a new framework for moral evaluation that would overcome the split between "objective" and "subjective" that has bedevilled Catholic moral theology for many centuries. To this end, he has deployed contemporary philosophical explorations of "the gift" to argue that the intrinsic morality of an action should be understood in terms of its capacity to be both given and received between persons. On this account, an "intrinsically evil" act is "a way of relating to others which damages or destroys their capacity to receive and give, and damages or destroys in the agent the capacity to be a giver and in the receiver the capacity to receive. It is an act of exclusion and domination . . ."[1]

Johnstone argues that the language of *acts* is inadequate to the intersubjective context of morality, whereas a *gift*, by contrast, invokes giver, receiver and the relationship between then. In this new framework, the "most basic sense" of the moral object is the other person as receiver, "while the object in the more restricted sense is the proposed gift."[2] Since a gift must be "something" can be given and received between persons, judging whether "a mode of interacting with others" can truly count as a giving or receiving, surely includes reflection on the nature of that act-become-gift along with its impact on persons and relationships.[3] However, one of the most neural-

---

1. Johnstone, "Intrinsically Evil Acts," 406.
2. Ibid., 403.
3. Cf., ibid., 405.

gic issues in Catholic moral theology concerns how the "nature" of human acts is to be understood. This issue is most intensely debated in the case of sexual ethics where the Church's teaching is commonly accused of privileging the supposed divinely-appointed, "objective" nature of individual sex acts over against people's "subjective" experience of sexuality and personal intimacy.

In this essay I will review a recent representative critique of Catholic teaching in order to clarify both the Church's teaching on sexuality and the approach to ethical reasoning it presupposes. The goal is to understand what a change in teaching would involve philosophically and theologically, and at what cost. I will do so with an eye to Brian Johnstone's critique of the split between subjective and objective morality. Sexual ethics may be taken as a test case for Johnstone's re-visioning of moral theology in terms of the gift. It will become evident that while the framework of the gift highlights "the [moral] object in the basic sense, as the other who is the receiver," it does not eliminate the traditional concern with the nature of moral acts, "the object in the restricted sense," which is the proposed gift.[4]

I. A Critique of Catholic Teaching on Sexuality

With a view to the 2015 Synod on the Family, Bishop Geoffrey Robinson noted that traditional Catholic teachings on sexuality are interconnected: "There is no possibility whatsoever of a change in the teaching of the Catholic Church on the subject of homosexual acts unless and until there is first a change in its teaching on heterosexual acts."[5] For Robinson, traditional teaching involves a questionable reliance on what is asserted to be the "God-given nature of the physical acts in themselves, rather than on these acts as actions of human beings."[6] In any case, he argues, the requirement that the unitive and procreative aspects of intercourse must be present on every occasion seems nothing more than mere assertion.[7] These familiar

---

4. Ibid., 403.

5. See Robinson, *The 2015 Synod*, 11. Defenders of the Church's teaching point to the same interconnection, arguing conversely that a change in the teaching on heterosexual acts would inevitably lead to change in the teaching on homosexual acts. For an early statement of this argument, see Elizabeth Anscombe's famous paper, "Contraception and Chastity," reprinted in Smith, *Why Humanae Vitae Was Right*, 121–46.

6. Robinson, *The 2015 Synod*, 16.

7. Ibid., 15–16.

criticisms direct our attention to "the nature" of human sexuality, its God-given meanings and, in particular, its link to procreation.

"Nature" and Other Presuppositions

There are few more ambiguous terms in moral theology than "nature." Distinctions are needed. First, there are *natural physiological processes* such as digestion, cardiac function, and ovulation. Sexual intercourse is *not* a "natural process" in this sense. Sexual intercourse occurs as the result of human choice. The ethical question, "What is *the nature of the choice* to have sexual intercourse?" uses "nature" not in the sense of a "natural" process, but with respect to understanding what a choice involves as a willed-knowing or known-willing.[8] Moreover, the related question: "What is the nature of sexual intercourse between a man and a woman?" is ambiguous because "the nature"—or more simply, *what*—we are concerned with depends on the sort of inquiry we have in mind: are we doctors, neuroscientists, psychologists, ethicists or theologians? Each discipline has its own subject matter; each investigates certain features of sexual intercourse, its "nature" in a particular respect. A psychologist might be interested in sex as a mutually pleasurable activity that bonds people together; a neuroscientist might be interested in the way sex leads to the secretion of certain chemicals in the brain which help account for this bonding effect; a theologian might be interested in the way sexual self-giving is a "sacrament" of Christ and the Church, and so on.

Ethics is concerned with sex as *a kind of human activity* and hence as an *object of choice*. An ethicist asks, *what* is one choosing to do in choosing to act sexually? What defines this activity "in its essence," as distinct from other kinds of voluntary human activity? Sexual morality cannot be read off from "nature" understood in terms of biology, psychology or anthropology—or Trinitarian theology, for that matter, but is developed on the basis of understanding how sexual activity fits within the activities that make for a good human life, and hence in terms of the point and good of the activity, the reasons for which people engage in it, with its results and consequences, and so on.

There is a further sense of "nature." Responsible human beings consider how their activity is partly or wholly determined by its various features

---

8. See Aristotle, *Nichomachean Ethics*, Bk. VI, 2 on the paradoxical character of choice.

and effects, be they physical, psychological, or spiritual, and also by *the end* towards which the activity naturally tends. In varying degrees, human actions have meanings and directions to an end that are prior to someone's particular purpose. It is difficult to see how a vicious slap across the face could be used as a greeting of friendship; conversely, it is easy to see why using a kiss as a signal of betrayal is especially offensive. Vicious slaps and affectionate kisses have meanings (a nature) prior to the intentions of particular agents.

Sexual actions also have their given meanings and directions. For example, *one* (but only one) obvious answer to the question, "what kind of act is sex between a man and a woman?" is, "the kind of act that leads to procreation." Clearly there are many reasons for having sexual intercourse which have nothing to do with procreation; nonetheless, when a man and a woman have intercourse they engage in the kind of act that naturally leads to procreation.[9] It always makes sense to ask, "might this act of intercourse lead to conception?" If someone does not know it is in the nature of heterosexual intercourse to be (among other things) the procreative kind of act, they literally know not what they do.[10]

It follows that a homosexual act is not a procreative kind of act, though it might "naturally" have some features in common with heterosexual intercourse (e.g., as an intimate, persons-bonding, kind of act). As yet I have drawn no ethical conclusions in this discussion, but an obvious ethical consideration appears on the horizon: if homosexual and heterosexual acts are—in a fundamental way—different kinds of acts, why should the former be judged by the ethical standard of the latter?

Does a Sexual Ethic Require Distinctive Criteria?

In Western culture today many are likely to adopt the ethical standard Geoff Robinson articulates: the condition for moral goodness is love and respect for the people affected by one's actions. For example, a sexual act will be judged "morally right when, positively it is based on a genuine love

9. On the difference between *end* and *purpose*, see Sokolowski, "What is Natural Law?"

10. Imagine a sex education course in which people were not told that intercourse is the kind of act that leads to conception; this would be a far more fundamental omission than failure to explain that intercourse can lead to infection. The latter can be an important piece of information in some contexts; the former is the essential information required if people are to understand what they are doing.

of neighbour, that is, a genuine desire for what is good for the other person. . . and, negatively, contains no damaging elements such as harm to a third person, any form of coercion or deceit, or any harm to the ability of sex to express love."[11] For the Catholic tradition, by contrast, the procreative aspect of sex is the overriding ethical consideration in relation to *all* sexual acts, including those that are not procreative in kind.

The contemporary claim that sexual morality should not give a decisive place to the link between sex and procreation is commonly associated with the charge that Catholic teaching is too "physicalist." Contemporary ethicists tend to emphasise not the physical, bodily reality of sex but its personal and psychological values. Thus Robinson, criticising consensual casual sex writes that, "because love is all-important and because sex is so vital a way of expressing love, sex is always serious . . . we must take the harm that can be caused by sexual desire very seriously, and look carefully at the circumstances than can make morally bad the seeking of sexual pleasure because they involve harm to others, to oneself or the community."[12]

It is worth noting the parallel between the so-called physicalism of the tradition and what might be called the "psychologism" of this contemporary approach. For, if it is a mistake to draw ethical conclusions from the biological structure of sex as procreative, why isn't it likewise a mistake to draw ethical conclusions from the psychological features of sex as capable of expressing intimacy and love? The short answer likely to be offered is that people's psychological experiences are more important than their bodily actions; in other words, the fact that a sexual act is not a procreative kind of act is nowadays thought to be of much less ethical significance than whether a sexual act expresses love and respect for the other.[13] This arguably inadequate answer draws our attention to the deepest issue in sexual ethics—how we are to understand the psycho-physical-spiritual unity of the human person. Are we persons who *use their bodies* in the service of psychological experiences, or are we body-soul unities—persons who *are living, sexually differentiated bodies*?

The modern, dualist understanding of persons gives such priority to our psychological lives that people can readily ignore the fact that human bodies are physiologically suited for heterosexual intercourse. By contrast, a more holistic view of the human person explains why people in other times

---

11. Robinson, *The 2015 Synod*, 21.
12. Ibid., 20–21.
13. See Gleeson, "Are People More Important?"

and cultures readily judged homosexual activity to be "unnatural"—not in keeping with the nature of the human person as a bodily creature. Likewise, solitary sexual acts used to be instinctively recognised as "unnatural"—not in keeping with the way sexual arousal is properly ordered to intimacy with another person rather than to private pleasure.[14]

II. Respecting the Procreative Nature of Sex

Moral Evaluation

Calls for change in the Church's teaching thus direct our attention to the link between sex and procreation within a Christian sexual ethics. Before addressing that issue, we must clarify the nature of moral evaluation more generally. It is tempting to think that moral evaluation consists in identifying the activity we are concerned with (e.g., sexual intercourse) and then evaluating that activity against our preferred moral standard (e.g., whether it respects the autonomy of the parties concerned; whether it is in accord with the teaching of Jesus, and so on, depending on one's preferred ethical theory). With St Thomas Aquinas as guide, however, we can see that this popular, seemingly innocuous approach to evaluation is misguided because it fails to appreciate the proper relationship between a natural description of human action (e.g., as sexual intercourse) and its moral description as chosen conduct (e.g., as marital intercourse, as adultery or as fornication).[15] The mistake is *to begin* by identifying an activity in *non-moral* terms, typically in the naturalistic terms of biology, physiology or psychology—for example, by identifying sex as a pleasurable activity (or, for that matter, as a procreative activity).[16] The popular approach then seeks *some additional* moral feature that would render the act good or bad (in line with one's preferred moral rule or ethical theory). Moral value (or

---

14. "Unnatural" is not a measure of moral gravity; it points to how the flaw in such acts is to be understood. Most people know why self-indulgent, solitary sexual acts, with or without the use of pornography, are not in keeping with (the nature of) human sexuality at its best.

15. The "Thomistic" approach to moral evaluation employed here builds on common ground shared by many recent interpreters of Thomas, including Johnstone, e.g., in "Intrinsically Evil Acts," 392–97.

16. The same mistake is made in some traditional expositions of Catholic teaching. Although I will be emphasising the often neglected truth that sex is the procreative act, I will not be arguing that moral evaluation should *begin* from this truth.

disvalue) is something added on to the "natural" (e.g., physical or psychological) reality of what we do.

However, moral evaluation should not begin with, nor focus on, some natural description of an action, for there are always many such natural descriptions available, and the choice of non-moral description may be quite arbitrary, and will likely prejudice the subsequent evaluation. In the present context, the issue is whether sexual activity should be described in a way that is neutral between heterosexual intercourse and other kinds of sexual activity. If sex is described merely as pleasurable activity, and a suitable moral standard is to be invoked, we may well conclude that love and respect are what really matter—they provide the added moral value. By contrast, if sex is described as procreative activity, we might well conclude that a parental context is required for it to be praiseworthy. The debate then reduces to one about the preferred natural description of sex. The so-called Naturalistic Fallacy looms as each side tries to build a moral conclusion on their own preferred—albeit valid—*natural description*. At the very least, we cannot and should not assume that we know in advance which natural description will be most relevant to the moral evaluation.

The key to circumventing such debates is to realise that moral evaluation is primarily concerned not with the physical or psychological features of an action, but with the "nature" of an action as an object of choice in relation to what is good, and—we might add—thereby as a gift to be given and received. St Thomas's approach to evaluation begins with the agent's goal or purpose—the good he or she wants to achieve.[17] The goodness or badness of an action depends on the kind of choice it embodies—on the purpose of the agent, on the quality of his or her reasoning about means to end or further ends, on the suitability of what's actually done to achieving the end, and on the virtuous or vicious disposition of the agent.

On a Thomistic approach, moral evaluation then, secondarily, examines the suitability of the particular action given its own qualities as a kind of act that tends to a certain end. The natural features of an action are relevant to moral evaluation, but only secondarily, and in subordination to the agent's intentions. At this point we might recognise that some actions are naturally and rightly suited to certain ends, but not to others. A slap across the face is suited to repelling an attacker, but not to welcoming a friend. In short, moral evaluation has a dual focus. Judging whether an action is a

---

17. For a masterly presentation of Thomas's "end focussed" approach, see Pinckaers, "The Role of the End in Moral Action."

rightly ordered means to an intended end concerns both the *intelligibility* of the means-end relationship and the *material suitability* of the particular means in the circumstances.[18]

The Priority of Goodness

Taking further guidance from St Thomas, moral evaluation does best to focus on when human actions are good or virtuous, since bad actions are always to be understood as, in varying degrees, departures from the good. The language of the virtues, like all moral concepts, are "open-textured"—not entirely reducible to the descriptive, but able to be descriptively articulated as the case requires.[19] Borderline disputes may remain: we might be unsure whether killing in this situation is murder, but the core description of murder as intentionally killing the innocent is clear. We typically, and rightly, move quickly from knowing a few facts about this killing or that sexual activity to its moral evaluation as murder or adultery. For Thomas, every human act is thereby a moral act: morality is not added on to the act, but is simply the act understood in relation to what it is to live a good human life and become a good human being.

In the case of sexual ethics, we do best to begin not by seeking a non-question-begging, natural description of sexual activity, but with what is not in dispute: that *marital sex* is good and mostly obviously so in the act of consummation. For the newlywed couple, intercourse expresses and celebrates their marital promises, the exclusive fidelity and openness to becoming parents together that jointly define marriage. Thus we speak of a couple entering into marriage as an "institution" with meanings, values and responsibilities that transcend the individual man and woman. The moral evaluation of *all* of a married couple's actions (not just their sexual actions) requires the dual focus already noted: primarily, whether their actions are intended to express and strengthen their marriage relationship, and secondarily, whether what they actually do to carry out their intentions is in keeping with the good of their marriage. Maintaining this dual

---

18. These two "objects" of focus correspond to what Thomas calls the "interior act" (the willing of an end by this means) and the "exterior act" (one's actual performance, doing this to achieve my end). As the example of organ donation by a living donor shows, an action which previously could not rightly be ordered to a good end (e.g., removal of a healthy kidney), is now able to be so ordered in the changed circumstances of modern medicine.

19. See Brennan, *The Open-Texture of Moral Concepts*, 105–24.

focus, it is easy to see why the psychological and biological features of sexual intercourse make it uniquely suited for embodying and deepening marital communion. That is precisely why only sexual union could constitute consummation in virtue of its unitive and procreative structure. As the kind of bodily union that naturally leads to conception, intercourse alone is capable of embodying the words, *I love you and I am willing to become a parent with you.*

On this account we do not derive the marital meaning from biological nature; rather we understand "the biology" in the light of the meaning of marriage. Of course, biology points in a marital direction—for sexual intercourse has natural features, both psychological and physiological, which make it apt for the embodiment of marital meaning. Nonetheless, understanding the goodness of marital intercourse begins with understanding marriage as the crucial ethical relationship between a couple (their context of giving and receiving), and then moves to consider why sexual intercourse is uniquely suited to being given and received as the expression of the twofold meaning of this relationship. It is in the light of the goodness of marital sex that fornication and adultery are known to be bad.

The most controversial part of the Church's teaching, however, is not that marriage requires sexual consummation, but that sexual intercourse requires the context of marriage. It might be objected that an explanation of the goodness of marital intercourse does not thereby show that every form of sexual activity should be marital. Since sex is valuable for numerous reasons quite apart from its procreative function, might not other forms of sexual activity have their own proper ethical standards, and be justified by their capacity to embody other (albeit non-marital) meanings?

The dual focus of moral evaluation enables us to state this objection more clearly. Thus, (primary focus) we might agree that—to put it in general terms—it is good for people to be physically intimate in keeping with the depth and quality of their relationship; the difficult question (secondary focus), however, is whether genital activity in particular is appropriate in a relationship that is not marital in the full sense. With respect to the Church's teaching, the critical question is not *why should every sexual act conform to a pre-given biological order,* but *why should every sexual act embody the meaning of marriage?* If it should, we will then have to address further questions about *what is required of a sexual act for it to have a marital meaning.* It will emerge that marital meaning does indeed require an act to have certain physical features, but this is not a case of deducing ethics from physical nature. On the contrary, nature acquires its true significance in the light of an ethical understanding of sex as marital activity. To this issue I now turn.

Catholic Sexual Ethics As a Distinctively Marital Ethics

The question is whether *those who are not married are free to give their genital activity a non-marital meaning*. Since procreation is one of the essential elements in marriage, the precise relationship between sex as personal intimacy and sex as procreative union needs to be clarified. We now know that intercourse is not the not the *per se* cause of conception. Rather, from the (scientific) observer's viewpoint, intercourse is the kind of act which can, but usually does not, lead to conception. For the observer, therefore, the link between sex and procreation might seem inconclusive: on the one hand, heterosexual intercourse "naturally" leads to conception, while, on the other hand, normally intercourse does not lead to conception. As observers we might be inclined to the popular idea that procreation should be regarded as an optional extra to sexual intimacy.

However, we are not primarily scientific observers of our sexual acts. We are the agents of our actions. Our perspective is first-personal: *I act* in and through what I do, and what I do sexually I do through (bodily) actions which reflect back on and shape who I am as a person. From the first-person, agent perspective, procreation is *always* an aspect of one's sexual activity, because genital actions prompt questions about their meaning and consequences as procreative. For both men and women, the progression of sexual arousal to climax reveals and makes available their potential fertility—irrespective of whether or not it can be actualised on a given occasion.[20]

It would obviously be wrong for a couple to engage in an act that could be procreative and yet not to take responsibility for its procreative consequences (and, likewise, for its propensity to spread infection)—hence the "safe sex" mantra of popular education programmes. There are, however, two ways in which people might take responsibility for the procreative aspect of sex: they might refrain from any sexual activity that could be procreative when it would not be right for a child to be conceived, or they

---

20. A man and a woman may be sure their intercourse will not be procreative, yet that certainty is subsequent to knowing their act is of a kind which could be procreative if certain conditions were met.

might use some form of contraception to ensure their sex will not be procreative. Because contraception renders the sexual act non-procreative, it thereby raises the same ethical issue as do sexual acts that are *of their nature* non-procreative (e.g., homosexual acts), viz. whether it is right for human beings to act genitally in non-procreative ways.

To clarify what is meant by a non-procreative sexual act, we can consider the frequent objection that abstinence in so-called natural family planning also involves trying to prevent intercourse from being procreative. The reply is that couples using fertility awareness and couples using contraception might well have the same goal, to avoid pregnancy. However, *what these couples actually do* is quite different. Couples using fertility awareness respect intercourse as the procreative act—from which they refrain at times of presumed fertility. Couples using contraception do something before, during or after intercourse to ensure it is not a procreative act; they thus treat their potential fertility as a problem to be dealt with by mechanical or chemical means, so that their subsequent decisions about when to have intercourse can be made quite independently of any consideration about its procreative nature.

I have not yet argued that contraception and homosexual activity are wrong. Contraception has been introduced only because it highlights the fundamental issue of how the procreative potential of heterosexual intercourse enters into our understanding of the nature of sex. There is a difference between choosing sexual acts of a kind that lead to procreation and choosing sexual acts that are essentially non-procreative, whether because of contraception or for some other reason (e.g., because they are homosexual acts). The former choice respects and accepts our bodily nature as sexual-procreative beings, whereas the latter involves changing our bodily nature in order to prevent sexual activity from reaching its natural end. It might be objected that homosexual activity does not involve *changing* the activity to become non-procreative, for it already is non-procreative. However, homosexual activity is *human activity*—it does not occur apart from choice. So those choosing to engage in homosexual acts are choosing to exercise their genital capacity in a non-procreative way; in this sense they *make* their sexual activity non-procreative.

In comparing the psychologism of contemporary approaches with the so-called physicalism of traditional teachings, we noted the underlying issue of respect for the psycho-physical-spiritual unity of the human person. This fundamental issue is likewise manifest when considering the way contraception and homosexual activity involve *changing* the nature of certain human acts. Here we reach the bed-rock of the Church's teaching: viz. that we are body-soul unities for whom God's plan for our happiness includes respect for the way we have been created.

A Holistic Understanding of Human Persons

The bed-rock of this teaching has been articulated in various ways. Firstly, traditional theology has focussed on respect for nature as God's good creation. Once we understand the choice to have sex as the choice to engage in the procreative act, and once we appreciate the value of new human life, we are led to respect the unique value of the sex act. In Janet Smith's terms, the human act which is naturally ordered to procreation shares in the intrinsic value of procreation itself. *Therefore,* it is wrong to impede the procreative power of actions ordained to assisting God in the creation of new human life.[21] The simple thought here will resonate with many people: understanding the sexual act as procreative prompts reverence for both the act itself and for the new human being it may bring about, and hence generates a moral reluctance to use this act in ways which fail to respect its procreative nature, or which make this act less than it ought to be.

Secondly, St John Paul II's "theology of the body" concludes that if a couple make their sexual intercourse non-procreative, they make it less than the full expression of their marital commitment; their act no longer says (as they did on their wedding day), *I give myself fully to you as spouse and potential parent*. On this account, contraception removes the power of intercourse as a "language of the body" to represent the mutual, total self-giving of spouses: the couple hold something back; they don't allow their act to be all it is suited to be. Again the simple thought will resonate with many people: the exercise of sexuality in non-procreative ways puts a person's actions and intentions at odds with the natural language of their bodies; such persons may wish to express their mutual self-giving but they do so in sexual acts whose natural parental meaning has been excluded.

Thirdly, we might invoke Brian Johnstone's gift methodology to argue that for sexual union to given and received as a free gift, it should be in such a way as to enhance the giving and receiving which is constitutive of the Christian tradition.[22] For Johnstone, the bed-rock of the tradition is "that

---

21. See Smith, *Humanae Vitae*, 100.
22. See Johnstone, "The Truth about Homosexuality."

form of mutual self-giving which can generate new life, new givers and receivers, who may carry on the community and its traditions across time." While abstinence may be in keeping with the logic of the gift, contraception involves "a form of dominion over the body" contrary to the freedom of gift-giving. Similarly, Johnstone concludes that "it has not been shown that the physical expression itself [of a homosexual relationship] might positively contribute to the tradition"—which "commends self-giving expressed in intercourse open to procreation, because this is the necessary, historical condition for the generation of new givers and receivers."[23]

These three lines of argument will not convince all and clearly require elaboration that is not possible here. In particular, they need strengthening by two insights of classical virtue ethics in order to address the widespread opinion among Catholic moral theologians that while sex is essentially linked to procreation, this link is not so strong as to require that marital intercourse *always* be ordered to procreation. First, the classical virtue perspective reminds us that morality is primarily about the underlying character and disposition of the agent. Authentic chastity, for example, is more than just *control* of one's inclinations. Rather, for the chaste person, the rightly ordered mastery of inclinations to what is pleasurable is embodied in his or her attitudes, emotional responses, habits, desires and choices. Ideally, a chaste person can literally trust their body to know and to feel what would be the right form of sexual intimacy in their particular circumstances. If procreation is an essential element in sexuality, then chastity must also embody procreative responsibility—so that, for example, a truly chaste person does not desire sexually someone with whom they cannot be a parent. In the case of a married couple, the practice of periodic abstinence can *embody* chastity and procreative responsibility because in this practice a couple integrate their sexual desires and actions in line with respect for the full meaning of sexual intercourse as unitive and procreative.

Secondly, even though growth in virtue is more important than individual acts, every act remains significant. A person doesn't become truthful by aiming to *generally* tell the truth! Occasional infidelity is still infidelity. Respect for the procreativity of sex should be embodied on every occasion of genital intimacy. A chastity which truly respects the link between sex and procreation will ensure that *each and every* sexual

---

23. Ibid. Echoing the critique of the dualist view of the person, Johnstone notes that arguments for the positive value of homosexual acts "seem to present a strangely disembodied, indeed a-sexual, notion of homosexuality."

act retains its procreative *meaning*, albeit not necessarily its procreative *function*. Accordingly, Humanae Vitae teaches that we *cannot* separate the unitive and procreative meanings of marital intercourse without undermining the marital act itself. "The Inseparability Principle . . . provides the very (anthropological) *rationale* that provides the reason *why* one *cannot* separate one meaning from the other . . . And because one *must not* destroy conjugal love (a point on which everyone agrees), this explains why *it is illicit* to effect such a separation."[24]

By contrast, "contraceptive acts render unnecessary the actions of periodic continence that contribute to the development of such habitual mastery through reason and will."[25] For those practicing contraception, respect for the procreative aspect of their sexuality will not be embodied in whatever otherwise respectful decisions they make about their sexual intimacy. Those who would justify homosexual activity will ask why the procreative aspect should be relevant in the case of people whose sexual activity of its nature cannot be procreative"? But this question returns us to the fundamental issue of whether human beings ought always to respect the procreative nature of heterosexual intercourse as *one* of the normative criteria for *all* good sex. A virtues argument does not address this question directly, for it presupposes the anthropological rationale of human body-soul unity that is central to the Catholic tradition. Yet, by drawing attention to the implications of this anthropological rationale, the virtues argument once again highlights the crucial significance of how we understand ourselves as human beings in relation to God as creator, and thus prompts a final question about the difference God should make to the moral life.

III. Why Should We Obey "the Law" of Our Nature?

The Catholic tradition holds that respect for the way God has made us, as male and female, as spiritual-bodily beings whose genital capacities are directed to procreative collaboration with him, means that rejection of one's procreative capacities is thereby a rejection of one crucial aspect of what we are and should become as virtuous men and women. However, someone might grant that it is reasonable to understand good sex as marital sex, and grant that this accords with a holistic understanding of what

---

24. Rhonheimer, *Ethics of Procreation*, 81. Cf. "each [meaning] receives its full intelligibility as a *human* reality . . . precisely *from the other*" (77).

25. Murphy, "Revisiting Contraception," 842.

it is to be human, and still ask: but why *should* we act in accord with this nature? Can't there be other more or less reasonable ways of understanding ourselves in which sex plays a different (and not necessarily marital) role? These questions raise the deeper question of the obligatory force of natural law reasoning.[26]

In the natural law tradition several key presuppositions are the basis for sound moral judgments: first, about the intelligibility of the world and the intelligibility of human nature as a coherent reality capable of being understood. This intelligibility underpins the universality of ethical truths about kinds of human action applicable to all human beings; secondly, about the capacity and the limitations of human reason to judge what is good and bad for us, and about the qualities of character required for sound moral judgments; thirdly, about our situation as creatures, dependent beings who are not the source of goodness, nor the autonomous judges of right from wrong; and, hence, fourthly, about God as creator and supreme source of being and goodness. Furthermore, as Peter Geach argued, if one believes there is a God, believes that God is all wise and all provident, believes that God commands us to do what is good and avoid what is bad,[27] and so concludes that God will give us sufficient guidance to assist our moral judgments, then we should further conclude that God would not want us to be always uncertain as to what is right and wrong in particular situations. God would not want us to be continually trying to work out if it would be permissible to lie, or to kill the innocent, in *this* situation—for that would mean that God has left us with no guidance at all! Hence, Geach argued, the imperfect knowledge we have that lying and killing the innocent are bad and therefore *generally* wrong is sufficient to be *in fact* the promulgation of God's law that lying and killing the innocent are *always* wrong, "even if [one] does not realise that this is a promulgation of the Divine law, even if [one] does not believe there is a God."[28]

An analogous argument can be offered as to the implications of our understanding of the goodness of some kinds of human action. Throughout this essay I have focussed on when sexual activity is good, and on why it is reasonable to understand sex as *the* marital act in virtue of its unitive

---

26. For a reminder about this point I am indebted to Lawrence Dewan, O.P., "St. Thomas, Natural Law, and Universal Ethics."

27. The first principle of natural law reasoning (see Thomas Aquinas, ST, I-II, 94.1).

28. Geach, *God and the Soul*, 117–29. He remarks that a local council No Parking sign is a promulgation of the law even if one falsely thinks it was erected by a neighbour who dislikes cars (125).

and procreative nature. In addition, the very nature of procreation as collaboration with God the author of life, further illuminates the goodness and dignity of sexual intercourse. Would it be reasonable both to affirm this vision of when and why sex is good, and also to affirm as good other non-marital uses of sex? Echoing Geach, I argue this would not be reasonable *for one who believes in God*: for if our understanding of the goodness of marital sex is not thereby a sufficient promulgation of God's law that sex *always* be marital, then God has left us with little insight into which actions compromise that goodness and so are forbidden.

That is to say, the vision of truly good human actions (e.g., marital union) includes within itself the obligation to avoid actions that destroy or undermine that goodness. While this truth can be grasped independently of belief in God, the reality of God explains why the good for us is obligatory.[29] "The vision of that reasonableness is the source of the obligation it presents to us."[30] Thus, for example, a couple who truly appreciate the goodness of sexual intercourse as the consummation of their marriage promises will feel obliged to reserve that intercourse until after they have actually made their promises.

More generally, by recognising what is good for us we also recognise what God wills for us, for the sake of our happiness, and conversely we recognise those evils we should avoid precisely because they detract from the goods proper to us as human beings. (To the question, why should we will God's intended happiness for us, we might agree with Geach that, "This is really an insane question."[31])

IV. Conclusion

The Catholic Church's teaching on marriage and sexuality are now wildly countercultural; the cognitive dissonance between official teaching and pastoral practice cries out for resolution. Nonetheless, I have argued that, despite its appealing simplicity, the proposal to judge all sexual activity against the standard of "love and respect for the other" is flawed by its approach to moral evaluation and by its assumptions about human nature and about God's role as creator. Yet, although the case for change has not

---

29. As Thomas says, if the end is good, whatever is necessary for that end obliges (see ST, I-II, 99.1).

30. Dewan, "St. Thomas," 746.

31. Geach, *God and the Soul*, 126.

been made out, it is true that understanding of the Church's teaching has long been distorted by an overly "objectivist" approach to morality, at worst by a kind of physicalism. The need for fresh insight into the Church's teaching is more urgent than ever.

Brian Johnstone's creative proposal for moral reasoning understands actions as gifts and persons as givers and receivers, rather than isolated agents. While this gift framework suggests fruitful ways of re-thinking traditional teachings, it does not entail radical change in teachings, as is clear from Johnstone's brief reflections on homosexual activity. This essay has sought to show why attention must be given to the moral object "in the restricted sense," and hence to the capacity of an action to be given and received in ways that enable further giving and receiving. The procreative nature of sexual activity will always remain crucial to understanding the gift that it is.

Bibliography

Brennan, J. M. *The Open-Texture of Moral Concepts*. London: Macmillan, 1977.
Dewan, Lawrence. "St. Thomas, Natural Law, and Universal Ethics." *Nova et Vetera* 9/3 (2011) 737–62.
Geach, Peter. *God and the Soul*. London: Routledge & Kegan Paul, 1969.
Gleeson, Gerald. "Are People More Important than Their Bodies?" *The Australasian Catholic Record* 82/2 (2009) 173–88.
Johnstone, Brian V. "Intrinsically Evil Acts." *Studia Moralia* 43 (2005) 379–406.
———. "The Truth about Homosexuality: A Reply to Gareth Moore, OP." *Australian EJournal of Theology* 4/1 (2005). http://aejt.com.au/2005/vol_4_no_1_2005/?article=395535
Murphy, William F. "Revisiting Contraception." *Theological Studies* 72/4 (2011) 812–47.
Pinckaers, Servais. "The Role of the End in Moral Action According to St Thomas." *Josephinum Journal of Theology* 17/2 (2010) 318–40.
Rhonheimer, Martin. *Ethics of Procreation and The Defence of Human Life*. Edited by William F. Murphy. Washington, DC: Catholic University of America Press, 2010.
Robinson, Geoffrey James. *The 2015 Synod—The Crucial Questions: Divorce and Homosexuality*. Hindmarsh, SA: ATF, 2015.
Smith, Janet. *Humanae Vitae—A Generation Later*. Washington, DC: Catholic University of America Press, 1991.
———, ed. *Why Humanae Vitae was Right: A Reader*. San Francisco: Ignatius, 1993.
Sokolowski, Robert. "What is Natural Law? Human Purposes and Natural Ends." *The Thomist* 68 (2004) 507–29.

it is to be human, and still ask: but why *should* we act in accord with this nature? Can't there be other more or less reasonable ways of understanding ourselves in which sex plays a different (and not necessarily marital) role? These questions raise the deeper question of the obligatory force of natural law reasoning.[26]

In the natural law tradition several key presuppositions are the basis for sound moral judgments: first, about the intelligibility of the world and the intelligibility of human nature as a coherent reality capable of being understood. This intelligibility underpins the universality of ethical truths about kinds of human action applicable to all human beings; secondly, about the capacity and the limitations of human reason to judge what is good and bad for us, and about the qualities of character required for sound moral judgments; thirdly, about our situation as creatures, dependent beings who are not the source of goodness, nor the autonomous judges of right from wrong; and, hence, fourthly, about God as creator and supreme source of being and goodness. Furthermore, as Peter Geach argued, if one believes there is a God, believes that God is all wise and all provident, believes that God commands us to do what is good and avoid what is bad,[27] and so concludes that God will give us sufficient guidance to assist our moral judgments, then we should further conclude that God would not want us to be always uncertain as to what is right and wrong in particular situations. God would not want us to be continually trying to work out if it would be permissible to lie, or to kill the innocent, in *this* situation—for that would mean that God has left us with no guidance at all! Hence, Geach argued, the imperfect knowledge we have that lying and killing the innocent are bad and therefore *generally* wrong is sufficient to be *in fact* the promulgation of God's law that lying and killing the innocent are *always* wrong, "even if [one] does not realise that this is a promulgation of the Divine law, even if [one] does not believe there is a God."[28]

An analogous argument can be offered as to the implications of our understanding of the goodness of some kinds of human action. Throughout this essay I have focussed on when sexual activity is good, and on why it is reasonable to understand sex as *the* marital act in virtue of its unitive

26. For a reminder about this point I am indebted to Lawrence Dewan, O.P., "St. Thomas, Natural Law, and Universal Ethics."

27. The first principle of natural law reasoning (see Thomas Aquinas, ST, I-II, 94.1).

28. Geach, *God and the Soul*, 117–29. He remarks that a local council No Parking sign is a promulgation of the law even if one falsely thinks it was erected by a neighbour who dislikes cars (125).

act retains its procreative *meaning*, albeit not necessarily its procreative *function*. Accordingly, Humanae Vitae teaches that we *cannot* separate the unitive and procreative meanings of marital intercourse without undermining the marital act itself. "The Inseparability Principle . . . provides the very (anthropological) *rationale* that provides the reason *why* one *cannot* separate one meaning from the other . . . And because one *must not* destroy conjugal love (a point on which everyone agrees), this explains why *it is illicit* to effect such a separation."[24]

By contrast, "contraceptive acts render unnecessary the actions of periodic continence that contribute to the development of such habitual mastery through reason and will."[25] For those practicing contraception, respect for the procreative aspect of their sexuality will not be embodied in whatever otherwise respectful decisions they make about their sexual intimacy. Those who would justify homosexual activity will ask why the procreative aspect should be relevant in the case of people whose sexual activity of its nature cannot be procreative"? But this question returns us to the fundamental issue of whether human beings ought always to respect the procreative nature of heterosexual intercourse as *one* of the normative criteria for *all* good sex. A virtues argument does not address this question directly, for it presupposes the anthropological rationale of human body-soul unity that is central to the Catholic tradition. Yet, by drawing attention to the implications of this anthropological rationale, the virtues argument once again highlights the crucial significance of how we understand ourselves as human beings in relation to God as creator, and thus prompts a final question about the difference God should make to the moral life.

III. Why Should We Obey "the Law" of Our Nature?

The Catholic tradition holds that respect for the way God has made us, as male and female, as spiritual-bodily beings whose genital capacities are directed to procreative collaboration with him, means that rejection of one's procreative capacities is thereby a rejection of one crucial aspect of what we are and should become as virtuous men and women. However, someone might grant that it is reasonable to understand good sex as marital sex, and grant that this accords with a holistic understanding of what

---

24. Rhonheimer, *Ethics of Procreation*, 81. Cf. "each [meaning] receives its full intelligibility as a *human* reality . . . precisely *from the other*" (77).

25. Murphy, "Revisiting Contraception," 842.

— 4 —

Gift as a Principle of Moral Action

Aristide Gnada

Introduction

At the present time, the concept of the gift is the object of various interpretations not only in the field of sociology and of anthropology,[1] but also in contemporary philosophy beginning with the contributions of Jacques Derrida (1930–2004) and of Jean-Luc Marion.[2] In the socio-anthropological discourse concerning gift, there is a conviction that the triple obligation to give, to receive and to give back constitutes the basis for social interactions. Derrida and Marion question this understanding of gift, because, according to them, the giver, the object given and the one receiving the gift each in their own way makes gift impossible, instead gift is transformed into a system of exchange and economy, rather than free as a gift ought to be. However, if according to Derrida true gift remains absolutely impossible, though being thinkable, desirable and speakable on account of its connection to ethics, for Marion, it is impossible only in the context of economy and exchange, but not from the standpoint of gift as reduced to giving and irreducible to exchange and/or to economy.[3]

Alongside the Derridian deconstruction of the concept of gift and the phenomenology of Marion on giving, we have the ontology of gift by

---

1. See Mauss, *Essai sur le don*; Godbout, *L'esprit du don*; Godbout, *Le langage du don*; Godbout, *Ce qui circule entre nous*; Caillé, *Anthropologie du don*.

2. Derrida, *Donner le temps*; Derrida, "Donner la mort," 11–108; Marion, "Esquisse d'un concept phénoménologique du don," 75–94. Marion, *étant donné*.

3. See Caputo, "Apôtres de l'impossible," 33–51.

Bruaire who considers gifting the essence of man's way of being spiritual.[4] For Bruaire, a human being, in so far as he is a spiritual being, is a gift of being in himself, destined to be a gift in his nature and gift for others. As such, one cannot negate one's nature which is an absolute gift, nor can one refuse one's ontological reality which is to be-gift, nor neglect one's manner of being which is to be a gift. The ontology of gift in Bruaire can approach the theology of gift in John Paul II who affirms that man can only be realized in the giving of oneself to another; this is the centre of his vocation and the source of his happiness. For John Paul II, gift is the way to pass from being an individual taken with himself to being a person open to God in order to be sustained in our gift of self to others; and human freedom means, in the perspective of evangelical freedom, the gift of self and the discipline of gift, a free initiative, and personal obligation.[5]

The hermeneutics of gift in the various disciplines reveals that with the gift we are in front of a multi-meaning and ambivalent term, in front of a complex and mysterious reality. Gift symbolizes affection, liking, love, comes across as a social, ontological and ethical bond, functions as a system of goodwill, of solidarity or a fundamental system of action.[6] The gift is a social fact that involves the economic, ecological, cultural, political, social, ethical and spiritual dimensions of man since moral theology has man and his actions as primary foci, it cannot be indifferent to the reality of gift.

Already A. Mattheeuws,[7] beginning with the assertion that gift is present in the universe, shows that gift is the basis of familiar ethics, but as Jean-Louis Bruguès says, it is really the whole of theology, and therefore moral theology as well would draw a definite advantage from considering this concept.[8] In this perspective and inspired by G. Richard,[9] I will attempt to show in the first part of this paper gift as a fundamental experience of being human; in the second part that moral life is fundamentally giving of self to the other as the Divine analogously gives of the Divine-self to humanity; and in the third part that gift is the principle of moral action.

---

4. See Bruaire, *Pour la métaphysique*, 258–66 ; Bruaire, *L'être et l'esprit*.
5. See John Paul II, *Letter to Families*, 14.
6. See Dumont, *Le Don*; Benveniste, *Problèmes de linguistique générale*, 316–23; Comito, "Dire 'dono' oggi," 27–28; Zanardo, *Il legame del dono*, 6–62 and 535–603. Godbout, *Ce qui circule entre nous*, 277–88 and 122–57.
7. See Mattheeuws, *Amarsi per donarsi*.
8. Ibid., 11.
9. See Richard, *Nature et formes du don*.

1. Gift as a Fundamental Experience of Being Human

If we consider experience as all that is grasped by the senses and makes up the stuff of human knowledge, a totality of known and knowable phenomenon, in other words, that which is applied to all that is gathered or has been undertaken by human beings obtained from another or communicated to another, we can ask: What is the fundamental experience of the person?

Reflecting on this question we realize that, before being able to discern, the human person has been in touch with the reality of gift, the gift of the possibility of being, and that, at the awakening of conscience, one tests the truth of gift at least under three forms: the ontic form or the gift of something determinate, the non-ontic form or the educational gift, and the ontological form or gift of personal being. In the first two forms, that we can call human gift, we test our capacity of gift in receiving and in giving, while in the third form we test the impossibility of gift for us and, therefore, the dependence of our being from a giving origin, called God in different religions.

In the ontic form of gift, we experience the three categories of gift that are destined to offer a possibility to the giver: gifts that allow the giver to simply be or to live, for instance procreation[10] or the gift of life, medical care and every activity that ensures the survival of another; gifts that allow the giver to be a person capable of focusing and aiming toward a purpose, for instance, everything that concerns instruction;[11] and gifts that allow the giver to consider himself in his personal dignity and not as diminished, for example, ones affect, ones cares, certain works of art and philosophical or theological doctrines.[12]

From our experience of education, we can say that education is more than transferring something determinate as in instruction, rather to educate is to draw out of the other that which is not really oneself, and to develop in him that which remains irreducible to a conglomerate influence of material reality. Education consists practically in a conversion of the other to the truth of his being, by which this always takes the form of a dispossession, always appears to the student as an undesirable, unexpected, unforeseen event and, consequently, possibly only in the spirit of the gratuitousness

---

10. It is necessary to distinguish the meaning of generation from creation: generation or the gift of life consists in giving the possibility of existence, of life, while creation or ontological gift consists in the giving of being itself.

11. To learn to speak, to write, to read, technical formation, scientific, etc.

12. See Richard, *Nature et formes du don*, 110–15.

of a gift calls the other to help him discover and live, in accordance with the truth of his being, to welcome a reality that precedes it and is offered to him.[13]

From these two kinds of phenomenon, it is possible to draw some characteristics of gift as a stark concept: the absence of compensation that we find in the common definition of gift as a transfer of something that is free; the threesome constitution of gift in giver, receiver and object given; the centrality and the primacy of the giver when we speak of gift; the impossibility of gift being required as a proof and criterion of what is demanded to the highest degree of being given; recognition of the other in his dignity of being in his own right and in the reality of limits and of need; the ideal giver as someone who appears not only as not having but who presents himself as someone who lets the other discover the truth of his own being; the indifference, in the sense of the gratuitousness or an act motivated by concern for the other, as a natural quality of gift.

Human experience helps us discover the true reality of gift, in virtue of its basic and fundamental nature, is effectively solid, stable and sure in its expression, and acts to arouse in the human person trust and fidelity, making one a being acting steadfast with gift, that is giver and receiver. Charity in truth, writes Benedict XVI, sets man in front of the amazing experience of gift.[14] In fact, from the beginning and always gift forms social bonds, it enters into interpersonal relations and is manifested in the reciprocity of gift. The human person is formed and shaped by the truth of gift, in order that his existential experience is essentially an experience of gift, an experience that is universal in space and permanent in time. The existence of the human person is inseparable from gift, and his history is a history of gift beginning with the ontological gift that he is.

That the human person is an ontological gift, can be deduced from the experience of gift itself and helps us discover the essential shape of the human not only as a giver but also equally as a receiver. Being giver, either in the sense of ontic gift or of educational gift presupposes a fundamental capacity to give, and to give to the other presupposes in the other a fundamental capacity to receive. Now the double capacity to give and receive presupposes in turn a giver distinct from man and a form of gift distinct from human gift: God and creation. Creation is a fundamental and primordial gift because in (creation) appears man who, as image of God, is

---

13. Ibid., 136–70.
14. See Benedict XVI, *Caritas in veritate*, 34.

capable of understanding the meaning of gift in the creation of existence from nothing.[15]

The experience of gift helps us to discover gift as the suitable concept to describe what personal being is really and essentially: The human person is gift to himself; he is a gift-being, whose identity returns to the creative action that was a free act and a free gift. The human person has, therefore, a gift origin that identifies him with the absolute gift: God. Because the person does not derive his origins from himself, he cannot but be *given*, and because he is given to *himself*, he cannot but be free. The human person is a given being given to himself, a free being in the image of his given origin: God-Creator. Gift, as an initial reality, describes the person and his actions in freedom.

According to Thomas Aquinas, "it ought to belong to a divine person to be given and to be Gift" and "from all eternity a divine person is said to be Gift."[16] When Saint John asserts that "God is Love" (1 John 4:16), he merely states that love, the gift of self, is the essence God, One, and Three. God is the infinite power of being in a unity of love, whose reality is expressed by fatherly generation, filial reciprocation, and spiritual confirmation.[17] "In his intimate life, teaches John Paul II, God "is love," the essential love shared by the three divine Persons: personal love is the Holy Spirit as the Spirit of the Father and the Son."[18]

In spite of its formal plurality—ontic, educational, and ontological—gift, in so far as it fulfills the other, is an unambiguous concept that we can understand as a means of one person relating to another fully destined for another, but incapable of achieving it by himself. In fact, the ontic gift is the unique concept of gift that preserves the physical integrity of the other. The educational gift is the unique form of gift that helps the other to find the truth of being human. The ontological gift is the unique kind of gift that establishes the human person as a gift given to himself, to the world and to God. Yet experience reveals that this being, fundamentally "made for gift," is not always recognized as such "because of a purely consumerist and utilitarian view of life."[19]

---

15. See John Paul II, *Uomo e donna lo creò*, 73.
16. See Aquinas, *Summa Theologica* Ia, Q. 38, Art. 1.
17. See Bruaire, *L'être et l'esprit*, 190–93.
18. John Paul II, *Dominun et vivificantem*, 10.
19. Benedict XVI, *Caritas in veritate*, 34.

In fact, the human person is a being who comes from gift, who lives in a universe of gift, who is a being open to gift, a being infused by the truth of gift and guided by the logic of gift, in such a way that to deny gift is enough to deny the truth and the logic of his existence. Did not moral evil from our origins spoken of in the Book of Genesis (Gen 3:1–13), enter into the heart of humankind by means of a false gift, or a false promise? Wasn't the fratricide committed by Cain (Gen 4:1–16) the consequence of a refusal, by Cain, of the logic of gift that implies freedom of the giver? In any case, the wickedness or the malice of a human action always lies in the negation of gift, under the guise of *anti-gift*[20] which consists in acting contrary to gift and under the appearance of *neglect*,[21] which consists simply in the refusal of responding to the call of the other.

In the first instance, the other is considered as an absolute center albeit negative of an action that tries to destroy his otherness and his ontological dignity as a finite being in his own right. Thus, the different forms of homicide and any other means of harming the well-being of another as such makes one opposed to the possibility of the gift of being and living. The lack of the educational gift prevents the possibility of the gift being realized within an individual responsible for himself and for others. Hatred, contempt, and indifference prevent the possibility of the gift being seen in the proper dignity of the person. In the second instance, we are talking about abandoning the other in her misery, in her suffering, and even her death. The negation of gift, therefore, under the form of neglect or refusal presents itself as a contradiction of gift. The other is considered as a simple part of an ontic reality. Even if it is, sometimes, the object of interest or of apparently generous busyness, it is, in fact, possessive and falls always into being considered an ontic reality, with nothing more than a state of relative and momentary concern.

The possibility of negating the gift of the other is in itself evidence that the human person, in so far as he is a given being and therefore free, finds himself, according to the logic of gift expressed in brotherhood and in the demands of giving as always with freedom and the possibility of accepting or refusing, affirming or denying gift. Left to himself, man is logically free of the logic of gift and at risk of becoming consumed in the isolation of refusal and the negation of the other through certain forms of violence and

---

20. See Richard, *Nature et formes du don*, 117–19.
21. Ibid., 119–20.

indifference, based on a utilitarian and egocentric conception of the human being, as we observe in the violation of fundamental human rights.

All the arguments or justifications that we are able to advance in favour of a violation of human rights, for instance, the violation of the right to life, are reduced unquestionably to self-centeredness and a tendency to be concerned exclusively with ones own pleasure and interests without any concern for the other. Now a morally good life, that allows man, who is in full possession of his ability to walk freely toward a profound fulfillment of himself, freed from any alienation, consists in accepting himself as gift and living in accordance with the logic of gift that essentially defines him. We are dealing here of a moral life that, in the perspective of Christian ethics, we can understand as a life of love or a gift to the other analogous to the mystery of the Incarnation: The Divine gift of God-self to man or divine love towards others.

2. The Moral Life as a Gift to the Other Analogous to the Divine Gift of God-self to Man

In light of the mystery of the Incarnation, understood as the mystery of God's self-giving to humanity (see Luke 1:26–38), love can be seen as a double desire both for the good of the other and of being united to the other: missing one or the other form of desire, that is the good of the other or that being united to the other, is not, to be precise, love in the full sense, but love in analogical sense. In love as desire for the good of the other and the desire for union with the other, the person who loves necessarily assumes that the good of the other is inseparable to this union and consists in being united to the other. The good of the other and the desire for union become one, as revealed in the mystery of the incarnation, as when God gives of Himself as one who is supremely desirable to fulfill man and who desires only the good of man.[22]

In the mystery of the incarnation that, from the point of view of love, is characterized by a total and irrevocable gift of self by God to man in Christ,[23] we are able to draw three conditions that form the legitimacy of love as gift of self or as one who gives. The first condition is that the person who gives must be capable of being a means to an end, while remaining an end himself. In fact, God, in the Son, has given Himself as an end in Him-

---

22. Ibid., 303–4.
23. See John Paul II, *General Audience* (September 29, 1982), 2.

self and as an adequate means of satisfying the desires of man. The second condition is that the person, that receives the other who gives, ought to be maintained in his identity in himself. In fact, it is insofar as an end in himself that man receives God. The third condition is that the good of the person who receives ought to be in harmony with the person who gives. In fact, the good of the person always consists in union with God. Thus, God is able to give of Himself as good to man without confusion of identity, without compromising us and without doing violence to man, for which, Jesus Christ, Son of the Incarnate God is true man and true God, according to our profession of Christian faith. Love in its truest sense is seen in a person desiring the good of the other and desiring to unite with the other, is received perfectly from God, and only derived from God through the inter-Trinitarian communion of God. Only God, because He is love and supremely desirable, is able to live out perfectly and legitimately love as gift of Himself or gift of His person to the other for the sake of the other.

In light of the mystery of the Incarnation, it is necessary to note the incapacity of man to live love in its most authentic meaning, whose purpose is to fill the human being with limitless desire. In actual fact, if man wants to be absolutely that which fills the infinite desire for the other, it will be at the cost of doing violence to the other. In fact, if man recognizing the limitless desire of the other, presents himself as someone who can fulfill these desires, this means he is forgetting that he is a creature, that he is forgetting his finiteness in order to be seen as the supreme desirable "object" of the other, and in this way he disfigures himself. But if instead man, recognizing his finiteness, presents himself as someone who fulfills the desire of the other, but will fulfill only a finite and limited desire, that is to say a desire which will have provoked or, however, accepted limitations, a desire which prevents an endless expansion, will in this circumstance do violence to the other.[24]

The gift of self to another makes sense and is real only if the self to be given is something the other has need of, only if the self is at the same time what is infinitely desired and fulfills every desire. In the case of man when we speak of love as gift of the self, the self refers to one or many aspects certainly meaningful, but not the entire being like the case of God. In fact, the gift of self in humans can have the sense of giving one's own life and is realized in the acceptance of sufferings and even death for another or in the name of another. The human gift of self can have the sense of consecrating

24. See Richard, *Nature et formes du don*, 307–8

one's own life to another and is realized in the entire and definite use of one's capacities, energies, resources, time, one's body and sexuality, for the other. The human gift of self can have the sense of conjugal love between man and woman and is realized in the union, body, and spirit, with the other. Then gift of self at the human level truly shows itself as gift of something that is not, to be precise, the self, even if there is the intention or the desire to give oneself. Human love, that is the human gift of self, is shown concretely in the gift of something and as educational gift, which are in actual fact imperfect forms of authentic love as gift of self expressed in the mystery of the Incarnation.

Nevertheless, these forms remain perfect forms that manifest the essence of gift of the human person and his participation in Divine Love, and by which it is always possible to lead the other to a communion with absolute gift, which is, in truth, the Trinitarian God who gives Himself as the supremely desirable good. In fact, human gift, in its various forms, reflects divine love, because divine love reveals a part of its mystery through every form of human gift. The analogy of human self-giving allows us to understand in a certain way the mystery of divine love, source and end of the moral life. The human person expresses gift through language, body, desire and freedom, in order to allow one to discover in himself and from himself gift as the principle of his moral actions that is a reality that is the uniting source, norm, and finality of moral action.

3. Gift as the Principle of Moral Action

A more careful consideration of human action shows that moral action is not distinct from human gift: gift of something and educational gift. Human gift and moral action are similar because they describe humanity and become realized in concrete actions that allow the other to simply be, to be capable of determining and moving toward a purpose, to consider himself as an end in his own right, and to discover and live in conformity with the truth of his being. To understand moral action as gift is to understand not only being in relationship, but the source of human responsibility towards others with respect to their rights and fundamental duties, and to understand human gift as a moral act means that the goodness of a human action resides in being an act of gift determined from the other as center, beginning and end in their own right, in view of adequately answering to their true, necessary and universal needs.

To acknowledge the human person as a gifted being is to recognize that, not only, is he free to cause whatever he himself does but also as a finite being who wants his dealings towards gift to be such that he cannot but give freely. Furthermore, because the human person is freely gifted as a person, he is infinitely in debt in his being[25] and, therefore, in the original state of surrender of himself at his beginnings.[26] But this surrender of self, or ontological conversion, that will be completed only in an interface with the original giver at the time of death,[27] this is already seen in the world as a moral conversion in the form of an opening towards the other and through the twin forms of ontic and educational gift (see Matt 25:32). The human person, because he is given to himself, is in debt within his being, and because he is in debt within his being, he is in a moral obligation, even if, thanks to his freedom he decides to deny it.

Human ethics, to be precise, cannot but be an ethic of gift as moral action, and every person, who follows the logic of gift, and truly leads a good moral life, because he is dealing with a logic which simultaneously includes every possible good and excludes evil: to give and to do good and avoid evil. Morality is duty in front of gift that each one has by the fact of existing. Abundance and gratuitousness constitute the substance of all moral objectivity.[28] Human action is morally good when it is an act of gift, an act that in the Christian perspective allows man to remain ever more in the image of God who is love and to participate in the love of God.

The believer in Christ is in fact called to be a witness to the generosity of God in Christ left to be moved by the spirit of gift as the motivating principle of his moral life which is concretized in acts of giving as a reply to the true, necessary and universal needs of others (see Matt 25:31–46; Jas 2:14–26; 1 John 2:7–11; 3:11–24). Gift is the natural locus of charity. Only within the logic of gift is the Christian able to show the greatness of their vocation in Christ and their duty of bringing charity to fruition

---

25. Debt is not a social or economic reality, nor a moral reality, but an ontological reality that places the human person as a dependent being and thus defined in his relationship with the original other.

26. See Bruaire, *L'être et l'esprit*, 60-61 ; Bruaire, *La force de l'esprit*, 27. Gift because it is free, is always open to a response under the guise of gratitude or of conformity to the gift received.

27. In the reciprocal gift of self to God, "man focuses and expresses all his energies that are part of his personal subjectivity together with his psychosomatic (reality)," see John Paul II, *Uomo e donna lo creò*, 270-71.

28. See Mattheeuws, *Amarsi per donarsi*, 334.

through their lives in the world. It is in this logic that the moral theologian is called to convey in the light of Jesus Christ's own commandment: "That you love one another as I have loved you" (John 15:12). The charity with which Christ has loved us overrides the juridical and moral demands that anyone could uphold. Charity takes in all good moral actions, including the chastisements, sanctions or punishments that we could legitimately set in virtue of the rights and duties of man, in justice.

Therefore, more than the spirit of justice, it is necessary to increase the spirit of gift for a livable world, a world where men worry and answer to necessary needs, true and universal needs of human beings in accordance with the logic of gift and of forgiveness which does not deny justice but surpasses it and completes it. "The earthly city is promoted not merely by relationships of rights and duties, but to an even greater and more fundamental extent by relationships of gratuitousness, mercy and communion. Charity always manifests God's love in human relationships as well, it gives theological and salvific value to all commitment for justice in the world."[29] A human society, beginning with the family, cannot live only from the works of justice that is to say of goods that derive from duty. What is necessary are actions flowing from gratuitousness that is actions that derive from the awareness of being tied into another who in a way forms part of my existence.

Gift shows itself not only as moral action but also as the principle of moral action that is as that which establishes it, directs it and orients it in all his dimensions: anthropological, social, economic, political, ecological. Gift is the beginning because it is not a reality invented by man, but a reality that man discovers as such in his existence and lived in the form of a gift of something and of education. In fact, in human existence, the person, from its conception to its death, receives from others the possibility of life, of tending to a goal, a bearer of dignity, and of discovering the truth of his being as someone who is an irreducible spirit within a corporeal dimension. Gift is, to be precise, an action of life that allows the human being to live, a law which naturally brings us to the goal of our being as humans, from which are expressed laws and rights and the answers of our natural inclinations: life, fertility, and sociability, and knowledge. The law of gift so structures human existence that no one can absolutely put it aside.[30]

---

29. Benedict XVI, *Caritas in veritate*, 6.
30. See Sagne, *La loi du don*, 5–8.

The fundamental law of gift as principle of moral action can be formulated this way: *moral action must be absolutely determined by reference to the other*. This law means that the determination of the circumstances of every moral action is deduced by the particular and determinate, universal and fundamental situation of the other as an end in itself. The other is presented, in light of the principle of gift, as one from whom one ought to consider doing moral action. This does not mean however submitting subserviently to the whims of the other. Rather, it determines to do moral action from the other as center and beginning demanding one to attenuate or at times defer one's desire, for instance in the case of a request that asks for euthanasia,[31] and as an education gift requires. In this gift, the educating subject is considered above all, in his identity as an end in himself, as a being irreducible in his contingent and particular needs that sometimes disguises his essential and true desires, and it is from this particular situation that the educator will help to find the truth of his being.

Application of the fundamental rule of moral behavior as gift requires, therefore, a moral criterion to follow. This criterion is based on the content of the action to be considered as gift that demands absolutely to be given: to be given, the thing must correspond to the necessary, true and universal need of the other. In accordance with this criterion, the absolute requirement of being given resides in its double character of being an end in itself and means: the thing to give must be at the same time be and not be an end in itself that is a *being-end* and a *being for* (for instance, a human organ). With respect to the first characteristic, the thing to give has neither price nor compensation, because the demands of being given are intrinsic to it. With respect to the second characteristic, the thing to give refers to the dignity of the person and, for this reason, cannot but be given to the other when it responds to necessary, true and universal need. In other words, without the character of finality in itself, the thing cannot absolutely demand to be given, but with the absolute character of a finality in itself, the thing demands absolutely not to be given, *a fortiori* to be sold or exchanged.[32]

---

31. Sacred Congregation for the Doctrine of the Faith, *Declaration on Euthanasia*: "The pleas of gravely ill people who sometimes ask for death are not to be understood as implying a true desire for euthanasia; in fact, it is almost always a case of an anguished plea for help and love. What a sick person needs, besides medical care, is love, the human and supernatural warmth with which the sick person can and ought to be surrounded by all those close to him or her, parents and children, doctors and nurses."

32. See Richard, *Nature et formes du don*, 106–9. A car can for example be sold or exchanged in so far as it is solely an instrument and a means, while a human being in so far as he is absolutely an end in itself, cannot be given to another.

In gift as a means of relating, the other is always in a situation of lacking what is necessary for being, a shortage of what is needed to be and, thus, is waiting to be fulfilled. But that which will fulfill the other will be truly a gift if what is demanded is not filling this or that condition, for example in expressing his need, but if the conditions of its realization have been left to the giver: the more a gift is truly gift, the less it demands the other to fulfill this or that condition in order to be a giver.[33] According to this criterion, we can make three observations: ontological gift is the far better gift because that which is received and the receiver one and the same, and therefore there are no expectations of getting something on the part of the giver; the educational gift is a greater gift when compared to the ontic gift, not only because it is assumed, but because all its demands, its conditions are dependent on the educator; the human embryo is the giver par excellence of the ontic form of gift, because the conditions demanded by it are reduced to the simple presence of the human person who does not ask anything other than affective, nutritional and medical care in order to live and grow.

In front of a certain ethical-medical discrimination of the human embryo with the excuse of avoiding the birth of abnormal children, the anthropology of gift and the theology of gift cannot but confirm that the human embryo, as every human person, is a given-being, a being that, in his weakness, poverty and fragility, necessarily has need of suitable gifts to exist.[34] We are dealing here of a moral challenge given to man who is in full possession of his own existential faculties and who can apply the law of gift as natural moral law. Rationality of gift alone seems able to deal with such a challenge. A human being, depending on age and circumstances, wants to preserve his life, to preserve his species, to live together with others and to know the truth, but the fundamental experience of gift reveals that the realization of these tendencies is possible only through gift and, thereby, inseparable and contingent upon the action of gift. Recognizing gift as the principle of moral action is really seeing not only gift as the beginning and end of human existence, but also as the as the unifying and universal instance of human actions and, thus, the norm par excellence that directs man on the way to a morally good life, in which one seeks to respect the human person in his identity of given-being, considering his otherness according to the logic of giving and in the spirit of love.

33. See ibid., 154–55.
34. See Mattheeuws, *Amarsi per donarsi*, 281–92.

Conclusion

If gift allows us to explain moral action in its source, norm, and finality, then it also reveals itself as principle of the moral theology that we can understand as a theological science that reflects on human behaviour in the light of divine revelation of love and the human experience of gift. Understood as such moral theology with the key of gift allows one to reaffirm, in the face of the ethical relativism, the existence of an universal ethics based on gift. The concept of gift which transcends every culture justifies not only the universality of moral theology but also its theological specificity that consists in the welcome and in the examination of divine revelation to answer humans who are always seeking the reasons for their actions. "Moral theology is a reflection concerned with "morality," with the good and the evil of human acts and of the person who performs them; in this sense it is accessible to all people."[35]

With gift, moral reflection is rooted in anthropology and in theology, because we are dealing with a concept that guarantees a link with ethics, anthropology, and theology, in which is recognized the truth of gift as the foundational, normative and orienting principle of moral theology and can thus help to facilitate a moral discourse much more rational and perhaps more acceptable to contemporary people. The category of gift opens the door to a true moral theological discourse, not only because it allows a connection between moral truths and ontological truths of man, but also because it expresses with clarity the means of realizing the fundamental precepts of natural moral law: namely, doing good and avoiding evil. From the point of view of universal ethics and within a strict fidelity to Christian ethics which is essentially an ethics of love, gift can not only serve as a criterion for a moral theological discourse but also help the moral theologian to forsake a picture that is too dry, even too rigid, with ought-to and obligations, to focus on laws of forgiveness and charity.[36]

The logic of gift as the principle of moral action is such that it establishes the full promotion of the human person in his identity and diversity as a given being. Man, however, whose ontological freedom we suppose, depending on age and circumstances, has freedom of choice and of action, can confirm or invalidate this logic. Yet if it happens that man invalidates this logic, acting in the opposite meaning of gift or contradicting gift, if it

---

35. John Paul II, *Veritatis Splendor*, 29.
36. See Mattheeuws, *Amarsi per donarsi*, 11.

happens that he acts in a-logical way, we can no longer speak of a moral good, but of a moral evil with all its consequences, not only to the victim but also to himself as author. In fact, in every action contrary to the logic of gift denies the infinite otherness of the other, hurting his true dignity as a gift-being.[37]

Yet gift, in its solidity and certainty, reminds us that, with forgiveness, it is always possible to reestablish all that has been denied and wounded. To forgive, that is to renounce punishing a lack or taking revenge for an offense, putting aside grudges towards another because of his wickedness, is demonstrated in the survival of infinite otherness and contemporarily it affirms the dignity of the other over and above his attitudes of violence or of indifference. Gift shows its omnipotence, victory, and overabundance through the person who has been negated by violence or indifference, turning him into a giver: a person who forgives, and through the person who has negated making him a receiver: a person forgiven.

Bibliography

Angelo, Comito. "Dire 'dono' oggi: tra linguaggio e significato." In *Il dono. Iniziatore di senso, di relazioni e di polis*, edited by Giacomo Panizza. Soneria Mannelli: Rubbettino, 2003.

Aquinas, Thomas. *Summa Theologica*. Translated by The Fathers of the English Dominican Province. New York: Benziger, 1947. http://dhspriory.org/thomas/summa/FP/FP038.html#FPQ38OUTP1.

Benedict XVI. *Caritas in veritate*. Encyclical letter on integral human development in charity and truth. June 29, 2009. http://w2.vatican.va/content/benedict-xvi/en/encyclicals/documents/hf_ben-xvi_enc_20090629_caritas-in-veritate.html.

Benveniste, Émile. *Problèmes de linguistique générale*. Paris: Gallimard, 1966.

Bruaire, Claude. *L'être et l'esprit*. Paris: Presses Universitaires de France, 1983.

———. *Pour la métaphysique*. Paris: Librairie Arthème Fayard, 1980.

Caillé, Alain. *Anthropologie du don. Le tiers paradigme*. Paris: de Brouwer, 2000.

Caputo, John D. "Apôtres de l'impossible: sur Dieu et le don chez Derrida et Marion." *Philosophie* 78 (2003) 33–51.

Derrida, Jacques. "Donner la mort." In *L'éthique du don. Derrida et la pensée du don*, edited by Jean-Michel Rabaté and Michael Wetzel, 11–108. Paris: Transition, 1992.

———. *Donner le temps, I. La fausse monnaie*. Paris: Galilée, 1991.

Dumont, Jean-Noël. *Le Don. Théologie, philosophie, psychologie, sociologie*. Lyon: l'Emmanuel, 2001.

Godbout, Jacques. *Ce qui circule entre nous. Donner, recevoir, rendre*. Paris: du Seuil, 2007.

———. *L'esprit du don*. Paris: Découverte, 1992.

---

37. Moral evil is precisely the evil of man as such, moral good is the good of man as such, see John Paul II, *General Audience* (July 20, 1983), 3.

———. *Le langage du don*. Québec: Fides, 1996.
John Paul II. *Dominun et vivificantem* [Encyclical letter on the Holy Spirit in the Life of the Church and the World]. May 18, 1986. Homebush: St. Paul, 1986.
———. *General Audience*. September 29, 1982. https://w2.vatican.va/content/john-paul-ii/it/audiences/1982/documents/hf_jp-ii_aud_19820929.html.
———. *General Audience*. July 20, 1983. http://w2.vatican.va/content/john-paul-ii/it/audiences/1983/documents/hf_jp-ii_aud_19830720.html.
———. *Gratissimam sane* [Letter to Families]. February 2, 1994. https://w2.vatican.va/content/john-paul-ii/en/letters/1994/documents/hf_jp-ii_let_02021994_families.html.
———. *Uomo e donna lo creò. Catechesi sull'amore umano*. Vatican: Libreria Editrice Vaticana, 2003.
———. *Veritatis Splendor* [Encyclical Letter Regarding Certain Fundamental Questions of the Church's Moral Teaching]. August 6, 1993. Boston: St. Paul, 1993.
Marion, Jean-Luc. "Esquisse d'un concept phénoménologique du don." *Archivio di filosofia* 1–3 (1994) 75–94.
———. *étant donné. Essai d'une phénoménologie de la donation*. Paris: Presses Universitaires de France, 1997.
Mattheeuws, Alain. *Amarsi per donarsi. Il sacramento del matrimonio*. Venice: Marcianum, 2008.
Mauss, Marcel. *Essai sur le don. Forme et raison de l'échange dans les sociétés archaïques*. Paris: Presses Universitaires de France, 2007.
Richard, Gildas. *Nature et formes du don*. Paris: L'Harmattan, 2000.
Sacred Congregation for the Doctrine of the Faith. *Iura et Bona* [Declaration on Euthanasia]. May 5, 1980. Boston: Pauline, 1980.
Sagne, Jean-Claude. *La loi du don. Les figures de l'Alliance*. Lyon: Presses Universitaires de Lyon, 1997.
Zanardo, Susy. *Il legame del dono*. Milan: Vita e Pensiero, 2007.

5

Natural Law Debates and the Forces of Nature

JAMES F. KEENAN, S.J.

In studying the force of nature, under the study of ethics, the natural law obviously arises as an important resource. This law however is seen under two very different contexts of interpretation. These differences must be studied if we are to see how (and under what interpretative key) natural law ethics is to help our approach to sustainability issues.[1]

For more than forty years, Catholic theological ethics has become deeply affected by two differing fundamental stances. These stances arose from theologians asking the question: how do we know moral truth? The question became particularly acute when in 1968, Pope Paul VI, published the birth control encyclical *Humanae vitae* where he insisted that church teaching on the prohibition was universal, absolute and incapable of being changed. One philosopher/theologian the Canadian Jesuit Bernard Lonergan offered a host of insights into a new epistemology concerning how we understand moral truth.[2] Foundational to his work was the turn to the subject.[3]

---

1. As a tribute to Brian V. Johnstone, I thought an article on method and nature seemed very appropriate. See some of his work on this: "A Proposal for a Method in Moral Theology"; "Moral Experience in the Test of History"; "From Physicalism to Personalism"; "The Revisionist Project in Roman Catholic Moral Theology"; and "Erroneous Conscience in *Veritatis Splendor* and the Theological Tradition."

2. Lonergan, *Insight*.

3. Lonergan, "Christ as Subject," 242–70.

As the church was trying to anticipate what the pope would teach, Lonergan published in 1967 three articles that profoundly influenced our understanding of articulating moral truth: "The Dehellenization of Dogma," "The Transition from a Classicist World-View to Historical-Mindedness," and "Theology in its New Context."[4] In them, Lonergan offered the distinction between the classicist and the historicist world-views and during the next forty years this distinction would provide two differing directions to moral theology.[5] Still, there is a significant caveat regarding this distinction; they are not differences in kind but in degree; no one can be a pure classicist or a pure historicist and sometimes scholars are classicist in one field and historicists in another.

For classicists, the world is a finished product and truth has already been revealed, expressed, taught and known. In order to be a truth it must be universal and unchanging. Clarity is key. Since principles are considered fixed and unchanging, moral logic is deductive: the classicists apply the principle to the situation and derive an answer as the conclusion of a syllogism.

The moral law is found then in that which is always true, never changes, and always applies. The truth claims of a statement are demonstrated when we can claim possession of the same truth for centuries: Consistency in historical transmission generates phrases like, "as we have always taught . . ." Change in moral teaching is, then, problematic; it suggests that at one point a teaching was right and, in a later (or earlier) instance, wrong. Similarly, classicists resist contextualization. The truth cannot be compromised by local claims; if it is, it is dismissed as culturally relativistic. The universality and constancy of the truth claim is central. While everyone knows that Church teachings have not unequivocally remained the same, classicists argue that these teachings "develop," but they do not change.[6] This is more a posited claim than a proven one. When considering the absolute prohibition against usury it is hard to call the foundation of the *Banco Santo Spirito* (Bank of the Holy Spirit) as simply a "development" of the teaching against usury.

---

4. Lonergan, "Dehellenization of Dogma"; idem, "Transition from A Classicist World View"; idem, "Theology in its New Context."

5. Keane, "The Objective Moral Order"; Melchin, *History, Ethics and Emergent Probability*; Gula, *Reason Informed by Faith*; Kopfensteiner, "Historical Epistemology"; Miller, *Living Ethically in Christ*.

6. See the important work on the church's teaching by John T. Noonan Jr., *The Church that Can and Cannot Change*.

Four other assumptions held by the classicists must be understood. First, classicists identify God's characteristics with those of God's will and God's law. As God is, so are God's teachings. God is eternal, unchanging, universally the same. Similarly, God's willed teachings have the same qualities. Second, the church is the guardian of that deposit of the truth; her leaders cannot change church teaching because they must not undermine God's will. Their role is to promote and proclaim again and again the constant teaching of the church. Third, for this reason the credibility of the church is invested in its constancy; were the church to change established teaching it would jeopardize the grounds of confidence that the faithful have in her. Fourth, the reason why people do not adhere to the truth is not because they do not or cannot understand it, or that it is unreasonable. Rather, the innate weaknesses and wickedness of human beings hinder their ability to follow the law of God. Thus call for reform of the law is a charade. No one wants to reform the law but rather to abandon its claim on us.

A fine example of these presuppositions being operative in church teaching can be found in Pius XI's encyclical *Casti Connubii* (1930) which upheld a clear classicism in the teachings on marriage, and in particular, the practice of contraception. The pope writes:

> Since, therefore, openly departing from the uninterrupted Christian tradition some recently have judged it possible solemnly to declare another doctrine regarding this question, the Catholic Church, to whom God has entrusted the defense of the integrity and purity of morals, standing erect in the midst of the moral ruin which surrounds her, in order that she may preserve the chastity of the nuptial union from being defiled by this foul stain, raises her voice in token of her divine ambassadorship and through Our mouth proclaims anew: any use whatsoever of matrimony exercised in such a way that the act is deliberately frustrated in its natural power to generate life is an offense against the law of God and of nature, and those who indulge in such are branded with the guilt of a grave sin.[7]

Elsewhere, the pope argued that the Church's teaching on the natural law is an embodiment of its trust from God.

> It is a divinely appointed law that whatsoever things are constituted by God, the Author of nature, these we find the more useful and salutary, the more they remain in their natural state,

---

7. Pius XI, *Casti Connubii*, para 56.

unimpaired and unchanged; inasmuch as God, the Creator of all things, intimately knows what is suited to the constitution and the preservation of each, and by his will and mind has so ordained all this that each may duly achieve its purpose. But if the boldness and wickedness of men change and disturb this order of things, so providentially disposed, then, indeed, things so wonderfully ordained, will begin to be injurious, or will cease to be beneficial, either because, in the change, they have lost their power to benefit, or because God Himself is thus pleased to draw down chastisement on the pride and presumption of men.[8]

As popes in the twentieth century tended toward classicism, so do a few of their theologians. Still, many other theologians raise concerns. Ann Patrick disputes the classical paradigm of Roman Catholic moral theology; she notes its defense of intrinsic evil (see below), its intolerance of circumstances and of particularity, its suspicion of the subject, and its promotion of moral objectivity as naively universal and unchangeable. By its constant teachings, the Church promotes a uniform identity for its members and at the same time inhibits the original competency of the individual conscience.[9]

Historical-mindedness theologians look at the world and at truth as constantly emerging. They argue that we are learning more, not only about the world, but about ourselves. As subjects we are as affected by history: we become hopefully the people whom we are called to become. What the world and humanity will be is not yet known, but rests on the horizons of our expectations and the decisions we make and realize. The moral law then looks to determine what at this period corresponds to the vision we ought to be shaping. It admits that the final word on the truth is outstanding but emerging.

Contrary to their detractors, historicists do not argue that truth is constructed or manufactured; rather truth is "discovered" in history by historical persons. Our grasp on truth is evolving and we need to update or modify our understandings of it. Truth has its objectivity, but it is only gradually grasped by us in our judgment over time, through experience, and with maturity. Our grasp of truth, then, is always open to reform.

Moreover, though historicists believe in the importance of the situation and of circumstances, they are not situational ethicists. Situational ethics developed by Joseph Fletcher argued that the moral agent has no

8. Ibid., 95.
9. Patrick, *Liberating Conscience*.

mediating norms between the self and the concrete: only the law of love is to be radically expressed in the here and now.[10] Thus, rather than norms for all sorts of issues, Fletcher held there was only one, love. Historicists, however, believe that there are multiple norms, but that our understanding of them is historically conditioned.

Experience differentiates the two perspectives of classicism and historicism. The classical manualists did little to recognize and incorporate human experience. Often, when it comes to moral teaching, classicists see experience as an attempt to diminish the truth claims of an evident teaching. Historicists are anxious, however, about whether they adequately grasp and understand human experience.

Historicists are suspicious of deductive logic; in their estimation, real truth is found through analogy. They believe that truth is found by comparing one situation to another. They are modest about their judgments and assertions, and usually quite tentative about many truth claims; they tend away from clarity and entertain circumstances as significantly and substantively relevant. The particularity of the situation is key.

Historicists, then, are much more inclined to context. Unlike the moral manualists of previous centuries, they accept change in teachings on usury, capital punishment, or contraception when that change illustrates a greater approximation to the law of love. They enjoy, therefore, studying the history of church teaching, to see how the community of faith tries to understand from one generation to another the values and visions of moral truth.

In sum, the classical worldview depends on what is already known; historical mindedness responds to the knower: our ability to recognize the truth as it emerges through the data of experience very much depends on our own moral nature. Following Aristotle, historicists acknowledge that we see reality as we are.

Second, if we remember that these are differences not in kind, but in degree, then we can appreciate that no period and no work is relentlessly attached to one perspective: while Plato was classically fixed on his ideas and forms, Heraclitus was very historicist-minded. When we turn to the bible, the texts seem fairly historicist, in part because each book unveils revelation and because humanity is slow to understand. Still, its basic truths are eternal.

---

10. Fletcher, *Situation Ethics*.

Unlike many of his predecessors, Pope John Paul II was fairly unpredictable regarding how the distinction affected his teachings. When he taught on women's ordination (see below) or on abortion, he was clearly classicist. But when he wrote on suffering and other topics, he wove in the differing schools of interpretation. The result would often be that historicists claimed the historical dimensions of the pope's teachings, while classicist accepted and promoted the classicist interpretations.

Third, the governing notions of objectivity are, nonetheless, very different, not only about history and universality but also about the human beings. For the classicist, the agent does not enter into the equation of moral truthfulness: the moral truth remains the same for all. If I want to know the truth, I should be as detached from the situation as possible. For the historicists, the agent is integrally involved in the morally objective judgment.

Finally, the church's identity is deeply affected by its self-understanding as moral teacher. Inasmuch as the church's hierarchy understands her in the classicist mode, they resist innovation as beyond her competency, where teachings have already been defined. These teachings sometimes limit the ambit of papal options. A fine example of this stance can be found in Pope John Paul II's teaching on women's ordination to the priesthood:

> Although the teaching that priestly ordination is to be reserved to men alone has been preserved by the constant and universal Tradition of the Church and firmly taught by the Magisterium in its more recent documents, at the present time in some places it is nonetheless considered still open to debate, or the Church's judgment that women are not to be admitted to ordination is considered to have a merely disciplinary force.
>
> Wherefore, in order that all doubt may be removed regarding a matter of great importance, a matter which pertains to the Church's divine constitution itself, in virtue of my ministry of confirming the brethren (cf. Lk 22:32) I declare that the Church has no authority whatsoever to confer priestly ordination on women and that this judgment is to be definitively held by all the Church's faithful.[11]

---

11. John Paul II, *Ordinatio Sacerdotalis*, para. 4. Cardinal Ratzinger reiterated this teaching adding that it was infallible: Congregation for the Doctrine of the Faith, "Reply to the *Dubium*," 401, 403.

The distinction between classicism and historicism plays out in the Catholic Church throughout the second half of the twentieth century. It has an enormous bearing on our understanding of the natural law.

Fundamental Understanding of the Natural Law

Whether one tends to be is an historicist or a classicist, there are fundamental assumptions about the natural law that are shared by both interpretive contexts. It is important to understand these points of agreement before we study the differences regarding these modes of interpretation as they pertain to the natural law. We will divide these fundamental assertions into two categories: scope and method.

In scope, the natural law is extraordinarily comprehensive. Catholic adherents to the natural law believe that God is the creator of the universe and of the human race. We also believe that in creation we can find indicators of God's will. Moreover, human reason is the most appropriate way to discern those indicators; human reason has therefore an enduring value for the natural law in understanding and further articulating the law itself. We believe through the natural law we can discover the purpose of human life and in fact the purpose of all created objects and beings. (This does not mean that historicists endorse intelligent design arguments). Finally, we believe that ethics is constitutive of the good life, that is, that ethics contributes substantively to human flourishing. Therefore, the natural law upholds for Catholics that in the pursuit of the creator's will, we follow human reason and pursue the purpose of human life and the world.

In method, the natural law is equally comprehensive. It first tries to articulate the indicators of the will of God by reading the inclinations in human nature. These incipient inclinations need to be understood and guided by human reason for its right realization and human flourishment. So for instance we are born with inclinations for human society and the virtues of friendship and justice are the ways reason guides us toward the right realization of those inclinations. Similarly, we have an inclination to eat and drink as well as inclinations to flee from danger and threat. To realize those inclinations rightly we need other virtues like temperance and fortitude, respectively.

Not all inclinations are good. The question is understanding which inclinations attain human flourish. An inclination to solitariness for instance would need to be carefully nourished. (Here we can think of the magisterium's teaching that homosexuality is an intrinsically disordered inclination that should not be realized because it is contrary to God's plan. But theologians like Stephen Pope ask, is that what we learn from human experience?)

Besides discussing inclinations and their right realization by the virtue, the natural law is dependent on human reason discerning which virtues we need and the proper way of developing them. Commonly we call this the work of prudence, the virtue of practical reason which helps us understand how to rightly realize the inclinations.[12]

Parents are constantly using prudence to teach their children. For instance, in the making of friends, parents help their children discern with whom their children should enter into friendship, what ways they should share so as to deepen and sustain those friendships, as well as learning the practices of reconciliation when the friendship suffers from misunderstanding or neglect.

Prudence then teaches us what to do in rightly realizing these inclinations. But these inclinations cannot be realized without actual practices or forms of conduct which help train our inclinations or dispositions in specific ways. We do not grow virtually in the virtues. Rather our dispositions to the good need to be exercised by right direction into regular practices or habits that shape us into developing virtues. To be temperate we need to practice discipline in eating and drinking, knowing when we are satisfied, what foods are good for us, and which are not, etc. We cannot sit at the dinner table, rapidly eat everything in sight, and claim to be engaging the right prudential practices for the development of temperance.

The most challenging practices to learn are those for the right realization of our relationship with the social good. What is the proper way of educating a citizenry into responsible lifestyles? What should be the expectation of how individuals should contribute to the welfare of the social structure? Should there be taxes, forms of service, a military draft? What constitutes right taxes and how should they be meted out? Should worship be required or how else should we acknowledge the relationship between the state and faith? How do we negotiate treaties and conflicts between differing societies?

Again, by looking at the inclinations we have toward the familiar and the suspicious one we have of the foreign, these too need to be prudentially

---

12. Nelson, *The Priority of Prudence*.

tempered when dealing with larger and larger societies. In sum, prudence articulates the multitudinous practices that we need to rightly reason about inclinations and about how those inclinations promote right human flourishing.

A short hand for understanding these practices are moral norms. A norm like obey and respect your parents is a short hand expression for placing children under the steady, prudential, loving care of parents.

We have an enormous number of these norms that are designed to guide us all, less by argument and more by summary judgment. Legal norms too are often pithy summary of prudentially rich legal opinions. Thus we are guided by prudence, our own as well as by prudential elders, mentors and friends. But the larger social order uses norms in order to communicate effectively the sum of moral wisdom. Thus no unjust wars, no abortion, no divorce are not simply stand-alone statements but rather norms that arise from a variety of practices and needs that have been expressed over centuries.

A final component to the natural law is its relation to the common good. Because we believe that the norms, practices and virtues that we determine are objectively right, we believe they hold for everyone. The natural law is not an individual set of virtues, practices and norms that solely govern the growth of private persons, but rather it guides a society toward its right realization in the common good. Just as it presupposes that the moral formation of child occurs within the context of the family *and* that in that context the child becomes a contributing member, so the natural law believe that it strengthens each person to become concerned for and promoters of the common good, the more they learn about virtues, practices and norms.

Interestingly, the more we are interested in the common good, the more historicist we turn out. This is in part due to the fact that those who write on the common good, heed empirical data and recognize how much the truth of their assertions depend on that data.[13]

History and the Natural Law

The natural law presupposes that God as Creator establishes within us these inclinations, and that God's will is deeply connected to our true flourishing. In the thirteenth century during the period of high scholasticism because

13. Charles Curran often notes this. See his *The Catholic Moral Tradition Today*.

human reason had to understand these inclinations within the person and because it had to guide human beings to the right understanding of the proper way of acting, discussions of the natural law were spirited, complex and dynamic. What inclinations, what goals, which virtues, what human nature, what moral law, etc., demanded attention? These debates last well into the sixteenth century.

After the enormous upheaval of the sixteenth century, which included the conquest of the Americas as well as greater trade with the East, later theological ethics settled into a highly classical format. These tendencies toward universal norms with less attention to virtues and practices were coupled with the legacy of the Council of Trent (1545–1563) which founded seminary education, organized courses into respective disciplines, and began publishing textbooks in these distinctive fields. Here contemporary understandings of human nature and moral reasoning became re-ified, classified and codified in these manuals. One could say that by the eighteenth century the dynamism of the natural law tradition came to a halt.

Natural law from the eighteenth to mid-twentieth century became a set of universal and unalterable prescriptions and prohibitions. No abortion, no divorce, no masturbation, no birth control, etc. all these absolute prohibitions were specific stipulations of the natural law and of what not to do in the realization of our tendencies. This eighteenth century understanding of the natural law is still found today with some teachings from leadership within the Catholic Church. Ironically, this most classicist period fails to recognize itself as an historical development.

Most people today, when they hear the phrase natural law, then, think of these fixed teachings with an established set of ends or what we call a fixed immutable teleology. For instance, several years ago when the Speaker of the House, Nancy Pelosi, visited Pope Benedict, the Vatican released this statement "His Holiness took the opportunity to speak of the requirements of the natural moral law and the Church's consistent teaching on the dignity of human life from conception to natural death which enjoin all Catholics, and especially legislators, jurists and those responsible for the common good of society, to work in cooperation with all men and women of good will in creating a just system of laws capable of protecting human life at all stages of its development." This understanding of the natural law is much more normative oriented and not emphatic about virtues, prudence, or conscience.

Though this understanding of the natural law as prohibitive, immutable, and universal is still the common understanding of the natural law, in theological circles, it is not. Still, because so many think of the natural law in this way, scientists especially are chagrined when someone like myself proposes the natural law as helpful. Scientists, among others say, that the end of human life, of human society, of the world and even the universe as we know it does not seem to have any fixed or even necessarily intelligible teleology. The very presuppositions about inclinations, ends, divine providence, intelligibility and teleology are precisely not validated by scientific research.

Natural Law and the Forces of Nature

How do these distinctions play out in considerations on the natural law itself. In answering this question it should become evident that scientists might find the historicist worldview of natural law congruent with scientific premises and research.

Though the distinction between classicist and historicist runs through much of ethics and theology, still few Roman Catholics believe that creation is incompatible with evolutionary theory. Only a small percentage are creationists, in part, I think, because Roman Catholics, unlike Christian Fundamentalists, do not see every utterance of the Scriptures as factual truth.

That being said, while both schools believe in God as creator, the immediacy of God's actions is more evident for the classicist, while the historicist sees in evolutionary theory the creative hand of God. Most historicists literally enjoy the findings of contemporary science which refer continually to a constantly unfolding universe. The possibility of understanding nature more and more and of not reducing it to an essence, a purpose, or a norm, makes historicists develop a natural affinity with contemporary scientists.[14] Still the theologians believe that at some point God as creator created the processes that we see unfold today, but when, what, and how that creation occurred and unfolded is beyond their claims. One could say that they believe that God willed us to be here.

The classicist has a fairly essentialist view of nature. To appreciate this, we need to understand there are two sets of action that in the

---

14. The Catholic theological ethicist Stephen Pope has consistently worked on evolution and Catholic Natural law, see *Human Evolution and Christian Ethics*.

classicist framework are prohibited as intrinsically evil, that is, they are always considered in themselves wrong, without exception.[15] Such actions are prohibited either because we have no right to do it or because the essence of a faculty is not to be used for that purpose. Regarding the first category, there are some actions that we cannot do because we would transgress God's domain. For instance, as Lord of Life and Death, only God determines when a life ends. Therefore, we have no right to take our lives or the lives of the innocent. Similarly, since God established marriage, we cannot by divorce tear it asunder.

The other set of activities are prohibited by the natural law because the so-called "telos" or purpose of certain natural "faculties" cannot be abused. Thus, according to essentialist, classicist our reproductive faculty is for procreation. Thus masturbation would be an illegitimate use of our genitals and is considered an intrinsic evil. Similarly, the faculty of speech is for truth-telling and any instance of lying contradicts the purpose of speech.

Underlying these latter teachings is evidently a deep essentialism. Scientists are particularly concerned with talk about essences; they find this language more metaphysical than real or empirical. What is the essence of nature, human nature, or the human being? Or what is the essence of our reproduction capabilities or our speech? These claims are riddled with presuppositions about the ability to determine the "nature" of a human faculty and they are very much an eighteenth century construct.

Many theologians in general and theological ethicists in particular argue against the deep "essentialism" of the eighteenth century; we do not accept that the nature of the human and the world have fixed essences that must be realized as such. In fact, we believe that the eighteenth century notion of the natural law is a considerable departure from what the scholastics of the high middle ages were arguing. Still, the order of being—understood in the context of a naive realist epistemology—was the foundation of moral obligation and moral action in the classicist natural law context.[16] Who we understood ourselves to be determined what we should do. This was not a turn to the person as subject, but rather an attempt to objectify human nature.

---

15. One of the best studies of what constitutes an intrinsic evil appeared in Ugorji, *The Principle of Double Effect*.

16. For a further treatment of these issues see Keenan and Kopfensteiner, "Moral Theology out of Western Europe."

This essentialism has been very influential when dealing with the laws of nature, which were seen as manifestations of the divine will.[17] But Catholic ethicists who are historicists (and, the majority are) argue today that to overcome essentialism and to retrieve a truer understanding of the natural law, we need an interdisciplinary approach to understanding nature and its role in moral reasoning.[18]

We do not see nature as a thing as it was in the essentialism of the eighteenth century; rather nature is a complex and unfolding system whose finality, development and ways of interacting are grasped only partially—though not arbitrarily—by human insight.

For historicist, natural law theologians, this understanding of nature offers the possibility of a reintegration of humanity and nature. This is a middle position, for while the classicist counterparts see nature as an essence with a discernible telos, on the other side is the offering of some in nineteenth science who naively viewed nature as nothing more than a value neutral background against which humans have the power to create value.[19] From this viewpoint, nature was seen as an empty space waiting for human freedom to fill it with purpose; nature was reduced to the raw material for human action. This worldview entailed an autonomous understanding of human freedom which believes we can either manipulate nature without limit or somehow escape nature; this worldview refused to acknowledge that human freedom and reason were always situated in nature.[20] Rather the human stood over and above nature. This notion of nature has caused incalculable harm to ourselves and our environment. And few scientists abide by it today.

The historicists' dialogue with the contemporary sciences then has important implications for moral epistemology. For instance, the appreciation of the role of the knower in the growth of scientific knowledge serves as a critical corrective to the essentialism of the classicist position. In dialogue with the sciences, we gain a more critical approach to the natural moral law in which the objective world is inseparable from the subjective aspects of knowledge. In other words, the natural world and humanity are

---

17. Autiero, "Zwischen Glaube und Vernunft."

18. Chiavacci, "Für eine Neuinterpretationen."

19. See also Fraling, *Natur im ethischen Argument*.

20 As Chiavacci points out ("Für eine Neuinterpretationen," 122), an appreciation of our being part of nature is at the heart of environmental concerns. This is made explicitly by Autiero, "Sozialethische Provokationen."

inseparable: we cannot imagine nature without humanity and we cannot imagine humanity without nature. As we understand ourselves we understand nature; as we understand nature, we understand ourselves. Nature is not independent of humanity, nor is humanity independent of nature, and therefore "Nature is not normative . . . in itself." Nature instead is an evolving and open source of normativity, dependent on the community's capability to rationally understand it.[21] Not only is our knowledge of nature and all its complex structures partial, relative, and open to revision but because the knowledge process is interactive, as we learn more about nature, we gain new perspectives from which to interact with it.

This renewed understanding of nature does not mean that humanity is passive before the processes of nature. The reintegration of humanity and nature does not diminish our ability to reflect on our place in nature and the possibilities we have of consciously intervening and directing it. Our interaction with nature will keep in mind that we are part of nature's process of development, are carried along and, in part, determined by it. Our interventions into nature will reflect both our responsibility for nature of which we are always a part, and our ability to mold nature in light of human purposes.[22] Our interventions into nature, in other words, will reflect our commitment to respect and enhance the conditions of future human action. This balance steers the necessary middle course between classicist and earlier, modern tendencies in natural law argument.

The reintegration of humanity and nature opens the way for the retrieval of the natural moral law as the participation of human reason in the wisdom of God the Creator. The divine will is not naively reflected in natural processes; rather, through our responsible and rational engagement with nature we participate in the plan of the Creator. By our responsible and rational engagement with nature, we are able to transform the created world of which we are always a part and so act as a secondary cause in the intricate processes of development initiated by the Creator. In this way, God is not conceived as one who intervenes in worldly affairs from "outside" history usurping human decision-making; the divine project of creation continues to unfold and develop through the conduit of human reason and agency.[23]

---

21. Chiavacci, "Für eine Neuinterpretationen," 126.

22. Demmer, "Natur und Person." Demmer is fascinating, see his student's work, Schockenhoff, *Natural Law and Human Dignity*.

23. Demmer, *Die Wahrheit leben*, 36–37.

As we conclude we might realize how the natural law concerns play out today. In the area of stem cell research, classicists argue that the essence of early embryonic life is unequivocally human. To destroy that life would be to violate God's law as Lord of Life and Death. Because such an act would be an intrinsic evil, the action could never be validated and in fact even the highest level of teaching in the church could not question it. Historicists always raise questions about what are we learning about the status of the early embryo. Moreover, the historicists' interests in the common good prompt them to ask about the possible benefits of such research for public health, while classicists firmly reject that appeal because stem cell research might not treat these embryos as persons. Still historicists wonder whether scientists who do this research have an adequate respect for the cells with which they are working. They would also ask whether we are adequately attending to the needs of our population that is grossly underinsured. Historicists ask, is this the right point in time for investing in stem cell research when so many citizens have no access to health-care? Should we not attend to immediate needs before we pursue long range research? While classicists have absolute prohibitions, historicists have concerns about the research and offer scientists arguments from their reservations, hoping that as the scientists advance that they are able to appreciate issues of human agency, the respect of human life, and attention to the common good. Still, the debates between historicists and classicists are considerable, even though church authority has quite clearly and consistently spoken against the research.[24]

While classicists are more likely to be concerned with threats to their teachings, whether stem cell research, gay marriage, abortion, or assisted suicide, still they address the ecological challenges though they think of nature essentially and of humanity's responsibility to maintain dominance over nature. Historicists do not see nature as essential and understand the human as belonging to and not dominant over nature. Threats to nature are threats to humanity and vice versa.

Historicists see that we need enormous perspectives to deal with the ecological crisis. We need interdisciplinary dialogue and research among departments of sciences and the humanities. We need to articulate virtues, practices and norms that can guide us to a healthier context. We need to think of humanity and nature as evolving and as unequivocally shaping one

---

24. Shannon and Walter, *Contemporary Issues in Bioethics*; see Keenan, "Casuistry, Virtues, and the Slippery Slope."

another. We need to further understand the evolving dynamics of nature and humanity but we need ethical insight to arrest many vicious practices that undermine the well-being of nature and humanity.

While those working for sustainability are looking to religion to help them, certainly there is great merit in encouraging classicists to summon humanity to greater responsibility, but in the long run, scientists ought to find a greater compatibility with historicists who share with them many presuppositions for understanding the challenges before us.

Bibliography

Autiero, Antonio. "Sozialethische Provokationen an eine anthropozentrische Moral. Das Beispiel der Umweltethik." *Theologie und Glaube* 37 (1994) 97–106.

———. "Zwischen Glaube und Vernunft. Zu einer Systematik ethischer Argumentation." *Ethik zwischen Anspruch und Zuspruch. Gottesfrage und Menschenbild in der katholischen Moraltheologie*, edited by Klaus Arntz and Peter Schallenberg, 35–53. Freiburg: Herder, 1996.

Chiavacci, Enrico. "Für eine Neuinterpretationen des Naturbegriffs." *Moraltheologie im Abseits?*, edited by Dietmar Mieth, 110–28. Freiburg: Herder, 1994.

Curran, Charles. *The Catholic Moral Tradition Today: A Synthesis*. Washington, DC: Georgetown University Press, 1999.

Demmer, Klaus. *Die Wahrheit leben*. Freiburgh: Herder, 1991.

———. "Natur und Person: Brennpunkte gegenwärtiger moraltheologischer Auseinandersetzung." In *Natur im ethischen Argument*, edited by B. Fraling, 55–86. Freiburg: Herder, 1990.

Fletcher, Joseph. *Situation Ethics: The New Morality*. Philadelphia: Westminster, 1966.

Fraling, Bernhard, ed. *Natur im ethischen Argument*. Freiburg: Herder, 1990.

Gula, Richard. *Reason Informed by Faith: Foundations of Moral Theology*. Mahwah, NJ: Paulist, 1989.

John Paul II. *Ordinatio Sacerdotalis*. 1994. http://www.vatican.va/holy_father/john_paul_ii/apost_letters/documents/hf_jp-ii_apl_22051994_ordinatio-sacerdotalis_en.html.

Johnstone, Brian V. "Erroneous Conscience in *Veritatis Splendor* and the Theological Tradition." In *The Splendor of Accuracy: An Examination of the Assertions Made by Veritatis Splendor*, edited by Joseph A. Selling and Jan Jans, 114–35. Kampen: Kok-Pharos, 1994.

———. "From Physicalism to Personalism." *Studia Moralia* 30 (1992) 71–96.

———. "Moral Experience in the Test of History." *Église et Théologie* 16 (1985) 319–38.

———. "A Proposal for a Method in Moral Theology." *Studia Moralia* 22 (1984) 189–212.

———. "The Revisionist Project in Roman Catholic Moral Theology." *Studies in Christian Ethics* 5 (1992) 18–31.

Lonergan, Bernard. "Christ as Subject: A Reply." *Gregorianum* 40 (1959) 242–70.

———. "Dehellenization of Dogma." *Theological Studies* 28 (1967) 336–51.

———. *Insight: A Study of Human Understanding*. London: Longmans, Green, 1957.

———. *The Subject*. Milwaukee: Marquette University Press, 1968.

———. "Theology in Its New Context." In *A Second Collection*, edited by William Ryan and Bernard Tyrrell, 55–67. Philadelphia: Westminster, 1975.

———. "Transition from A Classicist World View to Historical Mindedness." In *A Second Collection*, edited by William Ryan and Bernard Tyrrell, 1–9. Philadelphia: Westminster, 1975.

Keane, Phil. "The Objective Moral Order." *Theological Studies* 43 (1982) 260–78.

Keenan, James. "Casuistry, Virtues, and the Slippery Slope: Major Problems with Producing Human Embryonic Life for Research Purposes." In *Cloning and the Future of Human Embryo Research*, edited by Paul Lauritzen, 67–81. New York: Oxford University Press, 2000.

Keenan, James, and Thomas Kopfensteiner. "Moral Theology out of Western Europe." *Theological Studies* 59 (1998) 107–35.

Kopfensteiner, Thomas. "Historical Epistemology." *Heythrop Journal* 33 (1992) 45–60.

Melchin, Kenneth. *History, Ethics and Emergent Probability: Ethics, Society and History in the Work of Bernard Lonergan*. Lanham, MD: University Press of America, 1987.

Miller, Mark. *Living Ethically in Christ: Is Christian Ethics Unique?* New York: Peter Lang, 1999.

Nelson, Daniel Mark. *The Priority of Prudence: Virtue and Natural Law in Thomas Aquinas and the Implications for Modern Ethics*. University Park: The Pennsylvania State University Press, 1992.

Noonan, John T., Jr., *The Church that Can and Cannot Change*. Notre Dame: University of Notre Dame Press, 2005.

Patrick, Anne. *Liberating Conscience*. New York: Continuum, 1994.

Pius XI. *Casti Connubii*. 1930. http://www.vatican.va/holy_father/pius_xi/encyclicals/documents/hf_p-xi_enc_31121930_casti-connubii_en.html.

Pope, Stephen. *Human Evolution and Christian Ethics*. New York: Cambridge, 2007.

Ratzinger, Joseph. "Reply to the *Dubium* Concerning the Teaching Contained in the Apostolic Letter *Ordinatio Sacerdotalis*." *Origins* 25 (November 30, 1995) 401, 403.

Schockenhoff, Eberhard. *Natural Law and Human Dignity: Universal Ethics in an Historical World*. Washington, DC: Catholic University of America Press, 1996.

Shannon, Thomas, and James Walter. *Contemporary Issues in Bioethics: A Catholic Perspective*. New York: Rowman and Littlefield, 2005.

Ugorji, Lucius Iwejuru. *The Principle of Double Effect: A Critical Appraisal of its Traditional Understanding and Its Modern Reinterpretation*. Frankfurt Am Main: Peter Lang, 1985.

— 6 —

Jesus Ascends: An Expanding Horizon

Anthony J. Kelly, C.Ss.R.

Theologically speaking, the ascension has suffered some form of benign neglect compared to other aspects of Christian faith.[1] This has made it vulnerable to mythic fantasies that do nothing for faith or theology. On the other hand, it might be thought that the ascension of Christ is so obvious as not to provoke much questioning. For example, it is not often referred to in the work of the theologian this collection of essays is honouring. On the other hand, Brian Johnstone's pioneering work in connecting moral theology to the Resurrection and in presenting everything in the light of grace and gift-giving, suggest the horizon in which the ascension of Jesus is an all-defining dimension of Christian life and conduct. After all, the ascension and exaltation of Christ are the horizon in which the whole New Testament is set (John 20:17; Mark 16:19; Eph 4:8–10; 1 Tim 3:16; Heb 4:14; 9:27)—and so it continues in the life of Church today.

    Far from being a largely irrelevant item in terms of Christian experience, the ascension is that facet of the Christian mystery that is most near to those living the life of faith. St Paul, in emphasising his relationship to Christ in the present, declared, "even though we once knew Christ from a human point of view, we know him no longer in that way" (2 Cor 16).

---

1. See Kelly, *Upward*.

1. Resurrection and Ascension

Admittedly, the ascension is a liturgical feast of the Church, esteemed by some as the high point of the liturgical year. Today, however, there is a peculiar modern confusion of celebrating it in many places on the Sunday instead of the traditional Thursday, as the glow of paschaltide yields to the happy anticipation of Pentecost.

If Christ ascended, what does this mean for his presence to the Church on earth? What has changed, what is promised, and what difference does it make to the life of faith? These are big questions and, to some extent, embarrassing as well. Still, it is not unusual for theology to be goaded into new creativity when it suffers its greatest embarrassment. Christians, for the most part, have no trouble admitting that they do not see Jesus going up into the stratosphere after the manner of any number of gravity-defying objects such as balloons or rockets. In fact, in the present condition of faith, Christians have to admit that they see nothing of Christ with bodily eyes, and in the best biblical tradition see no point in scanning the sky for evidence of his going or return (Acts 1:11). In short, faith is no longer a matter of seeing in an ordinary sense—even if it is not blind, given the visibility of Christ through the mediation of sacramental symbols, biblical images, icons, and religious art—and in a kind of seeing that finds God or Christ in the neighbour (cf. Matt 25 and 1 John 4:20). On the other hand, faith implies a sense of personal intimacy with Christ, despite his invisibility. The words of the First Letter of Peter, in this respect, are especially striking:

> Although you have not seen him, you love him; and even though you do not see him now, you believe in him, and rejoice with an indescribable and glorious joy, for you are receiving the outcome of your faith, the salvation of your souls (1 Pet 1:8–9).

Something has ceased. He is no longer a visible, tangible presence as he once was in his earthly life.

If, with the ascension, something ends with a sense of completion and fulfilment, something also begins. What begins emerges as a new mode of presence characterising the time of the Church and the witness of the Holy Spirit in all times and places. Or as Augustine, a great champion of the ascension,[2] would put it in eschatological, ecclesial and moral terms,

---

2. For a succinct overview, see Geerlings, "Ascensio Christi," 475–79.

Just as he ascended into heaven without departing from us, so we, too, are already there with him although that which he promised us has not yet been accomplished in our body . . . Although he ascended into heaven, we are not separated from him. He who descended from heaven does not begrudge it to us; on the contrary, he proclaims it in a certain manner: "Be my members if you wish to ascend into heaven . . ." The body will be easily lifted to the heights of heaven if the weight of our sins does not press down upon our spirit.[3]

2. The Ascension and The Horizon of Christian Life

Clearly, in the various New Testament accounts and references, we are not dealing with flatly stated facts. For instance, in the imagination of faith, the ascension is the high point of Christ's mission—"mission accomplished," we might say. He has returned to the Father; and, at the same time, sends the Holy Spirit and promises the future return of Jesus.

From a Lukan perspective, the ascension is at once a looking back and a looking forward. It looks back in order to amplify faith's comprehension of the meaning of Jesus' life, mission, death and resurrection. However, it also looks forward. The disciples are not left impotently gazing into the heavens, but looking outward into the life and mission of the Church in its outreach to all peoples and all ages. As a result, Christian existence, retrospectively and prospectively, is deeply marked with the character of thanksgiving, waiting and hope. Jesus has gone before us. But in the present time, the faith of his followers must now wait, longing for his return as the Lord and judge of all. Though no longer in the world as he was before, he is neither absent nor disengaged from it. The numinous cloud accompanies his departure and his promised return (Acts 1:9–11). But he is carried upward to this divine realm with arms extended in blessing (Luke 24:50–53)—a gesture of effective solidarity with all who will follow him (cf. Luke 22:42–43). His departure in this way is a source of blessings and of the promised gift of the Spirit (Acts 1:6–8). In this sense, the ascension does not represent Jesus turning away from the community of faith, but rather an all-embracing turning to them from the height, depth and breadth of the mystery of God.

With John, the focus is less on the ascension as a discreet event and more on the action of the "ascending Jesus": "No one has ascended into

---

3. Augustine, *Sermons on the Liturgical Seasons*, 393–94.

heaven except the one who descended from heaven, the Son of Man" (John 3:13). True faith lives from a particular vision, seeing "the Son of Man ascending to where he was before?" (John 6:62)—an aspect of the "opened heaven" of communication between God and creation (John 1:51). In the two-way communication involved, not only does Jesus go to prepare a place for his followers, but he will also come again in order to gather them within the spacious hospitality of his Father's house (John 14:2–4). And the disciples will inhabit the world in a new way. In what his disciples already are, and through what they will later do, a new community based in the unity the Father and the Son comes into being (John 17:20–21). Jesus prays that the disciples given to him by the Father will be transported into a new sphere of existence—to be where he is and to share in his vision and glory (John 17:24a). By ascending to the Father and leaving the familiar world of his disciples, Jesus has in effect relocated them. Their world is changed. They live now in the heavenly realm of life and communion to which Christ has ascended, and in the atmosphere of the Father's house of many dwelling places (John 14:2–3). The Father's original love for Jesus is now overflowing to those identified with him: "that the love with which you have loved me may be in them, and I in them" (John 17:26b). United with Jesus in his return to the Father, the disciples are drawn into the universe of mutual love and self-giving communion (John 13:34–35; 15:12, 17). It follows that not only is Jesus ascended, but also that the disciples themselves are in a profound sense now "ascended" with him, and share in his communion with the Father. By ascending to "my Father and your Father, to my God and your God" (John 20:17), the ascended and glorified Jesus both transcends all worldly realities, categories and previous conceptions, and belongs to his followers in the deepest intimacy of his relationship to the Father.

Consequently, the ascension resonates in the consciousness of faith as an event (Luke-Acts) stimulating the mission of the Church, and as a field of communion with the Father and the Son (John).

From a Pauline perspective, the risen and ascended Christ is the source of gifts, building up of the body of Christ and bringing it to its fullest dimensions. After his self-emptying descent in lower parts of the earth, Christ ascends "above all heavens," not only that he might fill all things in a cosmic sense, but also that he might fill out the dimension of his Body with all the gifts necessary for its life, growth and up-building in love (Eph 4:7–16)—even in the teeth of adverse cosmic powers (Eph 6:11–12). In Colossians, the apostle prays to the Father who has raised Jesus from the dead, who has "rescued us from the power of darkness and transferred us into the kingdom of his believed Son, in whom we have redemption, the forgiveness of sins" (Col 1:11–14). Once more it is clear that faith in God's action in Christ means a relocation of struggling Christian existence into the realm that Christ occupies, and in which he communicates present deliverance and forgiveness. The impact of the ascension of Christ on the consciousness of faith finds expression in the exhortation to "seek the things that are above, where Christ is, seated as the right hand of God" (Col 3:1). The believer is called, beyond the limits of the mundane, to the heights (v. 2). When life is transformed through Christ's death and resurrection, it is "hidden with Christ in God" (v. 3) until its eventual glorious manifestation in him (Col 3:4). In the meantime, believers are clothed with the hidden reality of "the new self" (v. 9). Thus, the "lift up your hearts" of the liturgy is a summons flowing directly from the confession of Christ's ascension.

All this is obvious enough to the most basic Christian theology as it elaborates the articles of the creed in terms of a Christian vocation and conduct of life. Why say more? There can be only one answer: there is a continuing need to refresh our sense of the distinctiveness of Christian reality.[4] Today, all would admit, it is imperative that Christian faith be in dialogue with other versions of reality, religious, ethical, and otherwise. However, that communication will not bear fruit if Christian faith has lost its own distinctive sense of the real, and become somewhat flat, stale, and timid.

How, then, is the ascension to be interpreted? How is the ascension related to the resurrection of Jesus? How are both resurrection and ascension to be related to the incarnation itself? Does the ascension of Jesus mean that the incarnation—the Word become flesh—is somehow ended or made less real? What does the ascension mean both for Christ himself, and "for us and our salvation"?

3. THE FOCAL REALITY

We note, first of all, that ascension of Christ is a key event in the comprehensive sweep of the divine plan of salvation. The crucified Jesus rises from the tomb, and though transformed, appears to his disciples and is identified by them as the one who lived among them. He is then taken up into the luminous cloud of God's presence, no longer to be found in

---

4. See Kelly, "Refreshing Experience," 335–48.

the time and space of his earthly life in Palestine, nor any longer revealing himself through the episodic appearances that followed his resurrection. In his ascended existence, he now fills all time and space, and inhabits every dimension of reality, from the highest realm of the infinite Godhead to the mundane, agonising reality of created existence. The ascension opens the space in which Christian consciousness unfolds to embrace a new sphere of transformed existence. God has "made us alive together with Christ . . . and raised us up with him, and seated us with him in the heavenly places" (Eph 2:4–6). The ascension is not simply the end of the journey for Jesus alone. It is of universal significance; it is a new beginning for all who will follow him since he embodies the destiny to which all are called.

In Jesus' passing from this world to the Father, there is certainly an ending of his earthly mission and an experience of his absence compared to his previous manner of presence. But the consciousness of faith registers a new mode of presence: "Behold, I am with you all days . . ." (Matt 28:20). Faith, therefore, does not cling to Jesus as a localised cult object. By letting him go into the glory of the Father, the faithful receive him back, in every moment and place, in the celebration of the Eucharist and through the gift of the Spirit. As faith follows him ascending into the glory of the Father, it is lifted beyond the world of projections, beyond the fantasy of gazing into an imaginary heaven for a lost hero. The focus of faith is rather always on the crucified and risen Jesus, as the One who has come, and will keep on coming, from out of the luminous reality of God into the reality of this world. As the white-robed heavenly interpreters told the "men of Galilee," "This Jesus, who has been taken up from you into heaven, will come in the same way as you saw him go into heaven" (Acts 1:9–11).

The implication is that these natives of Galilee must now live as citizens of a much larger world. The whole of creation is filled with Christ's saving presence. From the glory of heaven, the Christ fills the space left by his earthly absence. He has opened our world to the hitherto impenetrable reality of heaven, as he had promised his disciples, "you will see heaven opened and the angels of God ascending and descending on the Son of Man" (John 1:51). Jesus will be the new Jacob's ladder (Gen 28:12–17), connecting what is above with what is below. He is in person the channel of communication between God and the world, so that his ascension opens up a God-given space for the unfolding of the whole history as it moves to its fulfilment. Because Christ has not shaken off the flesh of his humanity, human existence is already transfigured in him. The universe, and ourselves within it, has been drawn into the realm of God.

The ascension, therefore, manifests the boundless space in which Christ's victory over death and sin will be worked out. He is now "out of this world" in the sense that his absence, presence and return are defined only by the infinite creativity of the Spirit—the divine cloud that received him out of sight. The ascension means, therefore, that in rising from the dead, Jesus is not re-inserted into the fabric of the world that crucified him, and subject to its desires, expectations, plans and control. He is not resuscitated, but neither is he a kind of spiritual inspiration in a world unchanged and unchangeable. He has not ascended into the empty spaces that the world's calculations have left open, but "to the Father," to that realm in which the Father's will is accomplished, and the Kingdom of God is already realised. He lives and communicates with the world of faith from the hitherto unattainable and still uncontrollable "beyond" of God.

Big questions stir. In the ascension of the Lord, theology touches on an upper limit at which it is, for the most part, wisely silent. The ascended Christ, in carrying our humanity with and in him into the realm of God, is not subject to categories of the world from which he has departed. He now occupies a, ultimate realm compared to our usual sense of proportion. Our thoughts and feelings are inevitably anchored in the world of routine experience, and so, are reluctant to go further. But faith follows Christ into glory and shares his joy as he ascends from the passion of the Cross, from the terrible finality of his death and burial, to his present position as the right hand of the Father.

We must ask, therefore, whether the contrast is just too much, between his present state and our mortal humanity and the groaning of creation (Rom 8:19–25)? So great is the Christian sense of solidarity with suffering others –oppressed by disease, deprivations, political and economic powers and the systems that cause and support such miseries—that a celebration of the ascension cannot but appear as a fantastic distraction from the present world of grief. Are the glory and joy of the ascended Lord irrelevant to those committed to the struggle for freedom and flourishing in this present sphere? Dare a realistic faith follow him in his victory over death and in his return to the Father, to celebrate the glory that was his before the foundation of the world? In world of unfinished business, this side of the *eschaton*, can faith rejoice in his joy of completing the work that was his God-given mission?

Nonetheless, faith can find and maintain an essential and sober Christian joy. Without that joy, believers can be overwhelmed by the world of suffering—innocent or self-inflicted—that daily occupies our attention and shapes our sense of life as it is lived on this planet. Christ has come, and is now gone before us, order to find the joy and glory of divine life—for himself and "for us and our salvation"—the joy of love consummated, of life transformed, of evil radically vanquished. Christian sensibility appreciates that the ascension is an entry into the realm of joy (cf. Luke 24:50)—the joy that the world can neither give nor take away.

Such radical joy does not entail a repression of suffering and sorrow. It does, however, found the conviction that in the risen and ascended Christ, all sorrow can be met, named and even suffered, in hope and patience. One might suspect that a neglect of the resurrection—and its outcome in the ascension as the zone of joy and the realm from which the Spirit comes— has resulted in a certain depressive grimness in theology and perhaps even in Christian life. We cannot, and even dare not, speak too much of joy as Pope Francis reminds us.[5] Jesus is not forever transfixed in agony on the cross. That early Christian prophecy presents him as saying, "Do not be afraid; I am the first and the last, and the living one. I was dead, and see, I am alive forever; and I have the keys of death and of Hades" (Rev 1:17–18). Faith finds him at the centre of a new creation in which violence and death no longer rule, but are fated to be overcome entirely. Compared to the time-space configurations of the empirical world, the space and time of the ascension are now relative to Christ in glory, the source of life and communion with the Father in the Spirit. Though Christ is empirically speaking absent, we are not absent to him. Indeed, his present absence has a purpose: that faith open itself to his new mode of universal presence and to the time of salvation determined by his promised return. The words of Jesus addressed to the Samaritan woman in the Gospel of John are particularly relevant: "the hour is coming, when true worshipers will worship the Father neither on this mountain nor in Jerusalem" (John 4:21). In the hour of salvation, "true worshipers will worship the Father in spirit and truth . . ." (John 4:23). In this new era, true worshipers would not be confined to "this mountain or Jerusalem"—nor to Colombo, Paris, Rome, New York, or even Melbourne. To adore the real God is to live within the horizon of the Fathers' love for the *whole* world. In other words, Christ, by being absent from the limits of time and place that once structured his earthly life, has

---

5. See Francis, *Evangelii Gaudium*.

ascended into the divine all-inclusive realm of presence and action. As this new realm of relationship to the Father opens up, heaven itself has been opened (cf. John 1:51). The space and time of salvation is a reconciliation englobing all places, divisions and separations.

In this present era of interreligious dialogue, belief in the ascension is of great importance. This "departure" of Jesus from this world, and the consequent expansion of the Christ-Event beyond the dimensions of the earthly life of Jesus of Nazareth, serves to arrest the distortions and "idolic" propensities of religious projections and to allow for an epiphany by which the light of another world breaks through. If "in him all the fullness of the godhead was pleased to dwell" (Col 1:19), Christ is not simply *there* as our possession or under the control of faith. Rather, as demonstrably absent, he calls forth the ecstatic character of faith and the dispossession of the self that are conditions for entry into the Kingdom of the Father.

4. Distortions?

Our vision can be distorted. We can be so intensely focused on the classic doctrine of the incarnation as to reduce the resurrection and the ascension to being only a proof or manifestation of the basic reality of the Word made flesh. However, only by understanding the incarnation as an event expanding, as it were, into the resurrection and the ascension, can the full reality of the incarnation be appreciated. After all, Jesus is not less human after rising from the dead, nor does he shed his humanity by ascending to the Father's right hand. Clearly, the resurrection and the ascension are dimensions of the one expanding event of the transformed humanity of the risen and ascended Jesus.

There is the possibility of further distortion when the impression is given that the reality of the ascension is to be found, not in Jesus' ascent into heaven, but as his "ascending" into the Church. In effect, by identifying the reality of the Church with the ascended Jesus, the impression is given that the Church contains him on its level and in its structures, words and sacraments. The Church therefore must allow for the real *absence* of Christ in the glory of the Father—even while at the same time celebrating his real presence.[6] The Church continues on its pilgrim path, while Jesus has completed his journey and returned to the Father. In his ascended state, he is

---

6. This is the whole point of Farrow, *Ascension and Ecclesia*. See, too, idem, *Ascension Theology*.

the *head*—not a "member"—of his Body, the Church. In that capacity, he breathes his enlivening Spirit into his ecclesial Body and nourishes it with his eucharistic gift.

Given the danger of such distortions, the only course for theology is to keep the five articles of the creed in play, dealing respectively with the Word made flesh, his crucifixion, his resurrection from the dead, his ascension to the Father's right hand, and the promise of his return. Further, if this creedal framework is dismantled, the notion of God's self-communication in Christ and the Spirit is quickly lost. If, at the other extreme, the ascension swallows up the distinctiveness of the resurrection, the realism of salvation in Christ is undermined, and his victory over sin and death reduced to an abstract mythological significance. If however the ascension drops out of the picture, not only is a considerable range of New Testament references set aside, but eschatological, cosmic, sacramental and pneumatological dimensions of salvation in Christ are overlooked.

5. A Holistic Theology

In the ascended Jesus, time, space, body and nature are refashioned, and history, instead of being a concatenation of episodic events, is caught up in the updraught of all things being gathered into Christ. In this perspective, Christ's ascension and departure from this world amounts to the making of the Christian heaven. For Jesus ascends, not simply in his individual humanity, but as embodying a world, perfected, transformed, and offered to the Father, and diaphanous with the Light (Rev 21:23). According to explicit promise of Jesus to Nathanael—here representing all future disciples—"You will see the heaven opened, and the angels of God ascending and descending on the Son of Man" (John 1:51). The hitherto "closed heaven" is now opened in such a way that the glorified Son of Man is the new channel of communication between God and creation. Jesus will be the new Jacob's ladder (Gen 28:12–17), connecting what is above with what is below, what is at the centre and what at the circumference of existence (cf. John 3:13), the realization of a new communication between God and the world. Because he who is most intimate to the Father became accessible in the flesh of this world, believers can now find their way to the Father, and a dwelling in his house (John 14:1–4).[7] The ascended Christ is constituted as

---

7. Cf., Kelly and Moloney, *The Experience of God*, 287–89, and Balthasar, *Theo-Drama*, 376–79.

"being for" the world, ever active in his Eucharistic self-giving and breathing forth his Spirit.

That invisibility of the ascended Christ makes quite clear that Church does not possess, control or contain Christ. Rather, that totality is contained by him. Christ is not "in" in the sacraments, just as he is not "in" the world. Rather, elements of the world—the bread and wine, oil, water, and so on—are, through the action of the Spirit, assumed "into Christ," transfigured by him as anticipations of the new creation—so to become the sacraments of faith. The sacramental economy, being permanent, is guaranteed in the efficacy of its communication of the grace of Christ's presence. This is different from the episodic and privileged appearances of the risen Christ over the forty day period. The time of the sacraments has no end as long as history continues.

All this is to say that the ascension does not take Christ out of time, but is the condition for his complete immersion in it, as its fullness. Faith is the consciousness of having time "in him," so that he becomes the measure and goal of time. If time is "the measure of motion," the Body of Christ is the fullest measure of what is truly moving in history and in the universe itself, as gifts are poured out "for the building up of the body of Christ until all of us come to the unity of faith and of the knowledge of the Son of God, to maturity, to the measure of the full stature of Christ" (Eph 4:12–13). Jesus in his ascent to the Father brings time to its redemptive completion.

If Jesus has remained under the conditions of the previous economy, if he had not ascended to the incalculable realm of the Father, the receptivity and unreserved character of faith would be compromised. In the Pauline idiom, the ascension means not only that Christ fills all things but also that he is the source of all gifts necessary for the building up of his Body (cf. Eph 4:7–11). As gifts abound from the realm to which Christ has ascended, s So too does thanksgiving and serene longing for the promised return of Christ (cf. John 16:7; 16:24; 17:13). There is no desire to cling to the past as if faith were an endless reconfiguration of the recorded memories of Jesus of Nazareth within the dimensions of the present world (John 20:17). For Paul, the human point of view is a flatly horizontal perspective untroubled by the vertical disruption of his resurrection and ascension (2 Cor 5:16). Only an horizon enlarged by the resurrection and ascension of Jesus can appreciate that Christ embodies "a new creation: everything old has passed away" (2 Cor 5:17).[8]

---

8. For this section, see Granados, "The First Fruits," 6–38.

Nor does it mean inventing some form of celestial physics, nor, for that matter, taking the ascension to mean in effect an "excarnation" of the hitherto incarnate One. If the Word was made flesh (John 1:14), does the present situation of Christ, ascended into heaven, suggest that that his flesh, his bodily being, has been volatilised and so spiritualised that the incarnation ceases to be after his resurrection and ascension? The only possible solution is to be found in a more comprehensive theology of the incarnation so that it includes the resurrection and ascension—and indeed, the formation of the Body of Christ through time and space. When one considers the great "cosmic" Christological statements of John and Paul (John 1:3–5; 1 Cor 15:25–28; Eph 1:3–10; Col 1:15–17; Heb 1:1–4; Rev 1:12–16), it is clear that the overriding concern of the New Testament writers is not to locate Christ within the cosmos from which he has departed, but to view the totality of the world in its fabric and movement within the redemptive reality of Christ.

Christ will appear, as the fulfilment of all our knowing and hoping, as the Word Incarnate *in person* and in the universal inclusiveness of his identity. It would not be extreme to propose that the resurrection and ascension of Jesus "deconstructs" the categories and language of mundane thinking and even religious expression. The holding capacity of the old wineskins becomes inadequate in regard to the fresh wine of revelation (Matt 9:16–17; Mark 2:21–22; Luke 5:36–39).

In the experience of Christian life, although faith is not- seeing, neither is it blind. While there is no point in looking up to heaven, nor looking into the empty tomb, there is every reason within the consciousness of faith to look in other directions—within the corporate, sacramental, eschatological perspectives that have been opened up. In this respect, with all its symbolic retinue of metaphor and symbol, the ascension is the paradigmatic instance of imaginative expression going beyond all powers of expression, even while relying on the mediation of images (ascent, the cloud, the Father's right hand, heavenly figures, and so forth).[9] Faith follows the ascended One out of the world of experience, above the available world of representations and conceptual systems, to the unutterable reality of communion with him who will return, and who now draws the faithful into the

---

9. With regard to Luke's employment of the cloud symbolism, see Lohfink, *Die Himmelfahrt Jesu*. He remarks, "Die Wolke war bereits fur ihn ein biblisches Symbol, theologische Chiffre fur Dinge, die nur in Bild und Gleichnis anschaulich zu machen sind" (283). He concludes with a quotation from Maximus of Turin, Sermo XLIV 3 (CChrL XXIII, 179).

unity existing between himself and the Father.[10] Even though a new order of existence has been inaugurated, there is a distance, a hidden-ness and a radical demand inherent in it:

> . . . seek the things that are above where Christ is, seated at the right hand of God. Set you minds on things that are above, not on things that are on earth, for you have died and your life is hidden with Christ in God. When Christ who is your life is revealed, then you will be revealed with him in glory (Col 3:1–4).

As Bulgakov wisely remarks, the ascension, far from being a withdrawal or diminishment in terms of God's relationship to the world, it shows forth the God-world relationship in a clearer light.[11] In the ascent of the glorified humanity, time and space are newly configured. Chalcedon retains its validity in heaven. The hypostatic relationship of the divine person to humanity is not lessened but expanded. The continuance and expansion of the humanity of the ascended Christ makes clear that there is now no God without the world; and there is no world apart from God. To use a spatial metaphor, the world, owned, claimed, finalised in Christ, is now forever "in God." Aquinas considered that the ascension as the "cause" of salvation. In another idiom, it can be said that the ascension is not completed in the exaltation of Christ, but spills over, as it were, into the eventual ascension of all.[12] To that degree, it has the character of an unbounded event of universal effect. As Christ ascends and is glorified in his self-emptying surrender to the Father's will, his kenosis continues through all time and space. Though all things are now subjected to him, he is exalted in his subjection to the Father so that "God may be all in all" (1 Cor 15:28). Although he now possesses "the name that is above every name" (Phil 2:9), and all creation exalts the name of Jesus, he exercises his universal lordship "to the glory of God the Father" (Phil 2:11).

Any theology of the ascension must appreciate singular originality of the divine mystery. From one point of view, the ascension of Christ represents the most extravagant statement of positive theology. From another perspective, it demands a thoroughgoing negative theology, for Christ, even though he "means the world" to Christian faith—the world possessed by God and transformed by the divine Spirit—theologically speaking,

---

10. See Nancy, *Au fond des images*.
11. Bulgakov, *The Lamb of God*, 317–403, especially 398–99.
12. Ibid., 400.

he is "out of the world," in terms of any available analogies, concepts or symbols pretending to depict it. Positivity and negativity are intertwined. Each aspect impels toward the other, and both look beyond themselves to the singularity of the ascension itself. Thus, the ascension occupies a point outside all human experience, beyond the limits of death, beyond even our understanding of the resurrection-event itself, to be ultimately definable only by the mystery of God itself.[13]

6. The Ascension and Mary's Assumption

The mystery of Ascension suggests a connection with the Catholic doctrine of the Assumption of Our Lady, solemnly defined in 1950. This is one more point where, theologically speaking, the intentionality of faith has hurried past its powers of expression. If Mary is declared to be assumed, body and soul, into heaven, then the corporate, historical authority of the Catholic Church is thereby committed to a view of materiality, corporeality, and physicality in a way that is largely beyond our powers of expression, in either scientific or even imaginative terms. Here we can do little more than note that it would be of great ecumenical significance if our understandings of the Ascension of Christ and the Assumption of Mary interacted more positively. In the concrete liturgical unfolding of Catholic tradition, the ascension of Jesus would be deprived of its salvific significance if unrelated to the assumption of Mary as cause to effect. Likewise, the assumption, if more clearly connected to the ascension of Christ, would have a clearer ecclesiological and cosmic significance. Now assumed into the glory of Christ, she is the anticipation of the heaven of a transfigured creation.[14] In that regard, Mary is the paradigmatic instance of creation open to, collaborating with, and transformed by, the creative mystery of God in Christ. She symbolises the generativity of creation under the power of the Spirit. In her, as the Advent antiphon has it, "the earth has been opened to bud forth the Saviour." In its confession of the assumption, Christian hope finds a particular confirmation. In Mary, now assumed body and soul into the heaven of God and Christ, our humanity, our world and even our history have reached their divinely-destined term. She embodies the reality of our world as having received into itself the mystery that is to transform the universe in its entirety. In her, human history has come to its maturity, its age

13. Ibid., 393–98.
14. See Rahner, "The Interpretation of the Dogma," 215–27.

of consent, to surrender to the transcendent love for which it was destined. The ascended Christ has conformed her to himself, so that she embodies receptivity to the gift of the God who "has raised us up with him and seated us with him in the heavenly places in Christ Jesus, so that in the ages to come he might show the immeasurable riches of his grace in kindness towards us in Christ Jesus" (Eph 2:6–7).

Assumed into the heaven of her Son's ascension, Mary is no longer subject to the rule of death (1 Cor 15:42–58). Mary of Nazareth is the name of an historical person—the Mother of Jesus. Yet history has no record of her life except through the documents of faith, above all the Gospels of the New Testament. It is significant in the present context that she has become known to faith only through the immense transformation that took place in the resurrection and ascension of her Son, and its impact on human consciousness through faith, hope and love. The assumption enables faith to glimpse the "opened heaven" of Jesus' promise to the disciples in his conversation with Nathanael: "Amen, amen, I say to you, you will see heaven opened and the angels of God ascending and descending on the Son of Man" (John 1:51). Her Son embodies the open heaven of communication between God and creation.

Not to mention the assumption of Mary would leave the ascension of Christ without its more personal effect. It could quickly become a devotional "optional extra," and cease to be carrier of the universal and cosmic transformation of all creation in Christ. On the other hand, in the light of the ascension in which the presence and activity of Christ is viewed, belief in the assumption of the Mother of Christ, body and soul, into heaven cannot but continue to inspire a fresh hearing of this exhortation from the Letter to the Ephesians,

> So if you have been raised with Christ, seek the things that are above, where Christ is seated at the right hand of God. Set your minds on the things that are above, not on things that are on earth, for you have died, and your life is hidden with Christ in God. When Christ who is your life is revealed, then you will be revealed with him in glory (Eph 3:1–4).

Conclusion

In this postmodern context, the *sursum corda* of the ascension invites faith to be bolder and more confident in its commitment to the distinctive character of Christian revelation, the sense of reality it communicates and the moral conduct it inspires. When the shape of reality in all its guises has become so fluid in this post-modern era, it is a good time to rise to the challenge of witnessing to the singular reality of the Christ-Event, and to explore and communicate it in the largest hermeneutical and contemplative space—cosmic, ecumenical, interfaith and eschatological.

Caught up into the updraught of the ascension, Christian faith is drawn into the incalculable "more," into the inexhaustible excess of the mystery of God's self-giving in Christ. A "lifting up of hearts" is not an invitation to enter some unworldly zone in which the humanity of Christ is dissolved, or located in a "nowhere in particular," in a universe radically alien to the bodily humanity we share with Christ. In contrast, the faith of the Church prays and hopes for his return, for the full revelation and appearance of the crucified and risen One, Jesus of Nazareth.

The ascension draws faith into the realm that is proper to God—which only Christ can occupy. In all this, faith not a neatly packaged addition to ordinary life, nor is it an expression of human ambition and control. It is an open surrender, in and through Christ, to the infinities of God's love, grace, mercy and beauty. A continual alertness is necessary if faith is not to lose its self-transcending character by creating an attractive idol in Christian clothing. Faith moves with Christ ever upward, outward, and beyond itself to the realm of the Father. God is not like anything in the world, and the Kingdom of God surpasses the projections of human imagination and ambitions of human control and calculation.[15] On the other hand, the exaltation of the crucified One to the right hand of the Father, whom all creation must acknowledge as Lord, must have consequences for our way of looking at the world as it is, and for our way of treating those who are most disadvantaged and victimised within it. If social action on behalf of the poor loses its eschatological sense of direction, is deprived of its oxygen and its Spirit-given hope for the world.

The conclusion of John's Gospel reminds believers of every age that Christian faith is not a verbal formula of belief, nor even a particular program of action. The crucified and risen One has appeared in the fear-locked room of the disciples to send them forth on mission, and to breathe his Spirit on them. In every age, he comes into those places of dejection to send forth his followers, and to breathe into them his Spirit. This ongoing,

---

15. See Kelly, *The Resurrection Effect*, 159–67, and the chapter, "Beyond Locked Doors," 69–85. More extensively, Robinette, *Grammars of Resurrection*, 227–90.

inexhaustible event of his death, resurrection and ascension is not contained within the linear script of any book –nor in the sum total of all the books of the world (John 21:25). Christ's ascension to the Father means that his presence and action cannot be confined or restricted. It invites believers always "upward," and into this "other dimension." The writings of Brian Johnstone and the long witness of his theological life and work have consistently opened up wider horizons and pointed us in the right direction.

Bibliography

Augustine. *Sermons on the Liturgical Seasons*. Sermon 263, Translated by Mary Sarah Muldowney. New York: Fathers of the Church, 1959, 393–394.
Balthasar, Hans Urs von. *Theo-Drama: Theological Dramatic Theory*. Vol. 5, *The Last Act*. Translated by Graham Harrison, San Francisco: St. Ignatius, 1998.
Bulgakov, Sergius. *The Lamb of God*. Translated by Boris Jakim. Grand Rapids: Eerdmans, 2008.
Farrow, Douglas. *Ascension and Ecclesia: On the Significance of the Doctrine of the Ascension for Ecclesiology and Christian Cosmology*. Edinburgh: T. & T. Clark, 1999.
———. *Ascension Theology* (London: T. & T. Clark, 2011.
Francis. *Evangelii Gaudium: The Joy of the Gospel*. Vatican City: Libreria Editrice Vaticana, 2013.
Geerlings, Wilhelm. "Ascensio Christi." In *Augustinus Lexikon*, edited by Petrus C. Mayer, 1:475–79. Basel: Schwabe, 1986–1994.
Granados, José. "The First Fruits of the Flesh and the First Fruits of the Spirit: The Mystery of the Ascension." *Communio* 38/2 (Spring 2011) 6–38.
Kelly, Anthony J. "Beyond Locked Doors: The Breath of the Risen One." In *Violence, Desire and the Sacred: Girard's Mimetic Theory Across the Disciplines*, edited by Scott Cowdell, Chris Fleming, and Joel Hodge, 69–85. New York: Continuum, 2012.
———. *Upward: Faith, Church and the Ascension of Christ*. Collegeville, MN: Liturgical, 2014.
———. "Refreshing Experience: The Christ-Event as Fact, Classic, and Phenomenon." *Irish Theological Quarterly* 77/4 (2012) 335–48.
———. *The Resurrection Effect: Transforming Christian Life and Thought*. Maryknoll, NY: Orbis, 2008.
Kelly, Anthony J., and Francis J. Moloney. *The Experience of God in the Gospel of John*. Mahwah, NJ: Paulist, 2003.
Lohfink, G. *Die Himmelfahrt Jesu: Untersuchungen zu den Himmelfahrts-und Erhohungstexten bei Lukas*. Studien zom Alten und Neuen Testament 26. Munich: Kösel, 1971.
Nancy, Jean-Luc. *Au fond des images*. Paris: Galilée, 2003.
Rahner, Karl. "The Interpretation of the Dogma of the Assumption." In *Theological Investigations*, translated by C. Ernst, 1:215–27. London: Darton, Longman and Todd, 1961.
Robinette, Brian D. *Grammars of Resurrection*. New York: Crossroads, 2014.

7

The Rise and Fall of Normative Ethics in Recent Catholic Moral Theology

Terrence Gerard Kennedy, C.Ss.R.

The history of moral theology since the Second Vatican Council has yet to be thoroughly researched and documented. Professor Brian Johnstone belonged to the new generation charged with implementing the Council, like the master of a household who brings out of his treasure what is new and what is old (Matt 13:52). He embodied the Biblical ideal of a scholar. "If the great Lord is willing, he will be filled with the spirit of understanding, he will pour forth words of wisdom of his own" (Sir 39:6). His lecturing, directing dissertations, writing and research helped to open up and expand the discipline toward fresh horizons.

In 1960 moral theology and Christian ethics were defined in terms of normative ethics. The *Handbuch der Evangelischen Ethik* makes it unmistakeably clear what was meant: morality is nothing other than a system of rules or norms.[1] Such a conception is deeply rooted in European history and has dominated culture for seven centuries. Christendom had sketched out the rules for happiness, and good relations with God and neighbour. The Enlightenment was the first period to doubt this worldview. Since then situation ethics and cultural relativism have undermined every attempt to regulate personal behaviour in this manner. Morality had now to justify

---

1. Huber et al., *Handbuch der Evangelischen Ethik*, 15. "In der Moral geht es um die Regulierung des Handels durch Normen, und zwar der Tendenz nach um allgemeingültigen Normen. Moral ist ein System der Normen und Verhaltensregeln, die sich an den Grundscheidungen gut/bös oder schlecht, richtig/falsch, geboten/verboten (oder erlaubt) orientieren und für alle gelten."

itself before rationalism's tribunal. Pope Francis has highlighted the impact of this *Kairos* on contemporary history. It indicates not so much changing times but a whole era of rapid change characterised as post-modernity.

The Catholic Church experienced severe "culture shock" after the May 1968 riots in Paris. Post-conciliar tensions exploded when Paul VI published *Humanae Vitae* at the end of July, with protests and dissent against the natural law prohibition on contraception spreading internationally. Conflicts about decriminalising abortion and prohibited sexual practices in the USA were dubbed "culture wars." Theological infighting scandalised laity who put their trust in the Decalogue as God's revealed law, while priests became sceptical about their seminary education. Could morality really be defended purely on rational grounds? At this point moralists became divided about normative ethics. Some defended the magisterium at all costs, without any exception: many simply wanted *Humanae Vitae* overturned. But the new science of fundamental moral theology flourished. It was perceived as an adventure to confront and integrate modern critical philosophy into moral theology on its own grounds, witness the instant success of Franz Böckle's *Fundamentalmoral*.

Protestant ethicists had striven for decades to assimilate modern philosophies. Catholic intellectuals in countries like the UK, USA and Australia resisted such initiatives although they were not unfamiliar. Some German moralists were fascinated by them, and wanted to bring C. D. Broad's *Five Types of Ethical Theory*, the "is-ought" distinction, and the teleological—deontological classification of moral theories into service in moral theology. Bruno Schüller's rather simplistic identifying of casuistry with teleological reasoning resonated with many colleagues. In fact English analytic philosophy's findings were rarely received into mainline moral theology in their original meaning. Were these authors trying to rationalise their practice of casuistry, or were they propounding truly new theories? This study, therefore, takes up the alternatives facing moral theology in a secular age.

Two New Theories

The Decree on Priestly Training (*OT* 16) mandated moral theologians to expound their discipline in a systematic way, that is, according to the criteria of systematic theology. They set their minds on realising this programme of renewal. The main problem they encountered concerned the manualists' accounts of natural law which they understood as a normative ethic, a self-contained set of moral norms. Contemporary debate treated natural law as another moral theory in competition with others like those of Kant or Bentham. Natural law was also presumed to furnish a complete rationale for morality without reference to further outside principles. Dissatisfaction with the neoscholastic manuals in use, especially those inspired by Francesco Suarez, also motivated them. With little holding moralists together beyond the traditions to which they belonged, the reform proceeded in two radically different directions. One inclined to an empirical approach to justify norms from human experience, employing a hermeneutic favourable to changing their formulation. The other defended tradition and the magisterium's teaching authority. Its advocates lamented the lack of a clear proof for the existence of absolute norms, valid in all circumstances without exception and with whatever intention. They inclined to blame casuistry for the prevalence of moral scepticism in Catholic culture which they were convinced had compromised the true value of moral norms.

Germain Grisez rose to the challenge of remedying the perceived vacuum in natural law theory. He filled this gap up with a set of absolute norms that bound conscience in every situation. His book *Contraception and the Natural Law* provided new arguments against objections to the Church's teaching. In the seminal article "The First Principle of Practical Reason. A Commentary on the *Summa theologiae*, 1–2, Question 94, Article 2"[2] he laid down the foundations of his system. The basic goods were absolute requirements of reason that human action could never contradict or deny. Grisez denied that St. Thomas Aquinas's teaching that the exceptionless norms of natural law were valid "ut in pluribus" was true. For Thomas, a moral act is individualised by its matter. Circumstances thereby determine a norm's application. The more circumstances determine a moral act, the more precisely defined is the range of the norm applied. Grisez objected that physical circumstances could not limit a norm's binding force in this way. Physicalism contradicted Hume's "is-ought" principle and so committed an error modern philosophy would never condone. By making Hume's principle a mainstay in his conception of natural law Grisez deliberately distanced himself from what was being taught in seminaries. He asserted that "The Middle Ages were content to define natural law as 'participation in eternal law' but this did not satisfy contemporary questioning of the origin

---

2. Grisez, "First Principle," 168–201.

and apprehension of the most essential ethical and juridic principles."[3] Further, he criticised St. Augustine's notion of happiness as contemplating God, and the way he had molded the traditional understanding of natural law. Grisez postulated his theory on a double foundation: the goods that reason shows to be humanly fulfilling; and the modes of responsibility that guide human choice. He believed that his theory of absolute norms could prove *Humanae Vitae*'s thesis and other essential moral teachings irrefutably.

Natural Law had disappeared from English universities about two centuries ago. John Finnis, professor of international law in Oxford, made it respectable once again in the English—speaking world, and his *Natural Law and Natural Rights* showed that it could make sense and be rationally defended. His was a sort of apologetic suited to counties where Hume's thought was dominating intellectual life.

Finnis, like Grisez, thought of practical reason as the capacity to achieve the basic goods. He listed these as: 1. Life and health in all its aspects. 2. Knowledge. 3. Play. 4. Aesthetic experience and beauty. 5. Sociability. 6. Practical Reasonableness. 7. Religion as the sense of an ultimate order of things.

Finnis also classified ten modes of responsibility or prudential principles of practical reason.

1. Reasonableness structures our pursuit of every good.

2. A coherent plan of life derives from wisdom

3. No arbitrary preferences among values means that goods cannot be reduced to mere utility.

4. No arbitrary preferences among persons flows from the Golden Rule.

5. Detachment and commitment are complementary.

6. Consequences represent efficiency but cannot be weighed against each other. It is impossible to predict all of an action's long-term consequences.

7. Every basic good is to be respected in every act. Consequentialism sacrifices basic goods to other considerations, for example, killing an innocent person to save a hostage's life. Acts directly aimed at hurting, damaging or destroying basic goods are wrong, and fall under the absolute prohibitions sanctioned by natural law. Unintended,

---

3. Kennedy, "Originality," 128–29.

unavoidable side effects of an action are a different issue as is the principle of double effect.

8. The requirements of the common good mean that reason must provide the social conditions needed for persons to flourish as persons. Finnis believed that natural law follows a prudential method that functions as the foundation of law, authority and obligation.

9. Human rights are always an expression of duty and are the contemporary grammar for natural law thinking.

10. Morality results from applying these principles to our commitments and life projects. Moral terms take their meaning from these principles.

The "New Natural Law Theory," as it is called, is a genuine ethical theory with typically modern features. It is not based on a metaphysics of finality, nor on a hierarchy among the incommensurable basic goods. It is wholly dependent on the demands of practical reason to establish the norms that a free moral subject imposes on its action.

The alternative we are about to consider tells another story. It reacted strongly against the manuals and their rigorism in particular. It too aspired to the status of a normative theory. Described as a movement, work in progress in the renewal of moral theology, it arose about the same time as Grisez's initiative. It first came to USA moralists' attention in 1967 when the German fundamental theologian, Peter Knauer, published his groundbreaking article, "The Hermeneutic Function of the Principle of Double Effect."[4] Knauer had an utterly new insight: in itself the principle of double effect is a complete theory of action. This essay was destined to reconfigure and transform all the elements in the customary understanding of morality. Moralists had employed double effect for well over a century in the case of an action with two effects, one good and one evil. In the classic formula four conditions had to be fulfilled to permit an evil effect.

1. The action from which the evil would result must be good or at least indifferent.

2. The agent must intend the good effect. This is what the agent intends directly, the evil effect being permitting only indirectly.

---

4. Knauer, "Hermeneutic," 132–62.

3. The evil effect cannot cause the good effect, or at least the good and evil effects must be caused simultaneously.
4. There must be a proportionately grave reason for allowing the evil effect to occur.

If all these conditions were fulfilled, the evil caused by the contemplated action was judged indirect, and the agent was allowed to perform the action. This explanation of the principle was justified from the *Summa Theologiae*, II-II. q. 64, a. 7's treatment of self—defence against violent attack. The formula for the double effect became more complicated as it was extended to fresh cases troubling a changing society. Knauer pushed its boundaries even further. He, as it were, turned the principle on its head so that it absorbed every rule used to resolve hard cases,[5] concerning for example, scandal, cooperation, and solicitation of another to do evil.

Proportionate reason became the key insight for a new comprehension of moral theology. Its impact, the energy it released, has been described as a revolution. Its enemies invented the name that became its hallmark: proportionalism. In a chain reaction numerous noted moralists pleaded for its acceptance: J. Fuchs, B. Schüller, F. Furger, F. Böckle, L. Janssens, W. Kerber, C. Curran, J. Selling, E. Vacek, R. Grinters, K. Demmer, G. Hallet, B. Hoos and others. It was almost impossible to differentiat between them since no two had exactly the same ideas. But they shared one common concern, namely, the fonts or sources of morality by which an act's morality is assessed from its object, end and circumstances. Traditionalists took these terms separately and independently as self-standing, so that the object alone could determine an act's morality. Revisionists, as they were also called, would not ascribe morality to an act apart from its intention, the agent's proposed end and circumstances. This left the notion of intrinsically evil acts *ex objecto* in limbo. The revisionists found the terminology of the manuals so hard to apply that it started to appear unbelievable. For example, the idea that God had create certain organs with morally normative finalities written into their biology. This, they believed, had to bring Catholic teaching into disrepute.

More was at stake than the accepted implications of the double effect principle. The foundations of all prescriptive and proscriptive behavioural norms were being rethought in a novel manner. In order to reform the deontological norms that constitute natural law it was necessary to establish

---

5. Walter, "Foundation," 124–54.

"those features and characteristics that make acts morally right or wrong in the first place."[6] These concerned not an agent's goodness/badness, a pair of terms dealing not with a person's dispositions and attitudes, but the objective rightness/wrongness of acts.

Revisionists yearned for a wider better vision of morality than the restrictive double effect framework provided. They argued that the moral assessment of acts could not be achieved without considering circumstances. Nor could the object be separated out and judged apart from the complete act. Revisions never intended to deny the notion of intrinsically evil altogether, but held that it had to be determined concretely after considering all a situation's features.[7] Some attributed priority to the agent, evaluating the will's inner act as essentially constitutive of action, and as no mere external circumstance. If all circumstances were included, then consequences became relevant and had to be examined. What then determined an action's real confines and limits? Proportionalists were being accused of assessing the rightness/wrongness of an action solely by reference to the net total good produced. They rebuffed the charge of espousing consequentialism, and answered that moral reason always functioned teleologically to discern the proportionate reason that justified action.

They also affirmed that, despite terminological variations, all pre-moral or ontic values and disvalues had to be incorporated before arriving at a final judgement. Pre-moral disvalues are not merely physical evils, for example, the destruction brought about by a bush fire, but refer to the harms, lacks, pain, deprivation, and so on, that occur in or as a result of human agency. We have a moral duty in as far as possible to avoid pre-moral disvalues in our action. Proportionate reason was used to clarify the causing of pre-moral evils in conflict situations and could justify both the effect and the cause of such evil. The distinction between direct/indirect was not always decisive. It may be merely descriptive, indicating what the agent is doing, or what was aimed at, and with what means. Approval and disapproval were the appropriate categories to be applied in cases involving pre-moral evil. Traditional terms such as "to intend as a means" or "to permit" could denote an attitude of disapproval referring to a pre-moral evil. The revisionist exempted no moral terms from their project to refashion traditional moral theology using the teleological method. They

---

6. McCormick, "Notes," 86.
7. Yustinus, "Discussion," 113–26.

were determined to translate the natural law's deontological norms into teleological terms.

Richard McCormick wanted to engage the opponents of the new theory and to enlarge their perspective. At first he was quite sceptical about Peter Knauer's reworking the whole field of moral thinking. But after assiduously pondering the debate's progress and studying Knauer's later contributions he registered his reflections in "Notes on Moral Theology" in *Theological Studies*. These became a valuable thermometer for testing the temperature of the debate over the years. The Marquette Lecture 1973 *Ambiguity in Moral Choice* marked his conversion to Knauer's position, a profound change of direction in his thought that came close to identifying proportionate reason with choosing the lesser evil. The lesser evil became a standard of logical consistency to guarantee stability in the system. But he still aimed at enlarging the theory's perspective on the good. This he did by aligning it with John Finnis's list of the basic goods. Contrary to Finnis's intention and inspired by St. Augustine's order of charity he defined the moral order as a hierarchy of goods. Nevertheless an outstanding enigma persisted. How was an agent to choose when confronted with more than one negative value? Choosing a lesser evil over a higher one might cause more evil than necessary or acceptable. To resolve this dilemma McCormick turned to Knauer's suggestion that goods were not truly incommensurate but could be related by their functionality in a hierarchy of goods.

In 1979 the first volume in the series *Readings in Moral Theology*, edited by Richard McCormick and Charles Curran, collected together articles that had contributed to this project. As well it included the counter-positions by John Connery and Paul Quay who belonged to the same tradition as the theory's inventors. The title *Moral Norms and Catholic Tradition* touched a neuralgic nerve with those concerned for the future of moral theology. Could this proposal really be reconciled with the Church's moral teaching?

The debate continued fiercely until it reached an impasse with neither side conceding ground. The internal logic of both alternatives discussed above was flawed. The basic goods theory in fact reversed and in part dismantled the formulation of the first principle of natural law. Grisez raised its negative aspect to the supreme principle of morality. That meant that *malum est evitandum* overshadowed *bonum est faciendum et prosequendum*. The positive aspect of the first principle was left implicit and unacknowledged.[8] Absolute negative prohibitions were more important than striv-

---

8. Flannery, *Acts*, 48–49 and 212–17.

ing for the good. This newly coined theory thereby presented a basically defensive and inflexible morality. Proportionate reason, on the other hand, maintained that circumstances and intentions always had to be considered in the object of an action. This rendered the defining of moral terms quite impossible. This theory had got caught up in a series *ad infinitum*, where an action's definition could always change or mutate if further circumstances or intentions were added. In this case, there could be no definition of moral terms without condition, something that contradicts human experience. The basic question for moral theology now became: which philosophy did it need to truly support its systematic exposition?

Some Responses

Significant responses came from theologians and philosophers somewhat outside the tight circle of this debate. Taking rather different attitudes to the above developments, their reactions ranging from fervent support to outright scepticism, denial or indifference. Some felt that the Church's teaching authority had been compromised, while others hoped it would adjust to contemporary culture. In 1986 Servais Pinckaers's *Ce qu'on ne peut jemais faire* assailed the proportionate reason theory for its departures from St. Thomas, its dependence on nominalism, and its Suarezian approach to intrinsic evil. Martin Rhonheimer with others was convinced that the denial of any truly absolute norms would destroy natural law at its very core.

The Sydney philosopher, John Hill, examined the argument of *Doing Evil to Achieve Good* in his essay on "The Debate between McCormick and Frankena."[9] He put the crucial question: how would philosophers classify proportionalism as an ethical system? He regretted that one of Frankena's wise comments had been let pass unnoticed. "My impression has been that Catholic moral theologians," said Frankena, "have thought much harder about practices and cases than secular philosophers, while the later have thought harder about ethical theory." Hill noted how the theologians engaged in this particular dialogue appeared to form an "in-group," where philosophers hardly felt at home. He warned against a dangerous "intelligibility gap" growing up between the two parties. It soon became obvious that the philosophers could not position proportionalism on the deontological-teleological spectrum of ethical theories. Hill pointed out that moral theology did rely on philosophical procedures, and that if these were left

9. Hill, "The Debate," 121–23.

implicit and unrecognised then trouble would ensure. It should therefore be possible to translate this theory into terms comprehensible by the secular academy. Otherwise it would become a language complete to itself and dialogue with other disciplines would become untenable. Hill insisted that this stance obscured the task of moral theology. For example, Knauer had upheld the thesis that behaviour contradicting the value it sought to instantiate had to be morally condemned. Hill asked quite pointedly if this really added anything substantial to ethics. For Aristotle had taught that the end of moral science or ethics was not knowledge but action. Revisionist moral discourse seemed to have deviated from this aim, being tailored to dialogue with other university faculties. It had become forgetful of its pastoral function in service of the Church's mission in the world. For this reason Pope Francis has called for a "pastoral conversion" (*EG* 27) in Church thinking and practice.

Professional philosophers were often astounded that moral theologians seemed unaware of advances in moral theory. Elizabeth Anscombe's epoch making essay "Modern Moral Philosophy" was a case in point.[10] She underlined the historic origins of our problems in moral language. The modern senses of "ought" and "moral obligation" were remnants from a divine law conception of ethics where God was thought of as the Law-Giver. Today these terms refer to the *humanum* or inner worldly realities, and not to the context of divine law, outside of which they lose their meaning. Anscombe argued that "ought" has a non-emphatic meaning in ordinary language that contemporary ethics has unnecessarily complicated. She warned that consequentialism was a serious threat to society when it condoned the judicial condemnation of the innocent. Such a philosophy was incompatible with the Judeo-Christian ethic. She defended the logic of the proposition that "the prohibition of certain things simply in virtue of their description as such and such identifiable types of action, regardless of any further consequence" was essential to this ethic.

Revisionists seemed to display little interest in Alasdair Macintyre's *After Virtue: An Essay in Moral Theory*. In MacIntyre's analysis ethical theories had become entrenched and bogged down in senseless warfare with no end in sight. The reason for this conspicuous failure was that they had put aside the notion of *telos*. They could no longer connect what-we-are to what we-can-become, or what we-ought-to be. MacIntyre diagnosed, as it were, a blind spot, or better an inconsistency, in the very notion of normative

---

10. Anscombe, "Modern Moral Philosophy," especially 34, 36, and 42.

ethics as a self-standing system. He demonstrated that norms are inseparable from virtues, indeed both can only be properly understood in view of a *telos*, that is, the goods internal to virtues. These goods and the virtues embodying them are intelligible only in view of the end they seek. Outside this context moral norms do not make sense. This reinforced Anscombe's belief that norms were no longer roughly equivalent to law, and that they need a much richer moral psychology such as Aristotle's to support them.

Professor Johnstone entered this debate in 1985 with an essay on "On the Meaning of Proportionate Reason in Contemporary Moral Theology."[11] He summarised the historical and philosophical evolution of the principle of double effect, showing that the term "proportion" had three distinct meanings. 1. In the modern version deriving from Gury it compared effect with effect. 2. For St. Thomas the act had to be proportionate to the end in the context of self-defence. 3. For Knauer and the proportionalists the terms of comparison were pre-moral values and disvalues. This was a variant of the effect/effect comparison. Johnstone was sure that the quantitate interpretation could be traced to Gury who was credited with its systematic formulation. Johnstone then inquired what proportion could mean in terms of weighing values. Could it be influenced by considerations of urgency or counter indications? And on what scales might good and evil be compared? Could this be achieved by a hierarchy of values? Johnstone concluded that Knauer was optimising the long-term net gain of action and that redefining terms would only bring confusion. Proportion, therefore, has different meanings and different functions in different contexts. Two conceptions emerged as of crucial importance in the debate. In St. Thomas proportion meant the relationship of an act to the end to which it was directed. Proportionalists compared an action's good and evil external effects as seen by an objective, and it should be said, juridic observer. Johnstone foreshadowed the future direction of his research by calling for an integrated moral theory that satisfied the perspectives of both theories.

In 1993 St. John Paul II's encyclical *Veritatis Splendor* addressed "Certain Fundamental Moral Question in the Church's Moral Teaching." This document was the watershed in the whole discussion. The Pope praised moralists' attempts at renewal, but firmly criticised some errors without mentioning any authors by name. The central second chapter focused on moral theory. Its theme was that moral activity is directed to God as ultimate end. Its point of reference was stated as "*The relationship between the*

---

11. Johnstone, "Meaning of Proportionate," 223–47.

moral good of human acts and *eternal life.*" The Pope taught that "the moral life has an essential *'teleological' character,* since it consists in the deliberate ordering of human acts to God." This assertion seemed to be directed against some positions described above. The encyclical did not refer to the basic goods theory. But its conception of happiness as self-fulfilment, the enjoyment of the complex of basic goods, and not primarily of God as the ultimate end, appeared questionable. Themes relevant to normative ethics were: the dependence of natural law on eternal law; the moral order as established by the natural law; the body comes under natural law because of the body-soul unity of the person. This pivotal statement made the encyclical's teaching clear: "the negative moral precepts, those prohibiting certain concrete actions or kinds of behaviour as intrinsically evil, do not allow of any legitimate exception" (no. 67). As a result, the sources of morality (no 74) had to be interpreted in this light.

At the beginning of the new millennium Professor Johnstone offered courses in fundamental moral theology in the Alphonsian Academy, Rome. He examined various ethical systems, paying acute attention to the subject-object split that had penetrated deeply into modern philosophy. He stressed the profound influence of this worldview on moral theology and its history since the Middle Ages.[12] In his analysis the basic goods theory was developed from the side of the subject, with Kantian type reason declaring the norms of moral action. Proportionalism developed from the side of the object. It envisaged real existent objects, that is, an objective legal order in the external world, in which the good and evil effects of human action could be compared. Neither theory succeeded in relating the subject/agent with the object/world in an integrated way. Johnstone saw that they were already integrated and united by and in the *Ratio Divina,* God's Providence and Law governing both the order of Creation and of Redemption. The new proposals lacked an adequate metaphysics of creation to open and to point them to their ultimate end in God.

Bibliography

Anscombe, G. E. M. "Modern Moral Philosophy." In *Ethics, Religion and Politics,* 29–47. Minneapolis: University of Minnesota Press, 1981.
Böckle, Franz. *Fundamentalmoral.* Cologne: Kösel, 1977.
Broad, C. D. *Five Types of Ethical Theories.* Oxford: Oxford University Press, 1930.
Finnis, John. *Natural Law and Natural Rights.* Oxford: Clarendon, 1980.

12. Johnstone, "Argument," 139–55.

Flannery, Kevin. *Acts Amid Precepts*. Washington, DC: Catholic University of America Press, 2001.

Grisez, Germaine. *Contraception and the Natural Law*. Milwaukee: Bruce, 1964.

———. "The First Principle of Practical Reason: A Commentary on the *Summa theologiae*, 1–2, Question 94, Article 2." *Natural Law Forum* 10 (1965) 168–201.

Hill, John. "The Debate between McCormick and Frankena." *Irish Theological Quarterly* 49 (1982) 121–23.

Huber, Wolfgang, Torsten Meireis, and Hans-Richard Reuter, eds. *Handbuch der Evangelischen Ethik*. Munich: C. H. Beck, 2015.

John Paul II. *Veritais Splendor*. Vatican: Editrice Vaticana, 1993.

Johnstone, Brian V. "The Meaning of Proportionate Reason in Contemporary Moral Theology." *Thomist* 49 (1985) 2, 223–47.

———. "The Argument from Tradition in Catholic Moral Theology." In *Irish Theological Quarterly* 69 (2004) 139–55.

Kennedy, Terence. "The Originality of John Finnis's Conception of the Natural Law." In *Attualitá della teologia morale*, 118–39. Studia Urbaniana 31. Rome: Urbaniana Universiety Press, 1987.

Knauer, Peter. "The Hermeneutic Function of the Principle of Double Effect." *Natural Law Forum* 12 (1967) 132–62.

MacIntyre, Alasdair. *After Virtue*. Notre Dame: University of Notre Dame Press, 1981.

McCormick, Richard A. *Ambiguity in Moral Choice*. Milwaukee: Marquette University Press, 1973.

———. "Notes on Moral Theology: 1985." *Theological Studies* 47 (1986) 69–133.

McCormick, Richard A., and Charles Curran, eds. *Moral Norms and Catholic Tradition*. Readings in Moral Theology 1. New York: Orbis, 1979.

McCormick, Richard A., and Paul Ramsey, eds. *Doing Evil to Achieve Good*. Chicago: Loyola University Press, 1978.

Paul VI. *Humanae Vitae*. Vatican: Editrice Vaticana, 1968.

Pinckaers, Servais. *Ce qu'on ne peut jamais faire*. Paris: Cerf, 1986.

Walter, James. "The Foundation and Formulation of Norms." In *Challenges for the Future*, edited by Charles E. Curran, 124–54. New York: Paulist, 1990.

Yustinus, Yustinus. "The Discussion Regarding 'Intrinsice Malum' Before and After 'Veritatis Splendor.'" S.T.D. diss., Accademia Alfonsiana, 2006.

— 8 —

Moral Theology and Practice in Anglican-Roman Catholic Dialogue

Difference, Convergence, and Diversity

CHARLES SHERLOCK

Brian Johnstone: An Appreciation

Members of the *Second Anglican-Roman Catholic International Commission* (ARCIC II) gathered in Paris on 27 August 1991 for their annual meeting, a distinctive one in two respects. On the one hand, the topic the Commission was to work on was "morals in communion," the first ecumenical dialogue to take up this area. On the other hand, it was a substantially new group: eleven members joined five others who continued from the 1983–1990 Commission that had produced *Salvation and the Church* and *Church as Communion*—topics closely related to ecclesiology. An Anglican of evangelical outlook, I was one of the new members, whose theological expertise lay in systematic theology and liturgy more than ethics. Coming to this, my initial ARCIC meeting, from the other side of the globe, was thus a somewhat daunting prospect both culturally and theologically.

Another new Roman Catholic member was a skilled moral theologian, a fellow Australian—Brian Johnston. Being conscious of my Australian-accented English, it was a relief to find a colleague whose vocal expression rang with a familiar cadence. But more, Brian seemed to be familiar with every aspect of Christian ethics, and the Roman Catholic moral tradition in particular. Further, he would share his encyclopedic knowledge with no sense of superiority, and an evident humility. This allowed his many contributions to be assessed openly, with no defensiveness towards occasional gauche comments from uninformed Anglican from "down under." Brian Johnston not only made a major contribution to the successful completion in 1993 of *Life in Christ: Morals, Communion and the Church*, but played a large part in my own learning more of the Christian heritage of moral reasoning, for which I continue to be grateful.

But the agreements reached in *Life in Christ* have come under challenge in the two decades since it was issued in 1994. This article begins by reviewing the background to this Agreed Statement, analyzes the convergence it reached, reviews the responses made, and—not least in view of the significant shifts which have taken place since its publication—offer pointers on how the third phase of ARCIC might approach its mandate, "how in communion the local and universal Church come to discern right ethical teaching." In doing so, I am glad to acknowledge the significant part which Brian Johnston played both in the ARCIC process, and to own deeper education in Christian moral theology.

Anglican-Roman Catholic Dialogue on Morals: Difference

After nearly five centuries of division, Anglican-Roman Catholic dialogue opened up in the wake of the Second Vatican Council, sparked by the first meeting since the Reformation between an Archbishop of Canterbury (Michael Ramsey) and the Pope (Paul VI) in 1966. The ("Malta") Report of the *Joint Preparatory Commission* (1968) recommended that moral issues be taken up by a distinct Commission, alongside a body which attended to doctrinal questions. The latter were taken up from 1969 by the *Anglican-Roman Catholic International Commission* (ARCIC), but it would be a quarter-century before moral issues was considered, and then by ARCIC itself rather than by a distinct body.

In the years since 1969, ARCIC has significantly narrowed some doctrinal differences (and perceived differences), most notably concerning the eucharist[1] and justification.[2] By 2005 the Commission had published Agreed Statements covering all the doctrinal issues dividing the two traditions. These have had mixed official receptions, yet the dialogue continues, both through the *International Anglican-Roman Catholic Commission on Unity and Mission* (IARCCUM) and a third phase of ARCIC.

In grass-roots living, however, it is not so much doctrinal disagreement as differences over moral practice which are felt to be the biggest barriers to reconciliation. Only a generation ago, for example, the experience of an Anglican being married to a Roman Catholic in a vestry is still recalled with some bitterness, while the promise about children being brought up as Catholics were misunderstood and resented. This was the topic given to a *Joint Commission on the Theology of Marriage and its Application to Mixed Marriages* (its self-chosen title), which met from 1968. After two meetings the Commission agreed on "three fundamental theological principles." These are worth citing in full:

i. That Holy Baptism itself confers Christian status and is the indestructible bond of union between all Christians and Christ, and so of Christians with one another. This baptismal unity remains firm despite all ecclesiastical division.

ii. That in Christian marriage the man and the woman themselves make the covenant whereby they enter into marriage as instituted and ordained by God; this new unity, the unity of marriage, is sacramental in virtue of their Christian baptism and is the work of God in Christ.

iii. That this marriage once made possesses a unity given by God to respect which is a primary duty; this duty creates secondary obligations for the Church in both its pastoral and its legislative capacity. One is the obligation to discourage marriages in which the unity would be so strained or so lacking in vitality as to be both a source of danger to the parties themselves and to be a disfigured sign of or defective witness

---

1. ARCIC's first Agreed Statement was on the eucharist (1971), with an Elucidation a decade later: these were received by Lambeth Conference as acceptable to Anglicans. The official Vatican Response (1991) raised major issues, to which ARCIC II responded in *Clarifications* (1993), which were received positively by the *Pontifical Council for Promoting Christian Unity*. These and related texts can be found in Hill and Yarnold, *The Search for Unity*.

2. *Salvation and the Church* took up the issues around the doctrine of justification. This agreement was furthered by the 2001 *Joint Declaration on the Doctrine of Justification* by the Lutheran World Federation and the Roman Catholic Church.

to the unity of Christ with his Church. Another is the obligation to concert its pastoral care and legislative provisions to support the unity of the marriage once it is made and to ensure as best it can that these provisions be not even unwittingly divisive.

The Joint Commission then became aware that the 1966 Instruction *Matrimonii Sacramentum* was under revision in the light of Vatican II. It waited for three years before continuing work, until the outcome of the Instruction's review was issued, a Letter issued *motu proprio* by Paul VI in March 1970, *Matrimonia Mixta*. From an Anglican perspective this delay raised questions about how far dialogue takes us—but even so, convergence was beginning.[3]

The 1975 Report of the *Joint Commission on The Theology of Marriage and its Application to Mixed Marriages* was welcomed by Lambeth 1978 in Resolution 34, albeit with this rider:[4]

> The problems associated with marriage between members of our two Communions continue to hinder inter-Church relations and progress towards unity. While we recognise that there has been an improved situation in some places as a result of the "Motu Propio" [i.e., *Matrimonia Mixta*], the general principles underlying the Roman Catholic position are unacceptable to Anglicans.

A more positive outcome of dialogue—local rather than international—was the 1987 *Pastoral Guidelines* issued by the National Anglican-Roman Catholic Bishops' Dialogue in Canada. One notable development is the shift in language (in both English and French): the Guidelines do not speak of "mixed marriages" but of "inter-church marriages" throughout. This recognises the significant *ecclesial* reality in the marriage of two baptised Christians, even they are not fully not "in communion," whose life as "joint heirs" nevertheless signifies the union between Christ and the Church.

---

3. For a fuller account, see Sherlock, "Anglican–Roman Catholic Dialogue on Ethics."

4. This 1978 Resolution was more positive than Resolution 67 of Lambeth 1908: "We desire earnestly to warn members of our Communion against contracting marriages with Roman Catholics under the conditions imposed by modern Roman canon law." This 1908 Resolution was reiterated in Resolution 98 of Lambeth 1948.

Life in Christ—Morals, Communion and the Church: Convergence

Despite the programme proposed in the 1968 Malta Report which included reference to moral questions, it was not until 1990 that ARCIC took up this task. Even so, several indications of agreement in social ethics can be found in its earlier Statements. Thus

> [The Church] is called to affirm the sacredness and dignity of the person, the value of natural and political communities . . . to witness against the structure of sin in society, addressing humanity with the Gospel of repentance and forgiveness and making intercession for the world. It is called to be an agent of justice and compassion (*Salvation and the Church* §31).

What such agreement means in practice for relations between the Anglican Communion and the Roman Catholic Church has not been followed up until recently, precisely because it does not concern disagreement, the focus of the mandates for ARCIC I and II—a lacuna considered further below.

ARCIC II, having consolidated its insights into "communion ecclesiology" in *Church as Communion*, in 1990 began to take up moral issues. The outcome after four years' work was *Life in Christ: Moral, Communion and the Church*, the first Agreed Statement on morals to come from an ecumenical dialogue, and one to which Brian Johnson made considerable contributions. This statement is noteworthy on two fronts.

Convergence Rather than Agreement

Life in Christ works by recognizing the "new convergence" (§3) emerging between the Anglican and Roman Catholic traditions of moral reasoning: earlier ARCIC Statements aimed to reach full agreement about doctrinal questions.

This convergence is expressed in terms of a "Shared Vision" (Section B) of the "patterning power of the kingdom," based on a "Common Heritage" (Section C). Scholarly commentators find these Sections to be an accurate and hopeful portrayal of a shared vision of moral life, grounded in a set of agreed foundational values.[5] The Statement goes on to acknowledge "Paths Diverge" (Section D) following the sixteenth-century breach

---

5. Nilson, "Must Disagreements Divide?" and Clague, "On Agreeing to Differ."

of communion, as the two communions approached ethical questions in isolation, especially during the twentieth century. Yet ARCIC II was able to reach agreement sufficient to provide a basis for Anglicans and Roman Catholics to give joint witness to a secular world increasingly at odds with the Christian faith, and for approaching ongoing disagreements on moral issues between the two traditions. The Statement recognizes that "There is already a notable convergence between the two Communions in the witness they give, for example, on war and peace, euthanasia, freedom and justice" (§1). A recent example of such joint witness, grounded in Anglican-Roman Catholic co-operation but extending beyond this, is their joint participation in setting up the Global Freedom network to combat modern slavery.[6]

In the area of human sexuality, however, notably as regards divorce and contraception, there is documented disagreement between the Anglican Communion and Roman Catholic Church.[7] Section E of *Life in Christ* considers these matters in some detail, noting the historical circumstances in which distinct approaches developed, with differing patterns of government and decision-making involved. The Statement nevertheless argues that these differences derive from different applications of the "Shared Vision" which remains in place: the convergence behind them is more significant than the differences.

"Double Negative" Conclusion

Unlike earlier ARCIC Statements, whose "Agreements" were positive, *Life in Christ*, as a "convergence" text, works towards a "double negative" conclusion. This is the outcome of the recognition that

> Our two Communions have in the past developed their moral teaching and practical and pastoral disciplines in isolation from each other. The differences that have arisen between them are serious, but careful study and consideration has shown us that they are not fundamental (§88).

In the light of the key place of *koinonia* in ARCIC's work, it is significant that *Life in Christ: Morals, Communion and the Church* (the full title of the

---

6. This multi-faith network has its administrative base in the Anglican Centre in Rome: see www.globalfreedom.org.

7. When *Life in Christ* was drafted there were also "perceived" but not "official" differences between the Anglican Communion and the Roman Catholic Church over abortion and homosexual behaviour: these are discussed briefly in *Life in Christ* §83–87.

Statement) acknowledges the "deep desire" of both traditions "to find an honest and faithful resolution of their disagreements" as "itself evidence of a continuing communion at a more profound level than that on which disagreement has occurred" (§96). More fully,

> On the one hand, seeking a resolution of our disagreements is part of the process of growing together towards full communion. On the other hand, only as closer communion leads to deeper understanding and trust can we hope for a resolution of our disagreements (§99).

The interplay between these aspects is reflect in the "double negative" conclusions reached in *Life in Christ*. As the opening paragraph anticipates,

> Even on those particular issues where disagreement exists, Anglicans and Roman Catholics, we shall argue, share a common perspective and acknowledge the same underlying values. This being so, we question whether the limited disagreement, serious as it is, is itself sufficient to justify a continuing breach of communion.

And in the final paragraphs before the Conclusion:

> Confining ourselves to the two issues of abortion and homosexual relations, we would argue that, in these instances too, the disagreements between us are not on the level of fundamental moral values, but on their implementation in practical judgments (§83).

In sum, *Life in Christ* develops ARCIC's approach to acknowledging, sustaining and developing communion between Anglicans and Roman Catholics by its recognition of convergence and employing a "double negative" rather than "full agreement" conclusion as enabling and fostering it.

But that is not end of the story. In the two decades since its publication, events have transpired which would appear to put into question the convergence expressed in *Life in Christ*.

Anglican and Roman Catholic Responses to New Moral Questions: Diversity

Since the Commission completed *Life in Christ*, the context for ARCIC's dialogue has changed significantly. In 1993 electronic communication was in its infancy: today this has revolutionised people's access to ideas, and brought about a previously unimagined interactive dimension to learning.

In such contexts, the moral formation of a person is shaped by a range of influences in which scriptural, ecclesial and familial perspectives are regarded as one among many possibilities, and are increasingly unknown or disregarded.

The context has also changed within the churches. A number of teaching documents have been issued by the Roman Catholic Church, notably John Paul II's *Veritatis Splendor* (1994, published just before *Life in Christ*). Together with *Evangelium Vitae* (1995), the *Catechism of the Catholic Church* Part III: *Life in Christ* (1997), *Deus Caritas Est* (2005) and *Caritas in Veritate* (2009), the these documents provide a new Roman Catholic context for assessing and responding to the convergence reached by ARCIC II.[8]

As same-sex sexual relationships have become accepted in western societies, increasingly diverse ecclesial approaches to homosexuality have been taken. Debate in the Anglican Communion about this issue became divisive in the 1990s, and the 1998 Lambeth Conference passed the multi-part Resolution I.10 to address the variety of positions held. In the decades since, Provincial and diocesan relationships have been strained and impaired: while the Anglican Communion Covenant process has endeavoured to clarify how the Communion can maintain the highest degree of unity in the face of division about moral issues, debate continues.

Anglican-Roman Catholic dialogue was deeply affected by the 2003 consecration in The Episcopal Church of the USA of a bishop in a long-term same-sex relationship. Bishop Frank Griswold, the Presiding Bishop (Primate) of ECUSA, took part in the consecration, and subsequently resigned as Anglican Co Chair of ARCIC II.[9] IARCCUM—whose work was suspended for some years at the request of the Vatican—established a sub-commission whose report noted the far-reaching effects of this consecration:

> The decision of the Episcopal Church USA to proceed with the consecration despite sustained strong opposition from large segments of the Anglican Communion, calls into question significant portions of our agreed statements on authority and ecclesiology: the nature of ecclesial communion; the mutual interdependence of churches; the role of episcopal and collegial authority in

---

8. I acknowledge the assistance given to this section by Professor Janet Smith, Sacred Heart Seminary, Michigan USA, and a member of ARCIC III.

9. Archbishop Peter Carnley, Primate of the Anglican Church of Australia, took up the Anglican CoChair's position for ARCIC II's final meeting, in January 2004.

maintaining the unity of the communion; the process of discernment in the communion of the Church, and the decisive role of Scripture and Tradition therein. This decision also challenges our mutual claim that we uphold a shared vision of human nature and the same fundamental moral values.[10]

The issue not only divides the Anglican Communion, but indicates a shift away from convergence towards diversity between the Anglican and Roman Catholic traditions. This diversity can be seen as the personal as well as ecclesial levels, as the Anglican-Roman Catholic Committee in the United States (ARC-USA), responding to *Life in Christ*, noted:

> The sometimes sharply divergent specific teachings and practices of our Churches regarding divorce, contraception, abortion, and homosexuality are actually a frequently given reason why Roman Catholic and Episcopalian Christians leave one Church and enter the other.[11]

The ARC-USA response also took *Veritatis Splendor* into account, making an incisive comparison between the two documents. It drew attention to the contrast between ARCIC II's question, "What sort of persons are we to become?" (*Life in Christ* §6, 11), and that of *Veritatis Splendor*, "What ought we to *do*?" More fully, ARC-USA identified three major areas of moral life as needing greater attention:[12]

1. the significance of divergent Anglican and Roman Catholic positions on absolute moral prohibitions regarding specific categories of human action;

2. the contemporary influence of theological, geographical, and cultural diversity on the formulation of Anglican doctrines concerning moral questions, by contrast with the universal teaching that characterizes the Roman Catholic *magisterium* in such matters; and

3. the role of ecclesiastical authority in shaping the formation of moral judgments of individual Christians and by the whole Church.

Statements by the Lambeth Conference support the notion of universal moral law, but always with a discussion of how these work out in particular areas. Thus the 1930 Conference Report on "The Life and Witness of

---

10. IARCCUM, *Ecclesiological Reflections*, section E §44.
11. ARC-USA, "Christian Ethics," conclusion.
12. Ibid., §4.

the Christian Community" speaks of axiomatic moral principles, seeing abortion as "contrary to the law of God and man," while allowing the use of (non-abortive) contraception as a means of family planning within marriage (while holding procreation as its primary good).[13] Lambeth Conferences have passed similar resolutions on a wide range of moral issues, in all of which appeal is made to "fundamental principles" grounded in biblical teaching, the example of Christ, scientific data and the nature of humanity as made in the image of God. It is presumed that the Church can teach on moral issues because there are fundamental moral norms. Yet it is not the nature of these Reports, which have persuasive rather than canonical force in the Anglican Communion, to argue from basic moral concepts. They have considerable weight, yet Lambeth Conference resolutions are not binding on provinces, nor are they determinative for future decision-making.

Roman Catholics take into account prudential matters in ethical decision-making, but any action that violates an exceptionless norm is not subject to prudential consideration. Moreover, canon law upholds the same exceptionless norms as moral theology, but provides ways for the Church as a governing body to respond to such issues as the status of members in the Church who violate some of those norms. The magisterium of the Roman Catholic Church continues to teach that contraception, divorce, abortion and homosexual acts are always wrong, and *Veritatis Splendor* is directed against theories in moral theology which hold that there are no intrinsically evil actions. But it would appear that not all Anglican provinces do so. What is the nature and reasons for this disagreement, and how may it be addressed?

In sum, to what extent is it still possible to understand Anglican and Roman Catholic approaches to moral issues as the result of different emphases around "sharing the same fundamental moral values"? Or has the convergence reached by ARCIC II "died the death of a thousand qualifications," so that it is more realistic to speak of diversity?

Postscript: What *Life in Christ* Could Not Say

A number of responses to *Life in Christ* bewail its lack of attention to the many areas of moral teaching which are shared by Anglicans and Roman Catholics, especially on social questions. Thus the Briefing Paper for the

13. Lambeth Conference 1930, *Encyclical Letter*, 89–90.

July 2009 Church of England General Synod discussion of *Life in Christ* criticised it for this omission, noting that "ethical challenges already emerging when ARCIC did its work" are "now pressing . . . medical, biological, environmental and economic ethics and the ideology of human rights." *Life in Christ* alludes to issues such as these but does not discuss them (§94–95).

In this respect it is important to recognise that the mandate given to ARCIC II restricted it to addressing matters which divide the Anglican Communion and Roman Catholic Church: in the area of morals, these focus around human sexuality. The result was that wide areas of agreement on social ethics could only be given minimal attention. There is thus considerable room for the convergence reached by ARCIC II to be sustained and built upon—a key part of the mandate give to ARCIC III:

> To consider fundamental questions regarding the "Church as Communion—Local and Universal," and "How in communion the Local and Universal Church comes to discern right ethical teaching."

Why does pursuing the task of exploring the intersection of ecclesiology and morals matter? Because, as *Life in Christ* itself stated, "The crisis of the modern world is more than a crisis of sexual ethics. At stake is our humanity itself" (§11).

Bibliography

Anglican Communion Office. *Anglican Covenant.* www.anglicancommunion.org/commission/covenant/final/text.cfm.

ARCIC II. *Salvation and the Church.* London: CTS/SPCK, 1987.

ARC-USA. "Christian Ethics in the Ecumenical Dialogue: Anglican-Roman Catholic International Commission II and Recent Papal Teachings." www.usccb.org/seia/arc_ethics_1995.shtml.

Canadian Conference of Catholic Bishops. *Pastoral Guidelines for Interchurch Marriages Between Anglicans and Roman Catholics in Canada/Directives Pastorales pour Les Marriages Inter-Églises entre Anglicans et Catholiques au Canada.* Publications Service, 1987.

Clague, Julie, "On Agreeing to Differ: Some Reflections on the ARCIC Statement on Morals in Light of *Veritatis Splendor*." *Irish Theological Quarterly* 62/1 (1996) 70–74.

Hill, Christopher, and Edward Yarnold, eds. *Anglicans and Roman Catholics: The Search for Unity.* London: CTS/SPCK, 1994.

IARCCUM. *Ecclesiological Reflections on the Current Situation in the Anglican Communion in the Light of ARCIC.* 2004. http://iarccum.org/doc/?d=30.

Lambeth Conference 1930. *Encyclical Letter from the Bishop with the Resolutions and Reports.* New York: SPCK/Macmillan, 1930.

Lutheran World Federation and Roman Catholic Church. *Joint Declaration on the Doctrine of Justification*. 2001. www.vatican.va/roman_curia/pontifical_councils/chrstuni/documents/rc_pc_chrstuni_doc_31101999_cath-luth-joint-declaration_en.html.

Nilson, Jon. "Must Disagreements Divide? The Achievements and Challenges of ARCIC II's *Life in Christ*." *One in Christ* 3 (1995) 222–36.

Sherlock, Charles, "Anglican–Roman Catholic Dialogue on Ethics and Moral Theology— An Anglican Perspective." *One in Christ* 46/1 (2012) 89–107.

— 9 —

The Process of Formulating Official Catholic Teachings

Consulting the Laity and *Sensus Fidelium*

Vimal Tirimanna, C.Ss.R.

Introduction

At the time of composing this article (beginning of June 2015), Ireland that has traditionally been known as a Catholic country has just voted in a national referendum to recognize homosexual unions as "marriages." What was shocking was the overwhelming approval vote (62% approving such marriages) of the Irish, and that, in spite of the Catholic hierarchy actively campaigning hard to ask the voters to reject any civil move to recognize such unions as "marriages." As is well-known, traditionally, the Catholic Church upholds only heterosexual marriages, even though today she tolerates any civil union of homosexuals. Apparently, there is a vast gap between what the Church cherishes so dearly and teaches so resolutely and what the ordinary lay Catholics hold to be true, as is evident from the words of Archbishop Diarmuid Martin of Dublin in the aftermath of the referendum:

> It is very clear that, if this referendum is an affirmation of the views of young people, the Church has a huge task in front of it to find a language to be able to talk to, and get its message over to, young people not just on this issue but in general... The Church needs to do a reality check right across the board, to look at the things it is

> doing well, to look at the areas where we really have to say, "Have we drifted away completely from young people?" We need to have robust discussions and challenge one another and we are not doing that—we are becoming a Church of the like-minded and a safe space for the like-minded, rather than the Church which Pope Francis is talking about. That does not mean we renounce our teaching on fundamental values on marriage and family, nor does it mean that we dig into the trenches. We need to find as in so many areas a new language which is fundamentally ours, that speaks to, is understood and is appreciated by, others.[1]

This is not the first time in recent years that the hierarchy of the Church has openly admitted the existence of a gap between what the Church teaches officially and what the people believe and practice in reality. Even the *lineamenta* for the October 2014 Extraordinary Synod on Family (which itself was supposed to be the result of a wide ranging consultation all over the Roman Catholic Church) clearly acknowledged this ever growing gap. The purpose of this article is to draw the attention of the reader to the indispensable need to consult the laity with regard to important ecclesial issues, in general, and with regard to the process of formulating official Church teaching, in particular. Or else, the contention of this article is, the already existing gap between what the Church teaches and what her members really believe and live will further increase. In other words, gone are the days when the hierarchy could authoritatively wind up any discussion by simply saying: *Roma locuta est, causa finita est*!

The popular Catholic saying in the pre-Vatican-II era with regard to the main duties of the laity in the Catholic Church was: "to pray and pay"! In order to confirm the veracity of such a saying, it suffices for us to read what Pope Pius X wrote in an Encyclical in 1906:

> It follows that the Church is essentially an *unequal* society, that is, a society comprising two categories of persons, the Pastors and the flock, those who occupy a rank in the different degrees of the hierarchy and the multitude of the faithful. So distinct are these categories that with the pastoral body only rests the necessary right and authority for promoting the ends of the society and directing all its members towards that end; the one duty of the

---

1. Archbishop Diarmuid Martin of Dublin as cited by the Catholic News Update Asia, June 2, 2015.

multitude is to allow themselves to be led, and, like a docile flock, to follow the Pastors.²

In his Apostolic Exhortation, *Christifideles Laici* (1988), Pope John Paul II himself while recalling how the Council Fathers called for a definition of "the lay faithful's vocation and mission in *positive terms*," reaffirms such earlier *negative* sentiments within the Church with regard to the laity when he says: "In giving a response to the question 'Who are the lay faithful,' the Council went beyond previous interpretations which were predominantly negative."³

In fact, the official Church since Vatican-II[4] has radically changed her understanding of the role of the laity from that which prevailed in the pre-V-II era. The acknowledgment of the fact that the Church consists of the People of God (all the baptized),[5] the universal call to holiness of all the baptized,[6] the competence of the laity especially in secular matters,[7] the participation of the laity in the mission of the Church etc.,[8] are some of the salient features of this changed vision.

This article examines the challenge that the theological concept *sensus fidelium* (which was resurrected by V-II) poses with regard to consulting and listening to the lay faithful as an indispensable part of exercising the teaching office of the Church. We assume that more than any other concept this particular concept forms a firm theological basis as to why the laity need to be consulted and listened to within the Church, especially, in the process of the formulation of official Church teachings.[9] We will first briefly describe how *sensus fidelium* is understood in the Catholic tradition. Then, we will make a quick examination of how the conciliar and post-conciliar magisterial teachings treated the traditional Catholic concept of *sensus fidelium*. Finally, we will draw the attention of the reader to the ever-increasing

---

2. Pius X, "Vehementer," no: 8.
3. John Paul II, *Christifideles Laici*, no: 9.
4. Henceforth Vatican II will be denoted by V-II.
5. Cfr., *Lumen Gentium*, nos: 9, 11, in Flannery, *Vatican Council II*, 350–440. Hereafter, this document will be referred to as LG.
6. Cfr., LG, nos: 39–42.
7. Cfr., *Gaudium et spes*, no: 43. in Flannery, *Vatican Council II*, 903–1014. Hereafter, this document will be referred to as GS.
8. Cfr., LG, no: 31; *Apostolicam Actuositatem*, nos: 2, 7, in Flannery, *Vatican Council II*, 766–98.
9. Cfr., Rush, "Ecclesial Conversion," 799–802.

and glaring gap between what the Church officially continues to teach and what the majority of laity really believe and practice in the contemporary ecclesial reality, making a suggestion to take the Christian sense of the faithful (*sensus fidelium*) seriously so that such an unnecessary gap may be closed.

1. The Resurrection of the Concept Sensus Fidelium at Vatican II

1.1 What is *Sensus Fidelium*?

One of the most important theological teachings of V-II is its official recognition of what has traditionally been known as *sensus fidei*. As Sullivan points out, *sensus fidei* or "the sense of faith" is "a supernatural gift, an aspect of the gift of faith itself, a kind of God-given instinct by which believers are able to recognize the word of God for what it is, to discern truth from error in matters of faith, and to have sound insights into what they believe."[10] He further discusses the two corollaries of the same concept: *sensus fidelium* and *consensus fidelium*:

> The term *sensus fidelium* (sense or mind of the faithful) on the other hand generally has an objective meaning, referring not to the believer but to what is believed. Thus, if one asks: "What is the sense of the faithful on this matter?" one wants to know what people believe; what is the "mind of the faithful" on an issue. The term *sensus Ecclesiae* (mind of the Church) is often used with much the same meaning...
>
> The term *consensus fidelium* (agreement of the faithful) adds the element of universal agreement to the notion of *sensus fidelium*. It refers to the situation in which, on a particular issue of faith, the whole body of the faithful, "from the bishops down to the last member of the laity," share the same belief. As we have seen, it is in such a *consensus* that the Second Vatican Council says that the whole People of God cannot be in error.[11]

Having situated the intrinsic link among the above-mentioned three concepts (*sensus fidei, sensus fidelium* and *consensus fidelium*), we will now focus ourselves exclusively on *sensus fidelium* for the purposes of this essay.

---

10. Sullivan, *Magisterium*, 23.
11. Ibid., 23.

(The reader needs to note that at times this is also referred to as *sensus fidei fidelium* by some authors.¹²) Faith, as we know, is a gift of the Holy Spirit, and this faith is sustained and expressed through the *sensus fidelium*, by the same Spirit:

> The result of this gift of faith, through the Spirit in the church today, is the *sensus fidelium*, which is that pneumatic gift that enables the whole church to receive and transmit the deposit of faith—divine revelation—effectively and faithfully to new cultures and contexts.
>
> The *sensus fidelium* is given to all the faithful. That is why it is sometimes referred to as the ecclesial collective faith awareness, a "connatural, prethematic *sens*-itivity to what being Christian truly means." This collective "faith awareness" or, as Herbert Vorgrimler calls it, "faith consciousness," possessed by all the faithful enables them to understand the truth of faith under the influence of the Holy Spirit (*LG* no.12).¹³

The historical roots of the concept *sensus fidelium* in practice go back to the Apostolic Church.¹⁴ In the New Testament, we read how in the early Church communities all the believers together as a community played an active role in determining authentic Christian belief and practice. Chapters 1, 6 and 15 of the Acts of the Apostles render three classic examples of how the whole community of believers came together in agreeing as to what consisted of authentic Christian belief and practice. Thus, when Peter calls the community in Jerusalem to choose a replacement for the betrayer Judas, it is the whole community that suggested two names (1:15–26). Later, when there arose the question of the neglect of widows, "the Twelve summoned the body of disciples" (6:2), and "the whole multitude" chose the first seven deacons (6:5). When the crucial question of the continuation of the Jewish practice of circumcision even in the new gentile Christian communities arose, the Jerusalem community (together with Paul and Barnabas who had visited them to consult on this controversial issue) decides

---

12. See for example, the recent document of The International Theological Commission, on "*Sensus Fidei* in the Life of the Church," no: 3. Henceforth, this document will be referred to as ITC. See also, Rush, *The Eyes of Faith*, 215–19.

13. Ekpo, "The *Sensus Fidelium*," 338–39. For another more nuanced way of understanding what is conveyed through these crucially important theological concepts, see Rush, *The Eyes of Faith*, 215–19.

14. For a detailed discussion of the Biblical base (both OT and NT), see ITC, nos: 8–21.

to choose men from among them to be sent to Antioch and other gentile areas to convey the decision of the Twelve and the Elders in Jerusalem in this regard. What is important to note here is the phrase: "Then it seemed good to the apostles and the elders, with the whole church, to choose men from among them, and send them to Antioch with Paul and Barnabas" (15:22). Thus, there obviously was an inclusiveness of all the baptized in the decision-making, with regard to their Christian life. The underlying theological presumption for such an inclusiveness was their firm belief in the presence of the Holy Spirit in all the believers as a whole, as promised by Jesus. It was basing on this solid theological presumption that Congar could write:

> Tradition is what the ecclesiastical community believes, under its pastors, and is guaranteed by the Holy Spirit, who resides and operates in it. "And we are witnesses to these things, and so is the Holy Spirit whom God has given to those who obey him" (Acts 5:32; cf. John 15:26–27). However, if this rule exists in written documents—Creed, canons of Councils, writings of the Fathers, the liturgy—it is alive in the Church, inseparable from the *ecclesia*, its living subject. From this point of view, the objective meaning of the expressions *sensus fidei, sensus catholicus, sensus Ecclesiae* already signifies for the Fathers an interior disposition experienced within the fellowship of the Church—a sort of instinct or inner feeling.[15]

The crucial role the laity played in the Early Church is evident from the historical fact that during the Arian heresy when almost all the bishops at the time were trapped within the Aryan heresy and the controversies surrounding Arianism, it was the lay people who held on to the true orthodox Catholic faith, and eventually passed it on to future generations. This is rightly attributed to the *sensus fidelium*, and is well-documented by no lesser person than Blessed Cardinal Newman himself.[16] It is very important to note, however, that the simplistic equating of the profound theological concept of *sensus fidelium* to the exclusive sense of the faith of the laity is a serious mistake. By definition, as we have already seen, it refers to the sense of the faith of the community as a whole, laity included. We need also to mention here that lay participation in the official teaching process had been a cherished Catholic concept both in the East and the West from the time

---

15. Congar, *The Meaning of Tradition*, 79.
16. Cfr., Newman, *On Consulting the Faithful in Matters of Doctrine*, 75–101.

of the Early Church. That is why early Synods and Councils had not only bishops but also lay participants, often as voting members.

With regard to the presence of this concept in the Catholic tradition, the International Theological Commission in their recent study on *sensus fidei* has this to say:

> The concept of the *sensus fidelium* began to be elaborated and used in a more systematic way at the time of the Reformation, though the decisive role of the *consensus fidelium* in the discernment and development of doctrine concerning faith and morals was already recognized in the patristic and medieval periods. What was still needed, however, was more attention to the specific role of the laity in this regard. That issue received attention particularly from the nineteenth century onwards.[17]

However, by the nineteenth century the term "magisterium" or "the teaching office" of the Church gradually tends to be reserved exclusively to the hierarchy in the Western/Latin Church, implying thus, an exclusively teaching Church (*ecclesia docens*) and an exclusively learning Church (*ecclesia discerns*). Put simply, the hierarchy teaches actively and the laity learns passively! Dulles draws our attention to the historical roots of this unfortunate development when he writes:

> Beginning with Thomas Stapleton (d. 1598), many theologians divide the Church into components—the "teaching Church" which is hierarchical and the "learning Church" which is predominantly lay. The hierarchy is credited with active infallibility; the infallibility of the "learning Church" is regarded as merely passive. The duty of the faithful, therefore, is simply to accept what the hierarchy tells them. The "sensus fidelium" in this theory ceases to function as a distinct theological source.[18]

1.2 Vatican II and *Sensus Fidelium*

By the time of V-II, the existing official position was the same, namely, the hierarchy teaches actively (*ecclesia docens*) while the vast majority of the laity simply follow such teachings passively (*ecclesia discens*). There was no question of the laity having any role whatsoever in the official teaching

---

17. ITC, no: 22.
18. Dulles, *A Church to Believe In*, 112.

process of the Church. V-II corrected this erroneous development in the tradition, and recovered the practice of taking the lay voice seriously in the ecclesial decision-making, especially in its teaching process, when it resurrected the concept of *sensus fidelium*:

> The holy People of God shares also in Christ's prophetic office; it spreads abroad a living witness to him, especially by a life of faith and love and by offering to God a sacrifice of praise, the fruit of lips praising his name (cf. Heb.13:15). The whole body of the faithful who have an anointing that comes from the holy one (cf. 1 John 2:20 and 27) cannot err in matters of belief. This characteristic is shown in the supernatural appreciation of the faith (*sensus fidei*)[19] of the whole people, when, "from the bishops to the last of the faithful" they manifest a universal consent in matters of faith and morals. By this appreciation of the faith, aroused and sustained by the Spirit of truth, the People of God, guided by the sacred teaching authority (*magisterium*), and obeying it, receives not the mere word of human beings, but truly the word of God (cf. 1 Thess 2:13), the faith once for all delivered to the saints (cf. Jude 3). The People unfailingly adheres to this faith, penetrates it more deeply with right judgment, and applies it more fully in daily life.[20]

Basing itself on firm traditional Catholic roots, V-II made a further decisive break with the popular pre-V-II view that the hierarchical magisterium is the exclusive bearer of the Tradition when it taught:

> The Tradition that comes from the apostles makes progress in the Church, with the help of the Holy Spirit. There is a growth in insight into the realities and words that are being passed on. This comes about in various ways. It comes through the contemplation and study of believers who ponder these things in their hearts (cf. Luke 2:19 and 51). It comes from the intimate sense of spiritual realities which they experience. And it comes from the preaching of those who have received, along with their right of succession in the episcopate, the sure charism of truth.[21]

Gaillardetz and Clifford comment on this passage as follows:

19. With reference to this term, the English translation of Austin Flannery in a footnote says: "The *sensus fidei* refers to the instinctive sensitivity and discrimination which the members of the Church possess in matters of faith" (Flannery, *Vatican Council II*, 363). Kindly note that in this article, all references to V-II documents are taken from this work of Flannery.

20. LG, no: 12.

21. *Dei Verbum*, no: 8, in Flannery, *Vatican Council II*, 750–65.

> The text does mention the necessary role of the bishops but not before it first cites the contributions of believers who, through contemplation, study, and intimate experience, allow church tradition to progress. What is striking is the vision of the bishops and the lay faithful cooperating in this "traditioning" process. This shared responsibility presupposes that all Christians have a spiritual gift for discerning God's word that enables them to contribute to the "progress" of tradition.[22]

Interestingly, when the Council spoke about marriage and family (realities in which and on which the laity ought to have a major say), there was special reference made to this instinct or sense of the Christian faith of the laity:

> Christians, making full use of the times in which we live and carefully distinguishing the everlasting from the changeable, should actively strive to promote the values of marriage and the family; it can be done by the witness of their own lives and by concerted action along with all men of good will; in this way they will overcome obstacles and make provision for the requirements and the advantages of family life arising at the present day. To this end the Christian instinct of the faithful, the right moral conscience of man, and the wisdom and skill of persons versed in the sacred sciences will have much to contribute.[23]

In fact, the second part of GS was entitled "Some More Urgent Problems," and "The Dignity of Family and Marriage" was the first such "urgent problem" treated in that section (already in mid-1960s). How "the Christian sense of the faithful" could contribute to solving such an "urgent problem" is further highlighted by Mahoney when he comments on GS 52:

> As the Council explained, the Spirit of truth arouses and sustains in all the faithful who have received his anointing a supernatural "sense of faith," which is not exercised only in matters of dogma and doctrine but also in morals, enabling the People of God as a whole to penetrate the faith more deeply by accurate judgment and apply it more thoroughly to life. That this is not simply conscience as traditionally understood seems clear from the Council's later teaching, in concluding its treatment of marriage and the family in contemporary society, that a valuable contribution to the solving of modern difficulties in this area can be made by "the

---

22. Gaillardetz and Clifford, *Keys to the Council*, 42.
23. GS, no: 52.

Christian sense of the faithful and the upright moral conscience of men." It appears, then, that at least the Christian has more within him in the way of moral resources than just the conscientious use of reason.[24]

As the International Theological Commission correctly points out, when V-II strongly emphasized the importance of the sense or the instinct of the faithful in the life of the Church, it banished "the caricature of an active hierarchy and a passive laity, and in particular the notion of a strict separation between the teaching Church (*Ecclesia docens*) and the learning Church (*Ecclesia discerns*)."[25]

1.3 *Sensus Fidelium* in the Post-Vatican II Era

In spite of such eloquent teachings on the concept of *sensus fidelium* by an Ecumenical Council (i.e., the Pope together with the bishops—the highest authority of teaching in the Catholic Church), the post-V-II era has not witnessed much progress with regard to this concept. Of course, as fresh as he was with the spirit of the Council, Paul VI makes a passing reference to this when he writes in his post-Synodal Apostolic Exhortation, *Evangelii Nuntiandi* (1975):

> The Bishops' Synod of 1974, which insisted strongly on the place of the Holy Spirit in evangelization, also expressed the desire that pastors and theologians—and we would also say the faithful marked by the seal of the Spirit by Baptism—should study more thoroughly the nature and manner of the Holy Spirit's action in evangelization today (no: 75).

Pope John Paul II's Apostolic Exhortation at the end of the special Synod on the Laity, *Christifedelis Laici* (1988) clearly highlights the importance of lay participation as taught by V-II, but it does not speak about the same participation through the concept of *sensus fidelium*, except for a passing vague reference to it in no: 14.

During the post-V-II era, though there surely was more lay participation in the consultative bodies of the Church in contrast to the pre-V-II times, very rarely does one see the opinions of the laity taken seriously. The need for wider consultation within the Church especially in the writing of

---

24. Mahoney, *The Making of Moral Theology*, 207.
25. ITC, no: 4.

the controversial encyclical *Humanae Vitae* (1968) of Paul VI is often cited as a classic example of this:

> The painful experience of the reactions to *Humanae Vitae* in the Church as a whole points, rather, to the need for more thorough consideration and broadening of the sources of consultation and co-responsibility in the Church. In the body of episcopal teaching, comprising the encyclical and the resulting episcopal pronouncements which the Pope had invited in its support, it is possible to see a further expression of the Matthaean theology of authoritative teaching which we have already considered, with little reference to the positive functioning of what Vatican II also referred to as "the Christian sense of the faithful" having a contribution to make to the solution of difficulties of family life. It is true, of course, the Pope referred to the influence of the Holy Spirit in the minds and hearts of the faithful, but the role of the Spirit is seen by him as simply confirming what was being proposed by the papal *magisterium* rather than as making any more positive contribution to the contents of that proposal.[26]

Similarly, though there was lay participation in the Synods of Bishops of the post-V-II era, one wonders how much of their contributions ever entered into the official teachings pronounced in the form of post-Synodal Apostolic Exhortations of the Pope. A careful glance at the propositions voted by each Synod and the contents of the respective final papal Apostolic Exhortations show a clear gap between the two.

Often, the argument put forward in defence of not taking the voice of the laity seriously in the post-V-II era is simply to say that the Church is not "a democracy" or that the majority opinion of the laity is not what *sensus fidelium* really means. While both these assertions are certainly true, one also needs to take into account that the Church is not "an autocracy" either! According to V-II and the post V-II magisterial teachings, "communion" is the key-word in ecclesiology and participation of the laity in ecclesial life is a must, but such participation surely need not be in the exact fashion of a modern democracy. Similarly, while the majority opinions (even within the Church) need not always reflect what is true, active, sincere listening to such opinions may not be harmful at all whenever the Church is in the process of searching for the authentic contents that are in harmony with what the Spirit of Jesus wishes to teach the believers. The point at stake is neither democracy nor the majority opinion within the Church as such,

---

26. Mahoney, *The Making of Moral Theology*, 278.

but rather, providing adequate space for the active participation of the laity through the concrete forms of consulting the laity and the sincere listening to what the laity has got to say. These are morally obligatory if one takes the concept of *sensus fidelium* seriously, especially with regard to the process of official teaching in the Church. Put simply, while it is true that a simplistic equation of laity or public opinion to the rich theological concept of *sensus fidelium* is seriously erroneous, one has to acknowledge that both the laity and the public opinion may at least at times contain some elements of the *sensus fidelium*.

It is in this sense that one has begun to see a sudden glimmer of hope in the distant horizon during the past couple of years, with regard to the active participation of all the baptized, even with regard to the processes of formulating official Church teachings. Ever since his election, Pope Francis has clearly expressed his willingness to follow the conciliar teaching on taking *sensus fidelium* seriously. In his now well-known interview with Antonio Spadaro, the Pope said:

> The image of the church I like is that of the holy, faithful people of God. This is the definition I often use, and then there is that image from the Second Vatican Council's Dogmatic Constitution on the Church (no: 12). Belonging to a people has a strong theological value. In the history of salvation, God has saved a people. There is no full identity without belonging to a people. No one is saved alone, as an isolated individual, but God attracts us looking at the complex web of relationships that take place in the human community. God enters into this dynamic, this participation in the web of human relationships.
>
> The people itself constitutes a subject. And the church is the people of God on the journey through history, with joys and sorrows. Thinking with the church, therefore, is my way of being a part of this people. And all the faithful, considered as a whole, are infallible in matters of belief, and the people display this *infallibilitas in credendo*, this infallibility in believing, through a supernatural sense of the faith of all the people walking together. This is what I understand today as the "thinking with the church" of which St.Ignatius speaks. When the dialogue among the people and the bishops and the pope goes down this road and is genuine, then it is assisted by the Holy Spirit. So this thinking with the church does not concern theologians only.[27]

---

27. Francis and Spadaro, "Pope Francis' Interview," 298–99.

In his celebrated Apostolic Exhortation, *Evangelii Gaudium* (2013), the Pope while insisting that "the entire People of God proclaims the gospel,"[28] reaffirms his thoughts on the instinct of the whole People of God for the authentic tenets of Christian faith when he writes:

> In all the baptized, from first to last, the sanctifying power of the Spirit is at work, impelling us to evangelization. The people of God is holy thanks to this anointing, which makes it infallible *in credendo*. This means that it does not err in faith, even though it may not find words to explain that faith. The Spirit guides it in truth and leads it to salvation. As part of his mysterious love for humanity, God furnishes the totality of the faithful with an instinct of faith—*sensus fidei*—which helps them to discern what is truly of God. The presence of the Spirit gives Christians a certain connaturality with divine realities, and a wisdom which enables them to grasp those realities intuitively, even when they lack the wherewithal to give them precise expression.[29]

That the Pope does not limit these thoughts to mere words is evident from the fact of his launching of a "new"[30] more participatory process for the two Synods on Family. What is unique in this current Synodal process is its ability to attract the participation of all the members of the Church in her reflections to discern what the Holy Spirit is saying with regard to family in the contemporary world. Following the spirit of the Second Vatican Council, in launching this unprecedented Synodal process, Pope Francis has made sure not only to promote the collegiality of the bishops, but also to get the pulse of the entire People of God, thus, to enhance the traditional theological concept of *sensus fidelium*. Given below are the main elements of what we are referring here to as "the Synodal process":

- The Questionnaire about the Family in the Contemporary World that was sent to all the Episcopal Conferences in October/November 2013 for a feedback from their respective local churches.

- The feedback thus received was collated, and that became the Working Paper (*Instrumentum Laboris*) for the Extraordinary Synod of October 2014.

---

28. Cfr., Francis, *Evangelii Gaudium*, nos: 111–34. Henceforth, this will be referred to as EG.

29. EG, no: 119.

30. In fact, this is a return to the earlier more participatory Synodal system of the Church in the by-gone centuries of the first millennium, and in that sense, it is not "new"!

- The celebration of the Extraordinary Synod in October 2014, under the theme "The Pastoral Challenges of the Family in the Context of Evangelization." At the end, the Synod Fathers voted on each and every item of the Official Final Report (*Relatio*).
- The sending of the Official Final Report (*Relatio*) of the Extraordinary Synod back to the local churches for their further reflection and comments. These reflections, comments and recommendations are due to be gathered and collated, and eventually, they will become the Working Paper (*Instrumentum Laboris*) for the forthcoming Ordinary Synod of bishops which is due in October 2015.
- The celebration of the Ordinary Synod in October 2015, under the theme "The Vocation and Mission of the Family in the Church and in the Contemporary World." Hopefully, at the end, the Synod will once again vote each and every one of its own comments and recommendations that would be handed over to the Pope, as usually is done at the end of a Synod.
- These Synodal comments and recommendations will obviously serve as a basis for the would-be-official teaching of the Church which the Pope hopefully will declare through an Apostolic Exhortation.

2. The Gap Between What Is Officially Taught and Practiced in the Contemporary Church Reality

In launching the current Synodal process, more than changing doctrine with regard to marriage and family, Pope Francis seems to be preoccupied with getting the whole Church involved together in discerning what the Spirit says with regard to marriage and family in the contemporary world. What he seems to be mainly aiming at is a change of the magisterial teaching process (the method of arriving at official Church teachings), keeping in line with V-II's resurrection of the concept of *sensus fidelium*. A quick glance at the current Synodal process and the Pope's explicit encouragement to the participant bishops at the last Extraordinary Synod (October 2014) to speak out sincerely and openly even when they had opinions contrary to the Bishop of Rome, are clear signs of this. Unfortunately, quite a number of local Episcopal Conferences did not consult the laity in composing their responses to the original questionnaire that was circulated in October-November 2013. Then, there have also been complaints that even in countries where such consultation took place, the results were not published. Even during this current period between the two Synods which the Pope hoped would be a period of serious reflection of the whole Church on matters to do with family, very few Episcopal Conferences are reported to have taken the initiative to consult the laity. If such reports are true, then, that is a bad omen for what Pope Francis is aiming at because it shows that quite a number of bishops all over the world are not in favour of such a serious and transparent consultation of the laity. Could this be also interpreted as the latter's ignorance of or lack of faith in *sensus fidelium*? No wonder that the well-known Italian theologian, Archbishop Bruno Forte who was also the Special Secretary of the recent Extraordinary Synod admitted during a press conference held in-between the Synod sessions that the bishops are still learning how to get the voices of all the baptized involved in discussions to do with Christian faith and practice.

At the beginning of this essay, we mentioned the shocking revelation in "Catholic" Ireland with regard to homosexuality, as expressed in the recent referendum there. Should the Church's teaching authority take this seriously or should it simply dismiss it saying "public opinion has nothing to do with the truths taught by the Church"? Fortunately, Archbishop Diarmuid Martin of Dublin has called for a re-thinking of the ways in and through which the Church communicates her beliefs. This is surely a welcome sign in the sense that he seems to take public opinion seriously. But can the same be said of the world-wide episcopate? The common response of the majority of the hierarchy to such situations is expressed by one writer as follows: "So far church officials seemed to presume that the problem is situated almost exclusively at the level of the faithful themselves who are unwilling or unable to follow the moral law in their individual lives and relationships."[31] In the contemporary world that is dominated by Individualistic trends such as relativism and hedonism (especially with regard to sexual behaviour), such a presumption is surely justified. But the point is that "the problem" cannot be limited to a framework of such trends:

> What is more striking and alarming is that people no longer regard their deviance as aberration from and infringement of the moral law. The problem is thus no longer the gap between value and action but much more fundamentally the divergence between what Catholics discern as being morally good or bad and what the church teaches to be the moral norm. Although this is not true for

31. Le Roi, "Lay Perspectives," 170.

> every issue—with regard to adultery, rape and incest for instance most Catholics would concur with the moral judgment of the church—it is for central issues such as contraception and marriage that have dominated the debates among Catholics over the past decades and it undoubtedly will be in the future with regard to same-sex unions. To put it bluntly: while in the past the problem has been one of practice lagging behind the theory, it is for some time now theory itself that is put into question.[32]

The ever-widening gap between what the Church teaches and what her members really believe and put into practice is also evident from other recent surveys conducted in some parts of the world with regard to what the Church teaches officially and what the faithful really believe and practice. For example, Linda Woodhead, professor of sociology of religion at Lancaster University in England published the results of one of her surveys recently. This particular survey which was conducted in Britain between January and June in 2013 had 1,672 Catholics involved in it. Given below are just a couple of extracts from her report:

> When it comes to sex, British Catholics take a very positive view. Almost three-quarters say it is important for a fulfilled life, compared to 68 percent of the general population. Only 7 percent of Catholics disagree. On the basis of this and wider observation, it seems that traditional teachings about the value of celibacy have largely been abandoned. Catholics also depart from church teaching when it comes to contraception: only 9 percent say they would feel guilty using it, and 12 percent of weekly churchgoers.
>
> Although pre-marital sex has ceased to be something about which most Catholics would feel guilty (only one in five would), two-thirds say they would feel guilty about extra-marital sex—compared, for example, with 88 percent of Baptists, who are more guilt-prone than other Christians on most of these issues.
>
> Catholics are positive about the institution of the family, yet their views of what constitutes a family are now very broad. Marriage has ceased to be an essential element of the family in most Catholic minds, with only a quarter disapproving of unmarried couples raising children. Almost 90 percent agree that an unmarried couple with children is a family, and that a single-parent household constitutes a family; over half think the same about childless unmarried couples. When it comes to gay and lesbian couples, two-thirds of Catholics believe that a same- sex couple

32. Ibid., 170.

with children constitute a family, and almost half say the same of a same-sex couple without children. Over a third of Catholics disapprove of same-sex couples raising children, a figure that is slightly higher than in the general public.[33]

What are we to make out of such surveys? Is the Church to merely float along with such public opinion? Definitely not! The Church has to continue to teach what she has received from her Lord and His Apostles. In doing so, if and when necessary, she may also have to swim against all popular contemporary currents, given her cherished prophetic role. There is no doubt about that. However, does the Church's teaching hierarchy not have a moral obligation to speak to her faithful in a language they could understand, within a reality in which they actually live? As Archbishop Martin says, it is precisely here that the Church has to find a new way, a new language, a new idiom . . . etc. to express and teach her cherished beliefs. This would undoubtedly demand a serious consulting of and a careful listening to the laity, and their lived life situations. Or else, the Church will be teaching in an empty room, so to say; she may be teaching to non-real persons who do not exist in our contemporary real world! Whenever there is a gap between the audience which the hierarchical magisterium presumes to teach and the real people of this world, an indifference to such teachings may inevitably follow. That is why a serious consultation of the lay faithful is necessary as Beattie so clearly states:

> While some teachings are rejected because of a lack of faith or distorting cultural influences, sometimes it is because the Magisterium has failed to consult the faithful and to take into account their experiences before making decisions. Ultimately, doctrinal authority rests with the Magisterium, but those in authority must engage in consultation and dialogue with the people of God.[34]

Of course, as we ourselves have already insisted above, the *sensus fidelium* cannot be reduced merely to opinion polls, but this fact could not be used as an excuse to ignore public opinion completely, or still worse, not to consult the laity, in the Church's process of discerning and formulating her revealed truth to teach the contemporary believers. Of course, in any teaching process, the hierarchical magisterium ought to have the last word, but the same magisterium cannot be dispensed from its moral obligation to

---

33. Woodhead, "What We Really Think," 12.
34. Beattie, "Let the Laity," 9.

consult the whole Church, including the laity. It is in this sense that the current Synodal process as stipulated by Rome under the leadership of Pope Francis has enormous merits though (as already mentioned above) quite a number of local hierarchies did not follow that process.

Moreover, some of the recent unilateral decisions made by the Roman hierarchical magisterium have also come under serious questioning with regard to dialogue even between Rome and the local Episcopal Conferences, leave alone dialogue between the teaching authority and the laity. One of the glaring recent examples in this regard is the way the new English translation of the Roman Missal was imposed on the local churches in 2011, after having rejected the English translation that was approved by the English-speaking Episcopal Conferences worldwide.[35] Since the Eucharist is "the source and summit of Christian living" (LG, no: 11), and since laity too are expected to participate in it actively and consciously,[36] the inevitable question that needs to be asked is: did the laity have any say in this translation which is hardly intelligible to a contemporary decent English speaker? The uninterrupted series of articles and letters from the laity, published in various Catholic newspapers and journals are very negative about the unilateral process followed in bringing out this English translation.

Moreover, though the composition of lay participation at the recent Extraordinary Synod in Rome (October 2014) was relatively higher than the previous occasions, one wonders whether it ought not be even higher simply because the synodal theme was to do with family, something on which the laity ought to have a major say as they live it daily and have direct experience of it. As Rush points out, "*sensus fidelium* [the sense of the faith] ... exercises a truth-finding and truth-attesting function that has as its special character that it takes into account the faithful's experience of the world."[37] Selling, too, draws our attention to the indispensable role that experience plays in our moral behavior:

> Human experience also plays a role in directing moral behavior because it is necessary to take into account the precise life-situation of the acting person before most decisions could be made. For instance, carrying out certain tasks, such as teaching, offering psychological advice, or practicing medicine presumes, nay demands,

---

35. For a succinct account of this, Cfr., O'Collins, "Open Letter," 19. See also Ryan, "Mission Intelligible," 11–12.

36. *Sacrosanctum Concilium*, no: 48, in Flannery, *Vatican Council II*, 1–36.

37. Rush, *The Eyes of Faith*, 2.

that the person has developed competence in these specific fields. If one attempted to do these things without being competent they would be acting in a way that was wrong and unethical.[38]

Last but not least, in our contemporary world, there is another important reason why the "lay perspectives" need to be taken seriously in the teaching process of the Church. Today, there are lay people who may have more professional competence (than the clerical hierarchy) on certain matters, and as such, they need to be consulted and their opinions be seriously considered in formulating official Church teachings. In fact, V-II had already warned the laity not to depend on the clerical hierarchy for every solution to their day to day problems which inversely is also a hint to the clerical hierarchy not to presume to have all the answers to all the problems:

> For guidance and spiritual strength, let them turn to the clergy; but let them realize that their pastors will not always be so expert as to have a ready answer to every problem (even every grave problem) that arises; this is not the role of the clergy: it is rather up to the laymen to shoulder their responsibilities under the guidance of Christian wisdom and with eager attention to the teaching authority of the Church.[39]

Conclusion

The Church predominantly comprises of the laity. Should they not be listened to, even in exercising the teaching role of the Church which is exclusively reserved in the Catholic tradition to the clerical hierarchy? Of course, *vox populi* is not *vox dei*,[40] but as baptized persons, the lay believers, too, ought to be heard because they too are not only the "temples of the Holy Spirit" but the same Spirit speaks through them, too. V-II resurrected concepts like *sensus fidei* and *sensus fidelium*, precisely to indicate that all the baptized are sealed by the anointing of the Holy Spirit who continues to be active in and through them. Nowhere in the New Testament did Jesus promise his Holy Spirit only to the clerical hierarchy of the Church. If the Church is really serious about hearing and discerning the voice of the Spirit,

---

38. Selling, "Is Lived Experience?," 219.

39. GS, no: 43.

40. The celebrated saying *vox populi, vox dei* literally amounts to saying "the voice of the people is the voice of God"!

then, the clerical hierarchy and the laity invariably have to be in constant, sincere, healthy dialogue. When such a dialogue is missing, we end up in extreme positions wherein the Holy Spirit is surely absent. Such extremes emerge when on the one hand, the laity completely ignore the voice of the magisterium, and on the other hand, when the magisterium completely ignore the voice of the laity. Since by definition the Church comprises both of hierarchy and laity, and since the Holy Spirit acts in and through the whole Church (the whole People of God), listening to each other and taking each other seriously are indispensable moral obligations both of the hierarchy and of the laity, if they are sincere about discerning the voice of the Spirit.

Bibliography

Beattie, Tina. "Let the Laity Be Heard." *The Tablet* 16, August 2014, 9–10.
Congar, Yves. *The Meaning of Tradition*. Translated by A. N.Woodrow. San Francisco: Ignatius, 2004.
Dulles, Avery. *A Church to Believe In: Discipleship and the Dynamics of Freedom*. New York: Crossroad, 1982.
Ekpo, Anthony. "The *Sensus Fidelium* and the Threefold Office of Christ: A Reinterpretation of *Lumen Gentium* No.12." *Theological Studies* 76/2 (June 2015) 338–46.
Flannery, Austin, ed. *Vatican Council II: The Conciliar and Post Conciliar Documents*. Dublin: Dominican, 1975.
Francis. *Evangelii Gaudium*. Vatican City: Libreria Editrice Vaticana, 2013.
Francis, and Antonio Spadaro. "Pope Francis' Interview with Jesuit Magazines." *Origins* 43/19 (October 10, 2013) 293–306.
Gaillardetz, Richard R., and Catherine E. Clifford. *Keys to the Council: Unlocking the Teaching of Vatican II*. Collegeville, MN: Liturgical, 2012.
International Theological Commission, "*Sensus Fidei* in the Life of the Church." 2014. http://www.vatican.va/roman_curia/congregations/cfaith/cti_documents/rc_cti_20140610_sensus-fidei_en.html.
John Paul II. *Christifideles Laici*. Vatican City: Libreria Vaticana, 1988.
Le Roi, Thomas Knieps-Port. "Lay Perspectives on Marriage and the Family: Introduction to the Colloquium." *INTAMS Review* 20/2 (2014) 169–174.
Mahoney, John. *The Making of Moral Theology: A Study of the Roman Catholic Tradition*. Oxford: Clarendon, 1987.
Newman, John Henry. *On Consulting the Faithful in Matters of Doctrine*. Edited by John Coulson. London: Geoffrey Chapman, 1961.
O'Collins, Gerald. "Open Letter to the English-speaking Bishops." *The Tablet*, March 7, 2015, 19.
Pius X. "Vehementer." In *Keys to the Council: Unlocking the Teaching of Vatican II*, edited by Richard R.Gaillardetz and Catherine E.Clifford, 98. Collegeville, MN: Liturgical, 2012.

Rush, Ormond. "Ecclesial Conversion After Vatican II: Renewing 'The Face of the Church' to Reflect 'The Genuine Face of God.'" *Theological Studies* 74/4 (December 2013) 785–803.

———. *The Eyes of Faith: The Sense of the Faithful and the Church's Reception of Revelation.* Washington, DC: Catholic University of America Press, 2009.

Ryan, Michael G. "Mission Intelligible." *The Tablet*, November 29, 2014, 11–12.

Selling, Joseph. "Is Lived Experience a Source of Morality?" *INTAMS Review* 20/2 (2014) 217–25.

Sullivan, Francis A. *Magisterium: The Teaching Authority in the Church.* New York: Paulist, 1983.

Woodhead, Linda. "What We Really Think." *The Tablet*, November 9, 2013, 12.

10

LAS "OBRAS DE MISERICORDIA" Y LA TEOLOGÍA MORAL

La "Corrección Fraterna"

Marciano Vidal, C.Ss.R.

En el pontificado del papa Francisco la *Misericordia* se ha convertido en una de las mayores sensibilidades teológicas, morales, pastorales y espirituales del momento eclesial presente. Sin ser contrapuesta a la *Verdad* (es decir, a la coherencia teológica de la tradición eclesial), la *Misericordia* orienta nuevas propuestas eclesiales no solo en el campo del compromiso social (sensibilidad hacia los "marginados" o "descartados" de la sociedad) sino también en el ámbito eclesial (por ejemplo, la participación en los sacramentos de las personas cristianas divorciadas vueltas a casar).

La intervención del cardenal Walter Kasper, a petición del papa, en el consistorio del 21–22 de febrero de 2014 constituyó una expresión cualificada del nuevo énfasis eclesial sobre el valor cristiano de la Misericordia.[1] Dentro de ese mismo contexto ha sido recuperada la significación teológica, espiritual y pastoral de una obra previamente publicada por dicho cardenal alemán W. Kasper, *La misericordia*.[2] La proclamación del Año de la misericordia (Jubileo Extraordinario de la Misericordia, 8/XII/2015–20/XI/2016) ha de ser interpretada dentro de esta revitalización de la orientación teológico-pastoral misericordiosa.

---

1. El texto de la conferencia, aumentado con una introducción y un apéndice, ha sido publicado con el título: Kasper, *El evangelio de la familia*.

2. Kasper, *La misericordia*.

En el momento eclesial actual parece oportuno remozar y poner a punto la doble tabla de las obras de misericordia corporales y espirituales.[3] Por lo demás, no faltan libros dedicados expresamente a exponer tanto la espiritualidad de las obras de misericordia[4] así como el contenido moral que el esquema puede seguir expresando.[5]

En las páginas que siguen me propongo contribuir a la renovación teológico-moral de las obras de misericordia ofreciendo un conjunto de perspectivas, tanto histórica como actuales, sobre el esquema en general y, de forma más concreta, sobre una de las obras espirituales: "corregir al que yerra."

Dedico este trabajo al colega y cohermano prof. Brian Johnstone, C.Ss.R., sabiendo que los dos compartimos la tradición moral alfonsiana de la "moral misericordiosa."

Advertencia sobre el uso lingüístico: Soy consciente de que en el presente escrito utilizo, con frecuencia, un lenguaje no inclusivo desde el punto de vista del género. Pido al lector o lectora que, ya desde ahora, introduzca en su mente una permanente clave de inclusión semántica: super*ior*/super*iora*, *al*/*a la* que yerra, etc.

I. LAS OBRAS DE MISERICORDIA
en la teología moral

1.1 Perspectivas histórica

Las obras de misericordia (en adelante: OdM) constituyen un esquema organizativo (y orientativo) de la vida moral del cristiano, mediante doble tabla (como acaece en el Decálogo): obras corporales y obras espirituales. Sus elementos, sobre todo los correspondientes a la tabla de las obras corporales, se hallan básicamente en el examen ético del llamado juicio final de Matt 25, 31–36, al que hay que añadir el texto de Tobit 1, 16–17; más difícil es individuar los textos escriturísticos correspondientes a las obras espirituales de misericordia. Por otra parte, también es difícil precisar con exactitud cuándo se juntaron los dos grupos de elementos y configuraron el esquema de lo que los catecismos consagrarán como OdM.

---

3. Ver las orientaciones específicas sobre las obras de misericordia consignadas en la citada obra de: Kasper, *La misericordia*, 140–143, 193–194.

4. Grün, *Entrañas de misericordia*.

5. Keenan, *The Works of Mercy*.

Ya en el s. IV, el brillante escritor cristiano Lactancio sumó al citado texto de Matt 25, 35-36 otras situaciones de necesidades humanas construyendo así un frontispicio paradigmático de la práctica misericordiosa cristiana.[6] San Agustín aludió a muchas obras de misericordia, aunque en sus escritos no se halla un cuadro organizado de ellas.[7]

Muy probablemente, en la Edad Media se llegó a configurar la unión de los dos conjuntos temáticos de las obras espirituales y de las obras materiales. De esos conjuntos, sobre todo de las obras de misericordia corporal, hay testimonios tanto en escritos como en expresiones artísticas medievales, sobre todo a partir del s. XIV.[8] En el s. XIII, Tomás de Aquino no conoce el esquema de las OdM en cuanto tal y con ese nombre pero sí habla de las catorce obras concretas, organizándolas, mediante los dos septenarios conocidos, en torno a la categoría de *limosna*: siete limosnas espirituales y siete limosnas corporales.[9]

Fue en los catecismos postridentinos del s. XVI, sobre todo en los compuestos por autores jesuitas, donde quedó asumido el doble esquema de las OdM como un cauce expresivo más de las obligaciones cristianas. Así lo hizo Pedro Canisio en sus tres catecismos (1555, 1556, 1558), vinculando las OdM a la práctica de la justicia cristiana. Esa orientación fue seguida y consagrada por los catecismos de Gaspar de Astete (1591) y de Jerónimo Martínez de Ripalda (1591, 1618). Es de notar que el Catecismo Romano (1567) no se sirvió del esquema de las OdM para exponer el contenido de la moral cristiana. Sin embargo, en el siglo XIX se escribieron extensos comentarios catequéticos sobre las OdM, como los de J. Deharbe (1847)[10] y los de F. Spirago-R. F. Clarke (1899).[11]

---

6. Lucius Caelius Firminianus Lactantius, *Divinae Institutiones*, caput XII, "De generibus beneficentiae et operibus misericordiae": PL, 6, 676-684: "Praecipua igitur virtus est *hospitalitas* (. . .). *Captivorum redemptio* magnum atque praeclarum munus est (. . .). Non minus magnum justitiae opus est *pupillos et viduas* destitutos et auxilio indigentes tueri atque defendere (. . .). *Aegros* quoque, quibus defuerit qui assistat, curandos fovendosque suscipere summa humanitatis et magnae operationis est (. . .). Ultimum illud et maximum pietatis officium est *peregrinorum et pauperum sepultura*: quod illi virtutis justitiaeque doctores prorsus non attingerunt (. . .)» (los subrayados son míos).

7. Fitzgerald, *Misericordia, obras de misericordia*.

8. Sirna y Bonifazi, *Misericordia. Le opere di misericordia nell'arte*.

9. Tomás de Aquino, *Suma teológica*, II-II, q. 32, a. 2.

10. Traducción castellana: J. Deharbe, *Gran Catecismo Católico*, 4 vols. con otro volumen como *Apéndice*. Madrid, 1898.

11. Traducción castellana (de la parte moral): F. Spirago [profesor en el Liceo Imperial de Praga], *Catecismo Popular Explanado, Tomo II. Doctrina Moral*, traducido

Por lo que respecta al uso de este esquema de la OdM en la historia de la Teología Moral podemos señalar los siguientes momentos.

- En la Edad Media la moral fue expuesta preferentemente mediante el esquema de las virtudes, tal como aparece paradigmáticamente en la *Suma Teológica* (I-II y II-II) de Tomás de Aquino. En tal esquema son destacadas tanto la virtud de la *misericordia*, expresión interna de la caridad (II-II, q. 30) y parte potencial de la virtud de la *justicia*, como la virtud de la *beneficencia* (II-II, q. 31), expresión externa del dinamismo caritativo. Una y otra -*misericordia* y *beneficencia*- suscitan dos obras básicas de la caridad: la *limosna* (II-II, q. 32) y la *corrección fraterna* (II-II, q. 33).

- En la época de la Moral Casuística (ss. XVI-XVIII), orientada básicamente hacia la práctica del sacramento de la Penitencia, predominó el esquema de los mandamientos.

En este momento histórico, hay escritos que dan una importancia especial a las OdM. Así lo hizo, por ejemplo, el *Enchiridion confessariorum* o *Manual de confesores y penitentes* de Martín de Azpilcueta y Jaureguízar (1492-1586), también conocido como el Doctor Navarro. Esta obra, la más representativa de moral práctica del s. XVI, fue un libro muchas veces editado: en menos de 70 años, tuvo 81 ediciones y 92 más a modo de revisiones, de versiones y de compendios. Pues bien, el *Enchiridion* organiza la exposición de la moral en nueve libros:

1. El alma humana.
2. La confesión.
3. Los diez mandamientos de Dios.
4. Los cinco mandamientos de la Iglesia.
5. Los siete sacramentos.
6. Los pecados capitales.
7. *Las obras de misericordia.*
8. Los diversos estados particulares.
9. Las censuras y las excomuniciones. Según queda enfatizado por el precedente subrayado en letra cursiva, en la organización de la moral

---

directamente de la sexta edición alemana por R. Ruiz Amado, de la Compañía de Jesús. Barcelona-México, 1907.

cristiana hecha por el Doctor Navarro ocupa un puesto destacado el esquema concreto de las OdM.

Pero, esto no va a permanecer en los siguientes escritos de Teología Moral casuista. Para comprobarlo basta acudir a la exposición de la moral que hacen las obras más representativas. Por ejemplo, en las *Institutiones Morales* (1600-1611) del jesuita Juan Azor y en la *Theologia Moralis* (1749-1773) de Alfonso de Liguori apenas si se hace presente el esquema de la OdM.

Lo mismo se advierte en los libros de moral llamados *Confesionarios*, compuestos para orientar la práctica del sacramento de la Penitencia, durante los ss. XVII-XVIII. Mientras que en los *Confesionarios* del s. XVI (hemos aludido, anteriormente, al de Martín de Azpilcueta) se hace el balance moral del penitente en referencia a los 10 preceptos del Decálogo, los cinco Mandamientos de la Iglesia, las obras de misericordia y los siete pecados capitales, en los siglos siguientes "este esquema se irá simplificando progresivamente, desapareciendo los pecados cometidos contra las obras de misericordia y los siete pecados capitales, e incluyéndose en muchas ocasiones los mandamientos de la Iglesia en el interrogatorio relativo al tercer mandamiento del Decálogo. Al mismo tiempo, los mandamientos 9º y 10º del Decálogo serán incluidos en el 6º y 7º respectivamente."[12]

Esta situación permanece en los Manuales empleados en la Iglesia para exponer y para estudiar la Teología Moral durante los ss. XIX y XX. Ni que decir tiene que en la Teología Moral renovada posterior al concilio Vaticano II es prácticamente ignorado el esquema de las OdM, evidentemente no el contenido que expresa.

1.2 Situación presente

Al pretender actualizar el tema de las OdM se impone una constatación previa de carácter general: el escaso interés que el tema ha suscitado en la reflexión teológica reciente.

Es cierto que el concilio Vaticano II insistió, en numerosos pasajes de sus documentos, sobre la necesidad y sobre la importancia del compromiso del cristiano en la sociedad (*obras* [sociales] *de caridad y de justicia*):

---

12. A. Morgado, *Pecado y confesión en la España Moderna. Los Manuales de confesores*: Trocadero nn. 8-9 (1996-1997) 122.

- Un documento entero -la constitución pastoral *Gaudium et spes*- está prácticamente dedicado al tema.

- La constitución dogmática sobre la Iglesia, *Lumen gentium*, señala el compromiso social como un camino de santidad cristiana ("santidad a través de las actividades"), sobre todo de la santidad laical, y anima a los laicos a imbuir de espíritu cristiano la cultura y los espacio sociales ("las estructuras y las condiciones del mundo") (n. 36).

- El decreto sobre el apostolado de los laicos, *Apostolicam actuositatem*, sitúa las *obras de caridad y de misericordia* (en las que se incluyen tanto las privadas como las organizadas, así las de carácter voluntario como las vinculadas a las instituciones públicas) en el corazón de la actividad misionera de la Iglesia: "la misericordia para con los necesitados y enfermos, así como las llamadas obras de caridad y de ayuda mutua, destinadas a aliviar las necesidades humanas, son consideradas por la Iglesia con singular honor" (n. 8, remitiendo en nota a la encíclica *Mater et Magistra* de Juan XXIII); "las obras de caridad y misericordia ofrecen un testimonio excelente de vida cristiana" (n. 31).

Sin embargo, quedó fuera del horizonte comprensivo y expresivo de la teología conciliar el esquema tradicional de las OdM. Más concretamente, no existe, salvo error, ninguna referencia conciliar explícita a la tercera OdM "corregir al que yerra."

El actual *Catecismo de la Iglesia Católica* (1992) dedica un número a las OdM (n. 2447), que considera como "acciones caritativas mediante las cuales ayudamos a nuestro prójimo en sus necesidades corporales y espirituales (cf Is 58, 6–7; He 13,3)." El *Catecismo* retiene un dato tradicional al enfatizar la importancia de la categoría de la *limosna*, "uno de los principales testimonios de caridad fraterna" y "una práctica de la justicia que agrada a Dios."

Pero, el *Catecismo* no otorga un relieve especial al tema de la OdM, si bien recoge el esquema entre las "Fórmulas de Doctrina católica" con que concluye el *Compendio*. Por otra parte, en el citado número 2447, no retiene la 3ª OdM, objeto de la presente reflexión. El verbo *corregir* (*al que yerra*) no aparece en la secuencia de los verbos que expresan las OdM espirituales: *instruir, aconsejar, consolar, confortar, perdonar, sufrir* con paciencia. Bien es cierto que, al final del *Compendio* del Catecismo, entre otras *Fórmulas de doctrina católica*, se recoge el esquema de las OdM y en él se señala como 3ª OdM espiritual el *Corregir al que yerra*.

2. Función heurística y expresiva para la moral cristiana

Como todo esquema utilizado en Teología Moral, el de las OdM ha servido para descubrir valores (*función heurística*) y para formularlos (*función expresiva*). Por lo que respecta a las obras de misericordia espirituales, dejando aparte lo que diremos en la segunda parte de este escrito, apenas tuvieron funcionalidad ni para descubrir ni para expresar valores especiales de la moral cristiana.

La afirmación precedente cambia de sentido si tomamos en consideración la tabla de las obras de misericordia corporales. Las obras 2ª (*dar de comer al hambriento*), 3ª (*dar de beber al sediento*), 5ª (*vestir al desnudo*) de esa tabla tienen que ver con el justo reparto de los bienes económicos. Sus significados fueron concentrados, desde Tomás de Aquino, en la exigencia moral de la *limosna*. Esta ha constituido, en la literatura moral tradicional, la cifra y el compendio de toda ayuda prestada al prójimo por la caridad, actuante esta, internamente, por medio de la *misericordia* o compasión y, externamente, a través de la *beneficencia*.

Pero esta concentración moral en la acción de la limosna no ha de hacernos olvidar la gran funcionalidad heurística y expresiva que tuvieron las obras de misericordia corporal para el desarrollo de la moral cristiana. Desde ellas y en torno a ellas se fueron creando y formulando sensibilidades morales tan importantes como las que están a la base de toda comprensión moral cristiana de la economía:

- El principio del *destino universal* de los bienes económicos: *todos* estos bienes están en función de *todas* las personas.
- El *derecho a la propiedad privada*, aunque es válido y necesario, no anula el valor del principio recién formulado sobre el destino común de los bienes económicos: la propiedad privada "no constituye para nadie un derecho incondicional y absoluto"[13]; sobre ella "grava una hipoteca social" (Juan Pablo II).[14]
- La *comunicación de bienes* es una afirmación moral que precede a la posesión exclusiva y al uso privado de los mismos. "El hombre no debe tener las cosas exteriores que legítimamente posee como

---

13 Pablo VI, *Populorum progressio*, n. 23.

14 Juan Pablo II, *Laborem exercens*, n. 14; *Sollicitudo rei socialis*, n. 42; *Centesimus annus*, n. 30. Ver, además: Celam, *Documento de Puebla* (1979), n. 492.

exclusivamente suyas, sino también como comunes, en el sentido de que no le aprovechen a él solamente, sino también a los demás."[15]

- De los principios precedentes se deducen las orientaciones éticas siguientes[16]:

    a. "quien se halla en situación de necesidad extrema tiene derecho a tomar de la riqueza ajena lo necesario para sí";

    b. "los hombres están obligados a ayudar a los pobres y por cierto no solo con los bienes superfluos";

    c. "el hombre no debe tener las cosas exteriores que legítimamente posee como exclusivamente suyas, sino también como comunes, en el sentido de que no le aprovechen a él solamente, sino también a los demás."

Para algunos autores, estas exigencias éticas del destino universal de los bienes es lo único que tiene de "cristiano" la propiedad privada.[17] En todo caso, son estas exigencias éticas las que están a la base de la doctrina cristiana de la *limosna* y las que confieren a esta la máxima importancia moral tal como consta en la historia del pensamiento social cristiano.

3. la 3ª obra espiritual de misericordia: "CORREGIR AL QUE YERRA"

3.1 Orientaciones de la Moral casuística

La tradición moral católica, sobre todo la que comenzó a configurarse en la Edad Media y que encontró su autonomía disciplinar teológica al comienzo del s. XVII, desarrolló notablemente—en espacio y en precisiones conceptuales—el contenido de la 3ª obra de misericordia espiritual: *corregir al que yerra*. Así como la limosna tendió a concentrar las OdM corporales, la corrección fraterna cobró el máximo relieve entre las OdM espirituales. De hecho, la corrección fraterna constituyó uno de los capítulos importantes de la moral casuística.

---

15. Concilio Vaticano II, *Gaudium et spes*, n. 69.
16. Ibidem.
17. F. Rodríguez, *La propiedad en la doctrina social de la Iglesia*: Varios, Curso de doctrina social católica. Madrid: Bac, 1967, 611.

En este momento nos interesa tomar nota de dos aspectos que aparecen en el desarrollo histórico del tema: en primer lugar, de las coordenadas teóricas en que fue planteado; en segundo lugar, de las orientaciones más sobresalientes en que fue concretado.

Para presentar estos dos aspectos me sirvo de las exposiciones hechas por una serie de autores que, situados a lo largo de la tradición teológico-mortal, representan secuencialmente el conjunto de ella: Tomás de Aquino[18], Alfonso de Liguori[19], Bernhard Häring (en la etapa anterior al concilio Vaticano II, 1954)[20] y Antonio Royo Marín.[21]

Por lo que respecta a las coordenadas en que fue planteado el tema de la 3ª obra de misericordia espiritual es fácil advertir lo siguiente:

- El horizonte acotado para descubrir y señalar el error (*al que yerra*) es netamente religioso. No se tiene en consideración el *error humano*, por ejemplo: la equivocación lingüística (en el hablar), el fallo de cálculo (en el actuar), la inexactitud en la ponderación de posibilidades (en el proyectar), etc.

- El error religioso que se considera es de carácter moral: es tenido como *pecado*. De ahí que a veces se cambia la formulación convencional de la 3ª OdM espiritual (corregir al *que yerra*) por esta otra: corregir *al pecador*.

- A fin de determinar con precisión la situación y de proponer la correcta orientación se tienen en cuenta dos grupos de variables:

    1. Si el responsable de la corrección es un igual o es un superior del que precisa de ella: en el primer caso será corrección meramente fraterna; en el segundo caso será corrección de un superior (en cuanto padre, pero no en cuanto juez).

    2. Si la corrección es solo corrección o si ha de suponer también la delación del fallo moral al superior. Aun en esta segunda variante, la corrección se mantiene en los límites propios y no entra en el

---

18. Tomás de Aquino, *Suma Teológica*, II-II, q. 33: "La corrección fraterna."

19. Alfonso de Liguori, *Theologia Moralis*, lib. II, tract. III, cap. I, dub. IV, nn. 34–42: "De Misericordia spirituali, seu praecepto Correptionis fraternae": Edición L. Gaudé, Romae, 1905, I, 331–335.

20. Häring, *La ley de Cristo*, II, 410–415.

21. Royo Marín, *Teología de la Caridad*, 452–460; Id., *Misericordia*; Id., *Teología moral para seglares*, 394–395.

horizonte de la justicia penal ya que la delación se hace al superior *ut patri*: en cuanto padre, y no *ut iudici*: en la condición de juez.

En cuanto al contenido de la exigencia moral de la corrección fraterna, la Teología Moral casuista parte de la regla de la comunidad del capítulo 18 del evangelio de Mateo (18, 15-17), asume las definiciones de la teología escolástica acerca de las virtudes y, a continuación, ofrece una valoración detallada de situaciones y de casos.[22] Recogemos únicamente tres grupos de aspectos.

La corrección fraterna es un acto de caridad que tiene como finalidad el remedio del mal moral -del *pecado*- del prójimo. Es un deber de todos, no solo de los superiores -prelados- respecto a sus súbditos. En los destinatarios de la corrección entran todos, sin excluir a los mismos superiores.

La corrección ha de ser hecha siempre y cuando sea previsible la enmienda del pecador y por medios adecuados que conduzcan a ella. De ahí que:

- sea necesaria la prudencia;
- haya que evitar el constituirse en inspectores de las vidas ajenas;
- tenga que salvaguardarse la fama del hermano a quien se corrige;
- lo cual exige que la amonestación sea secreta y que deba preceder a la denuncia pública cuando esta sea exigida por el bien común.

Las condiciones dichas se refieren a la corrección fraterna como acto de caridad. Otra cosa es la corrección cuando proviene de la obligación de justicia, situación que acaece cuando el fallo moral perjudica el bien común que ha de ser protegido mediante la virtud de la justicia.

4. Pistas de actualización: La "corrección fraterna" en el ámbito cristiano

La concreción más conocida de la 3ª OdM ha sido históricamente—y todavía sigue siendo, en bastantes ambientes—la llamada *corrección fraterna*, expresión proveniente de 2 Tes 3, 15: "corregidlo como hermano."[23] La cor-

22. Puede verse una casuística detallada (con las citas correspondientes de bastantes moralistas) en: Blanc, *Correction fraternelle*.

23. Para una breve síntesis: Juliá, *Corrección fraterna*; Gennaro, *Corrección fraterna*. Presentaciones más amplias: Noble, *Correction fraternelle*; Costello, *Moral Obligation of Fraternal Correction*; Palsterman, *La correction des autres*.

rección fraterna es un acto de *beneficencia* (dimensión externa) y de *compasión* (dimensión interna) nacido de la *misericordia* en cuanto virtud que concreta la *caridad* hacia el prójimo y que tiene por objeto sacar al hermano de una *situación fallida*. Los subrayados indican la riqueza de significados teológicos, morales y espirituales que conlleva la corrección fraterna.

La corrección fraterna también ha de ser considerada como un medio o instrumento de perfección espiritual del sujeto que corrige. En efecto, la corrección fraterna "es un medio de formación para quien la practica, ya que el corregir a los demás ayuda a arrancar de nosotros mismos los posibles hábitos que quizá descubrimos mejor y más claramente cuando los vemos en el prójimo."[24] Además, "así como nuestro amor propio y tan a menudo nuestros mismo carácter no nos permiten descubrir nuestros defectos, la corrección fraterna es un remedio a dicha deficiencia y por ello un instrumento de progresión y perfección espiritual."[25]

El pensamiento teológico siempre ha visto la razón y el modelo de la corrección fraterna en el texto de Matt 18, 15-17: "Si tu hermano peca contra ti, ve, amonéstalo a solas entre tú y él. Si te escucha, has ganado a tu hermano. Pero, si no te escucha, toma aún contigo a uno o dos para que por boca de dos o tres testigos sea establecido todo asunto."

En la tradición eclesial -con validez en la actualidad- el horizonte de la corrección fraterna no se limitó a la situación de "si tu hermano peca *contra ti*": se refirió a toda situación negativa o fallida. Por otra parte, además del citado texto principal de Matt 18, 15-17 hay que tener en cuenta otras referencias bíblicas tanto del Antiguo (Lev 19, 17; Eccl 19, 14-15; Prov 10, 12) como del Nuevo Testamento (Lc 17, 3b-4; Gál 6, 1; 1 Tes 5, 14; 2 Tes 3, 15; 1 Ped 4, 8; Sant 5, 19-20; 1 Tim 5, 1-2), las cuales enriquecen el mundo motivacional y orientan el modo de actuación de la tercera OdM.

Señalo a continuación las orientaciones que, encarnadas en la peculiaridad psicológica y sociológica de cada situación, pueden ayudar a la práctica de la corrección fraterna en el mundo de hoy.

- El *error* a corregir no ha de ser supuesto sino probado, según el axioma *nemo malus nisi probetur*. La auténtica corrección fraterna no nace de una interpretación maliciosa de la conducta del prójimo sino de una relación empática hacia él. "La clarividencia y el sentido común son tanto más necesarios en esta materia, cuanto más fácil es a nuestra

---

24. Juliá, *Corrección fraterna*, 533.
25. Gennaro, *Corrección fraterna*, 499-500.

naturaleza pensar más en el lado negativo que en el positivo de las personas."²⁶

- Quien se propone corregir al hermanos no ha de pensar tanto en los errores cuanto en el *acercamiento al hermano*. "En una comunidad -como, por ejemplo, en nuestra comunidad monástica- siempre existe el peligro de que se hable de los demás: '¿No has visto lo que ha hecho, cómo vive? ¿No has oído lo que ha dicho?'. Con tales habladurías sobre los demás los herimos. En cambio, se necesita valor para acercarse al otro y dirigirle la palabra. Pues sé de fijo que tampoco yo me encuentro de manera completamente correcta y que no todo es bueno en mí."²⁷

- La forma de hacer la corrección precisa en el sujeto que la realiza unas *calidades de humanidad* nada comunes, calidades que, si se poseen, reciben un notable acrecentamiento mediante el ejercicio activo de la corrección. Así, pues, "hay que evitar la pedantería, es decir, el hacerse intolerables por quererlo juzgar y criticar todo. [Por otra parte], el no hacer las cosas como nosotros creemos o el tener un punto de vista distinto del nuestro, y obrar en consecuencia no nos da derecho a juzgar y corregir ni mucho menos a imponer nuestro modo de ver a los demás, ya que, evidentemente, no es nuestro modo de ver lo que constituye la norma suprema de las acciones ajenas."²⁸

- La corrección fraterna será efectiva y constituirá un ejercicio de auténtica caridad si se realiza con humildad sincera y si conlleva un sincero esfuerzo de corregir en la propia vida del que corrige los fallos que se denotan en el hermano. A este respecto son de recordar las cualidades que se pedían en la literatura moral casuista a la corrección fraterna: *caritativa, paciente, humilde, prudente, discreta, ordenada*.²⁹

5. ¿Cuándo y cómo la "corrección fraterna" ha de pasar a "denuncia"?

En algunas situaciones la corrección ha de llegar a ser también *denuncia* al superior correspondiente. Es el caso en que la situación fallida repercuta

---

26. Ibid., 500.
27. Grün, *Entrañas de misericordia*, 89.
28. Gennaro, *Corrección fraterna*, 500.
29. Royo Marín, *Teología de la Caridad*, 457–459.

notablemente en el bien de la comunidad y no pueda lograrse la corrección mediante la amonestación fraternal. Hay que tener en cuenta que "cuando la denuncia se hace al superior tan solo como a *padre*, no puede él de ninguna manera proceder como *juez*."[30] Lo que se comunica al superior con el único fin de procurar el bien del prójimo no puede ser utilizado como motivo o justificación de cualquier forma de actuación canónica penalizadora.

Aunque las faltas públicas no han de ser ocultadas al superior, es de anotar que las denuncias anónimas no han de ser admitidas, ni mucho menos fomentadas. Por lo demás, "el superior ha de sopesar las declaraciones y del carácter del denunciante. Y en lo posible ha de dar ocasión al denunciado para defenderse (. . .). El superior no puede denunciar a otro de más categoría cosas que deben darse por terminadas."[31]

En el caso de que se trate de un *delito*, de que se abuse de personas débiles (niños, deficientes, etc.), o de que entre en juego de forma grave el bien común de la institución, en tales situaciones es obligatoria la *denuncia* en el sentido jurídico fuerte. Hoy día somos muy sensibles a los fallos en el campo del abuso sexual de menores (pederastia). Si se hubieran seguido las orientaciones de la moral, no se hubiera llegado a situaciones que hoy día lamentamos. Sirvan de recordatorio las dos apreciaciones siguientes:

Según A. Royo Marín, "en un colegio o comunidad es obligatorio, bajo pecado moral, denunciar al superior a los corruptores ocultos, por el daño gravísimo que están haciendo al bien común y el peligro de grave infamia para toda la comunidad o colegio. El que, conociendo con certeza aquella corrupción, se negase a denunciarla, es indigno de la absolución sacramental."[32]

En apreciación de B. Häring, "ni en comunidades, ni menos en establecimientos de educación ha de erigirse la denuncia en sistema de gobierno. En cambio, todos han de tener presente que cuando no basta una advertencia y corrección fraterna, ha de denunciarse a los corruptores, o a cualquiera que sistemáticamente socave la autoridad, el buen espíritu o la buena reputación del establecimiento o comunidad."[33]

---

30. Ibid., 460.
31. Häring, *La ley de Cristo*, II, 415.
32. Royo Marín, *Teología de la Caridad*, 459-460.
33. Häring, *La ley de Cristo*, II, 415.

6. La amonestación "de" los superiores y "a" los superiores

6.1 La corrección de los superiores.

Es obvio que sigue siendo actual -y necesaria- la función orientadora y amonestadora de las personas que han sido constituidas en el servicio de animación y de dirección de los diversos grupos humanos y eclesiales. Es lo que denominamos: amonestación *de* los superiores, la cual constituye una de las vertientes de la tercera OdM "corregir al que yerra." Entran en este grupo: las autoridades eclesiásticas, los superiores de las comunidades religiosas, los agentes de pastoral (sacerdotes, predicadores, catequistas, etc.) y todos cuantos tienen la función de dirigir un grupo sea del carácter que sea y tenga la finalidad que tenga.

También es obvio que la forma de realizar esta obra de misericordia por parte de los superiores ha de acomodarse a la altura de los tiempos antropológicos y teológicos del presente. Por razones antropológicas y teológicas, están superados los modos *prepotentes*, los gestos *altaneros*, las palabras *sin posibilidad de réplica*, el recurso a las *amenazas* para contrarrestar la debilidad de las argumentaciones.

Hay modelos neotestamentarios de amonestación, que constituyen otros tantos paradigmas para la actuación de los superiores[34]:

- Ahí están las "correcciones" de Jesús a sus discípulos: 1) El conjunto de las que recoge Lucas y que engarza en su relato del "camino hacia Jerusalén" (9, 51-19, 28) o camino del discipulado: 9, 55; 12, 22; 17, 5-6; 17, 7-10. 2) Las correcciones sobre la falta de fe y de confianza, transmitidas por Mateo: 8, 26; 14, 28-31; 16, 6-8. 3) Las amonestaciones de Marcos sobre el discipulado como "servicio": 8, 27-33; 9, 33-37; 10, 32-35.

- También constituyen formas paradigmáticas del *Corregir al que yerra* las amonestaciones que el Espíritu dirige a las Iglesias en Apoc 1, 4-3,22, no solo por razón del contenido de las advertencias sino también por la forma de realizarlas:

  3. desde el amor: "Yo a los que amo, corrijo y reprendo";

---

34. Ver el desarrollo que ofrece: Contreras, *Corrección fraterna*, 149-156.

4. partiendo de lo positivo que se posee para denotar la carencia de la plenitud: "conozco tus obras" (buenas)—"pero tengo algo contra ti."

6.2 La corrección a los superiores.

Los superiores también han de ser tenidos como destinatarios del *Corregir al que yerra*. "Según la enseñanza común de los teólogos (precisamente en consonancia con Gál 2, 11: [la advertencia de Pablo a Pedro acerca de que la observancia de la ley ritual judía podía perjudicar grandemente a la misión entre los paganos]) hay apremiante deber de caridad de *corregir a los superiores* cuando de veras lo necesitan. Solo que al hacerlo no se ha de olvidar el debido respeto (cf. 1 Tim 5, 1). La corrección pública de un superior solo sería lícita por faltas evidentes y escandalosas cuyos perjuicios no pudieran remediarse de otro modo."[35]

Bajo la expresión de *superior* entiendo aquí no solo ni principalmente las personas constituidas en autoridad sino sobre todo las instituciones directivas de una determinada institución; por ejemplo, los capítulos (generales, provinciales) de la Vida Religiosa. En estos ámbitos donde se ejerce la autoridad de forma colegial es donde hoy cobra mayor sentido el *corregir al que yerra*.

Los teólogos medievales, concretamente los franciscanos, llamaban *peccatum taciturnitatis* (pecado de silencio) a la omisión de este deber. Creo que en los ámbitos colegiales de la autoridad se ha faltado más *por silencio* que por palabras o por textos escritos.

Dentro de esa misma orientación se sitúan algunos *dictámenes* recogidos de la boca de san Juan de la Cruz por el padre fray Eliseo de los Mártires, el primer visitador del Carmelo reformado que pasó a las Indias y el primer provincial carmelita descalzo en México.[36] En varios de esos dictámenes el místico carmelita critica los *silencios* culpables en capítulos y la *altanería* de algunos superiores. Sobre el último supuesto: "Fue enemigo de que los superiores de religiosos, y más reformados, mandasen con imperio (. . .)" (dictamen 1).[37] Sobre los silencios en los capítulos: "Y decía que se podía temer ser traza del demonio el criar los religiosos de esta manera ["criar

---

35. Häring, *La ley de Cristo*, II, 414.

36. Lo tomo de: san Juan de la Cruz, *Obras completas*, 1318-1325: "Dictámenes de espíritu recogidos por Eliseo de los Mártires"

37. Ibid., 1319.

a los religiosos con rigores irracionales": dictamen 16][38]; porque, criados con ese temor, no tengan los superiores quién les ose avisar ni contradecir cuando erraren. Y si por ese camino o por otro llegare la Orden a tal estado que los que por las leyes de caridad y justicia, esto es, los graves de ella, en los Capítulos y Juntas y otras ocasiones no osaren decir lo que conviene por flaqueza o pusilanimidad o por miedo de no enojar al superior, y por esto no salir con oficio, que es manifiesta ambición, tengan la Orden por perdida y del todo relajada" (dictamen 17).[39] Y esto sucede "claramente cuando en los Capítulos nadie replica, sino que todo se concede y pasan por ello, atendiendo a solo sacar cada uno su bocado; con lo cual gravemente padece el bien común y se cría el vicio de la ambición, que se había de denunciar, sin corrección [probablemente con mejor lectura: sin compasión], por ser vicio pernicioso y opuesto al bien universal."[40]

Una amonestación paradigmática a superiores fue la que se atrevió a dirigir el papa Francisco a la Curia Romana el 22 de diciembre de 2014, señalando en ese "cuerpo" 15 posibles (y, muy probablemente, reales) "enfermedades"[41]:

1. El sentirse inmortal, inmune o incluso indispensable.
2. El martismo (de Marta) o la excesiva laboriosidad.
3. La fosilización mental y espiritual.
4. La planificación excesiva y el funcionalismo.
5. La mala coordinación.
6. El Alzheimer espiritual.
7. La rivalidad y la vanagloria.
8. La esquizofrenia existencial.
9. Los chismes y la murmuración.
10. Divinizar a los jefes.
11. Indiferencia hacia los demás.
12. La cara de funeral.

38. Ibid., 1323.
39. Ibid., 1324.
40. Ibidem.
41. Traducción castellana (del texto original italiano) en: Ecclesia n. 3.760–61 (3 y 10 de enero de 2015) 31–35.

13. La acumulación.
14. Formar círculos cerrados.
15. La enfermedad del beneficio mundano y del exhibicionismo.[42].

7. La crítica de instituciones y estructuras

Una conveniente—y hasta necesaria—actualización de la 3ª OdM espiritual es la que incluye en el horizonte de la amonestación a las instituciones y a las estructuras, tanto las de carácter religioso como las profanas. Este ensanchamiento de la corrección es correspondiente al ensanchamiento de la toma de conciencia y de la categorización teológica del mal moral. Teniendo este como sujeto siempre a la persona, su concreción primaria -en lenguaje técnico, "primer analogado"- acaece hoy en las instituciones y en las estructuras.[43] El papa Francisco, en la carta apostólica *Evangelii gaudium*, siguiendo el magisterio pontificio reciente (*Sollicitudo rei socialis*, n. 36; *Centesimus annus*, n. 38), ha asumido la categoría de "estructuras de pecado" (n. 59).

Pertenece hoy a la OdM de *Corregir al que yerra* realizar una crítica, severa en el contenido aunque suave en el tono, a las instituciones y estructuras injustas. En el mundo secular, abundan esas estructuras e instituciones. Por ejemplo:

- En el ámbito económico: el sistema financiero actual, reducido (en más de un 70%) a especulación monetaria sin entrar (en menos de un 30%) en la economía real.

- En el ámbito político: el sistema de partidos que necesariamente genera corrupción (uso del interés público en beneficio privado).

También se dan estructuras e instituciones fallidas ("de pecado") en el ámbito religioso cristiano. Es obra de misericordia hoy *corregir el error* de:

- Estructuras eclesiásticas contrarias a los derechos humanos.

- Instituciones que, además de ser "ridículas" por estar fuera de tiempo, contradicen genuinos valores evangélicos. Las hay: en el orden del pensamiento (por ejemplo, seguir midiendo *temporalmente* el efecto de las indulgencias), en la forma de *re-vestirse* para las celebraciones

---

42. Ver una presentación en: Teología Espiritual 59 (2015) 49-56.
43. Vidal, *El mal moral estructural*.

cultuales, en los modos de *tratamiento* oficial, en el rechazo de las normales y justas exigencias del *feminismo*, etc., etc.

Final (por exigencia del guión).

Por lo que acabo de señalar, no ha quedado sin trabajo la obra de misericordia espiritual del *Corregir al que yerra*. Utilizando una expresión de raíz platónica y de sabor orteguiano (del filósofo español J. Ortega y Gasset) todavía le queda pendiente una *segunda navegación*. Ojalá los dioses -y los vientos- sean propicios y al autor de las presentes líneas le quepa en suerte embarcarse en tan venturosa nave.

He tratado el tema en clave ético-religiosa. Pero, soy consciente de que tiene otra interesante clave de desarrollo: corregir el *error meramente humano* (en el hablar, en el razonar, en el ponderar, en el proyectar, en el ejecutar, en el evaluar). También esta tarea queda pendiente para la *segunda navegación*.

Bibliography

Blanc, G. *Correction fraternelle*. In: DThC, Paris, 1911, XIII, 1907–1911.
Costello, J. A. *Moral Obligation of Fraternal Correction*. Washington D. C., 1949.
Fitzgerald, A. *Misericordia, obras de misericordia*. In: A. D. Fitzgerald, A. D., Diccionario de San Agustín, Burgos: Monte Carmelo, 2001, 898–905.
Gennaro, C. *Corrección fraterna*. In: E. Ancilli, E., Diccionario de espiritualidad, Barcelona: Herder, 1983, I, 499–500.
Grün, A. *Entrañas de misericordia. Caminos para transformar el mundo*. Santander: Sal Terrae, 2009.
Häring, B. *La ley de Cristo. La teología moral expuesta a sacerdotes y seglares*. Barcelona: Herder, 1968, II, 410–15.
Juan de la Cruz, San. *Obras completas*. Revisión textual, introducción y notas al texto por José Vicente Rodríguez, introducción y notas doctrinales por Federico Ruiz Salvador. Madrid: Editorial Espiritualidad, 1980, 1318–1325: "Dictámenes de espíritu recogidos por Eliseo de los Mártires."
Juliá, E. *Corrección fraterna*. In: Gran Enciclopedia Rialp, Madrid: Rialp, VI, 1972, 532–33.
Kasper, W. *El evangelio de la familia*. Santander: Sal Terrae, 2014.
———. *La misericordia. Clave del Evangelio y de la vida cristiana*. Santander: Sal Terrae, 2014.
Keenan, J. F. *The Works of Mercy. The Heart of Catholicism*. New York: Sheed and Ward, 2005.
Noble, H. D. *Correction fraternelle*. La Vie Spirituelle 19 (1929) 411–20.
Palsterman, J. *La correction des autres d'après saint Thomas d'Aquin*. Ephemerides Theologicae Lovanienses 37 (1961) 503–56.

Royo Marín, A., *Teología de la Caridad*. Madrid: Bac, 1960, 452–60.

———. *Misericordia. II. Virtud y obras de misericordia*. In: Gran Enciclopedia Rialp, Madrid: Rialp, XVI, 14–17.

———. *Teología moral para seglares*. Madrid: Bac, 1973, 394–395.

Sirna, G., y Bonifazi, Mª. L., *Misericordia. Le opere di misericordia nell'arte*. In: EC, Città del Vaticano, 1952, VIII, 1082–85.

Vidal, M., *El mal moral estructural. Lugar hermenéutico de la responsabilidad y de los valores éticos*. In: Varios, *Misterio del mal y fe cristiana*. Valencia: Tirant Humanidades, 2012, 261–92.

Bibliography for
Brian Johnstone, C.Ss.R.

1. "Eschatology and Social Ethics: A Critical Survey of the Development of Social Ethical Theory in the Ecumenical Discussion, 1925-1968." *Bijdragen* 37 (1976): 47-85.

2. "New Order of Penance." *Compass Theology Review* 10 (1976): 3-10.

3. "Privacy and Intrusions: A Discussion from the Viewpoint of Some Christian Beliefs on Human Rights." *The Australasian Catholic Record* 59 (1982): 318-331.

4. "The Moral Status of the Embryo." In *Test-Tube Babies: A Guide to Moral Questions, Present Techniques and Future Possibilities*, ed. William A. W. Walters and Peter Singer, 49-56. Melbourne: Oxford University Press, 1982.

5. "The Right and Duty of Defense." *Studia Moralia* 22 (1984): 63-87.

6. "The Experience of Conversion and the Foundations of Moral Theology." *Église et Théologie* 15 (1984): 183-202.

7. "Nuclear War: Asking the Moral Questions." In *Moral Studies: Science-Humanity-God.* Terrence Kennedy, ed. 28-46. Melbourne: Spectrum Publications, 1984.

8. "Moraltheologische Fragen zum Thema: Atomkrieg." *Theologie der Gegenwart* 29 (1986): 113-118.

9. "A Proposal for a Method in Moral Theology." *Studia Moralia* 22 (1984): 189-212.

10. "The Right to Privacy: The Ethical Perspective." *The American Journal of Jurisprudence* 29 (1984): 73-94.

11. "The U.S. Bishops and the Bomb: What They Said and Why." *Doctrine and Life* 35 (1985): 75-79.

12. "The Meaning of Proportionate Reason in Contemporary Moral Theology." *The Thomist* 49 (1985): 223-247.

13. "Moral Experience in the Test of History." *Église et Théologie* 16 (1985): 319-338.

14. "In Vitro Fertilization and Ethical Dualism." *Linacre Quarterly* 53 (1986): 66-79.

15. "Non-Combatant Immunity: The Origins of the Principle in Theology and Law." *Studia Moralia*: 24 (1986): 115-148.

16. "The Structures of Practical Reason: Traditional Theories and Contemporary Questions." *The Thomist* 50 (1986): 417-446.

17. "Noncombatant Immunity and the Prohibition of the Killing of the Innocent." In *Peace in a Nuclear Age: The Bishops' Pastoral Letter in Perspective*, ed. Charles J. Reid, 305-322. Washington: The Catholic University of America Press. 1986.

18. "The Theory and Strategy of the Seamless Garment." *Social Thought* 12 (1986): 19-27.

19. O'Brien, Mary Elizabeth, Rosemary Donley, Mary Jean Flaherty and Brian V. Johnstone. "Therapeutic Options in End-Stage Renal Disease: A Preliminary Report." *ANNA JOURNAL* 13.6 (December, 1986): 313-31

20. "Justice and Cost Containment in End-Stage Renal Disease." *The Journal of Contemporary Health Law and Policy* 3 (1986): 65-84.

21. "Evangelical Counsels." *The New Dictionary of Theology* (1987), 355-357.

22. "Casuistry." *The New Dictionary of Theology* (1987), 160-161.

23. "Fundamental Option." *The New Dictionary of Theology* (1987), 407-408.

24. "Probabilism." *The New Dictionary of Theology* (1987), 801-803.

25. "Should Australia Maintain the U.S. Alliance? Some Perspectives from Christian Ethics." In *U.S. Alliance: On What Terms*, Brian Johnstone and Senator Michael Tate, 1-27. Melbourne, Australia: Spectrum Publications. 1987.

26. "Human Rights, Justice and Theology." In *Culture, Human Rights and Peace in Central America*, ed. George F. McLean, Raul Molina and Timothy Ready for the Council for Research in Values and Philosophy. Lanham, MD: University Press of America, 1988.

27. "The Instruction 'Donum Vitae' and its Reception." *Studia Moralia* 26 (1988): 211-229.

28. "Learning through Suffering: The Moral Meaning of Negative Experience." In *History and Conscience*, Studies in Honour of Sean O'Riordan, C.Ss.R., ed. Raphael Gallagher C.Ss.R. and Brendan McConvery C.Ss.R., 144-160. Dublin: Gill and MacMillan, 1989.

29. "La tecnologia genética: perspectiva teológico-moral," *Moralia* (Madrid) 11 (1989):297-314.

30. "Organ Transplants." *New Catholic Encyclopedia*. Supplement (1989).

31. "The Significance of the Moral Theology of St. Alphonsus: The Redemptorist Focus Today." *Studia Moralia/Supplement*, Recentre de Moralistes Redemptoristes, Aylmer, Québec, Canada, 26-30 June 1989, Actes/Acts, 77-98. Rome: 1990.

32. "From Physicalism to Personalism." *Studia Moralia* 30 (1992): 71-96.33. "The Revisionist Project in Roman Catholic Moral Theology." *Studies in Christian Ethics* 5 (1992): 18-31.

34. "The European Synod: The Meaning and Strategy of Evangelization." *Gregorianum* 73 (1992): 469-487.

35. "Verzicht auf die Theorie vom 'Gerechten Krieg': Zur Entwicklung des Friedengedanken bei Bernhard Häring 1954-1989." In *Christus zum Leben befreit*, ed. Josef Römelt and Bruno Hidber, 205-224. Freiburg, Basel, Wien: Herder, 1992.

36. "Erroneous Conscience in *Veritatis Splendor* and the Theological Tradition." In *The Splendor of Accuracy: An Examination of the Assertions made by Veritatis Splendor*, ed. Joseph A. Selling and Jan Jans, 114-135. Kampen-The Netherlands: Kok-Pharos, 1994.

37. "Methodology, Moral." *The New Dictionary of Catholic Social Thought* (1994),

38. "Die Enzyklica 'Glanz der Wahrheit.'" *Ethica* 2 (1994): 43-55.

39. "Personalist Morality for a Technological Age: The *Catechism of the Catholic Church* and *Veritatis Splendor*." *Studia Moralia* 32 (1994): 121-136.

40. "Abandoning the Just War Theory: The Development of B. Häring's Thought on Peace, 1954-1990." *Studia Moralia* 33 (1995): 289-309.

41. "Solidarität und Gewissen: Eine theologische und pastorale Herausforderung." *Theologie und Glauben* (1995): 163-178.

42. "Life in a Culture of Death." *Priests and People* 9 (1995): 409-413.

43. "The Encyclical *Veritatis Splendor*." *The Ecumenical Review* 48 (1996): 168-172.

44. "The Dynamics of Conversion." In *Spirituality and Morality: Integrating Prayer and Action*, ed. Dennis J. Billy and Donna Orsuto, 32-47. New York/Mahwah, NJ: Paulist Press, 1996.

45. "Transformation Ethics: The Moral Implications of the Resurrection." In *The Resurrection: An Interdisciplinary Symposium on the Resurrection of Jesus*, ed. Stephen T. Davis, Daniel Kendall, S.J. and Gerard O'Collins, SJ, 339-360. Oxford: Oxford University Press, 1997.

46. "Faith and Reason in Morals: A Polyphony of Traditions." *Studia Moralia* 35 (1997): 261-281.

47. "The Resurrection as the Source for a Theology of Peace." *Studia Moralia* (1998): 441-460.

48. "Proportionalism." *Dictionaire Critique de Théologie* (1998)

49. "Scandale." *Dictionaire Critique de Théologie* (1998)

50. "Utilitarisme." *Dictionaire Critique de Théologie* (1998)

51. "Responsibility in Catholic Moral Theology." In *Proceedings of the Fourth International Congress of Redemptorist Moral Theologians*; Krakow, 4-9 July, 1999. ed. Raymond Douziech, C.Ss.R., Rome: Redemptorists, 99-112.

52. "Can Tradition be a Source of Moral Truth? A Reply to Karl -Wilhelm Merks." *Studia Moralia* (1999): 431-451.

53. "Resurrection and Moral Theology." *Josephinum Journal of Theology* 7 (2000): 5-17.

54. *The Christian Faith in the Doctrinal Documents of the Catholic Church*, ed. Jacques Dupuis. Seventh Revised and Enlarged Edition, chapters 20, 22. Bangalore: Theological Publications in India, 2001.

55. "AIDS Prevention and the Lesser Evil," *Studia Moralia* 39 (2001): 197-216.

56. "AIDS Prevention: A Response to Drum," *Studia Moralia* 39 (2001): 586-590.

56a Drum, Peter. "Aids Prevention and the Lesser Evil:" Response." *Studia Moralia* 39 (2001): 883-585.

57. "The Debate on the Structure of the Summa Theologiae of St. Thomas Aquinas: from Chenu (1939) to Metz (1998)." In *Aquinas as Authority*, ed. Paul Van Geest, Harm Goris and Carlo Leget, 187-200. Leuven: Peeters, 2002.

58. "The Definition of Life: Its Role in Ethics." In *Fundamentals of Life*, ed. Gyula Pályi, Claudia Zucchi and Luciano Caglioti, 553-561. Paris: Elsevier, 2002

59. "The War on Terrorism: A Just War?" *Studia Moralia* 40 (2002): 39-62.

60. "Le frontiere morali di Potere e Salute." *Dolentium Hominum* 49 (2002): 60-64.

61. "Political Assassination and Tyrannicide: Traditions and Contemporary Conflicts." *Studia Moralia* 41 (2003): 25-46.

62. "¿Qué es la tradición?" In *La ética cristiana hoy: horizontes de sentido*: Homenaje a Marciano Vidal, ed. Miguel Rubio, Vicente Garcia and Vicente Gómez Mie, 25-46. Madrid: Instituto Superior de Ciencias Morales, 2003.

63. "Zngazowanie Jana Pawla II na rzecz pokoju," *Homo Dei* 3 (2003): 13-24.

64. "The Status of the Human Embryo: Catholic Teaching and the Role of Reason," http://www.lifeissues.net/writer.php (2003-08-11). (Consult under "Abortion.")

65. "Pope John Paul II and the War in Iraq," *Studia Moralia* 41 (2003): 309-330.

66. "Conscience and Error." In *Conscience, Readings in Moral Theology* 14, ed. Charles E. Curran, 163-174. New York: Paulist Press, 2004.

67. "Keeping a Balance: Contemplation and Christian Meditation." *Review for Religious*, 63 (April, 2004): 118-133.

BIBLIOGRAPHY FOR BRIAN JOHNSTONE, C.SS.R.

68. "The Gift: Derrida, Marion and Moral Theology." *Studia Moralia* 42 (2004): 411-432.

69. "The Argument from Tradition in Roman Catholic (Moral) Theology." *Irish Theological Quarterly* 69 (2004): 139-155.

70. "The Ethics of the Gift According to Aquinas, Derrida and Marion." *Australian EJournal of Theology* 4 (August 2004): 1-33. http:77dlibrary.acu.edu.au/research/theology/ejournal/aejt_3/johnstone.htm

71. "The Truth about Homosexuality: A Reply to Gareth Moore." *Australian EJournal of Theology* 4 (February 2005): 1-16. http://dlibrary.acu.edu.au/research/theology/ejournal/aejt_4/johnstone.htm.

72. "'Objectivism,' 'Basic Human Goods,' and 'Proportionalism:' An Interpretation of the Contemporary History of Moral Theology," *Studia Moralia* 43 (2005): 89-118.

73. "What is Tradition: From Pre-modern to Postmodern." *Australian EJournal of Theology* 5 (2005): 1-45. http://aejt.com.au/2005/vol_5_no_1_2005

74. "Intrinsically Evil Acts," *Studia Moralia* 43 (2005): 379-406.

75. "The Human Embryo: Person and the Gift." In *Life and Learning. Proceedings of the Seventeenth University Faculty for Life* conference at Villanova University 2007, ed. Joseph W. Koterski, S.J. (Washington, DC: University Faculty for Life, 2007): 489-505.

76. "Christian Faith in Redemption: Source of Moral Attitude." *Journal of Law Philosophy and Culture*, 3:1 (Spring, 2009): 421-428.

77. "What Does it Mean to be a Person." *Studia Moralia* 48 (2010): 125-140

78. "Abortion: The Person as One to be Loved," *Studia Moralia* 49/2 (2011): 419-438.

79. "The Presumption against Violence and War." In *Catholic Theological Ethics: Past, Present, and Future: The Trento Conference*, ed. James F. Keenan (New York: Maryknoll: 2011):160-166.

80. "The Resurrection in Phenomenology Jean-Luc Marion on the 'saturated phenomenon par excellence'." *Pacifica* 28.1 (February 2015): 23-39.

www.ingramcontent.com/pod-product-compliance
Lightning Source LLC
Chambersburg PA
CBHW051744230426
43670CB00012B/2147